MA

g

D0578216

Growing Fragrant Plants

by Rayford Clayton Reddell and Robert Galyean

photographs by the authors

HARPER & ROW, PUBLISHERS, *New York*
Philadelphia, Grand Rapids, St. Louis, San Francisco,
London, Singapore, Sydney, Tokyo

COPYRIGHT © 1989 BY RAYFORD CLAYTON
REDDELL AND ROBERT GALYEAN
All rights reserved. Printed in the United States of
America. No part of this book may be used or
reproduced in any manner whatsoever without
written permission except in the case of brief
quotations embodied in critical articles or reviews.
For information address Harper & Row, Publishers,
Inc., 10 East 53rd Street, New York, NY 10022.

FIRST EDITION

A YOLLA BOLLY PRESS BOOK
Growing Fragrant Plants was produced in association
with the publisher at The Yolla Bolly Press, Covelo,
California, under the supervision of James and
Carolyn Robertson. Editorial and design staff:
Barbara Youngblood, Diana Fairbanks, Nancy
Campbell. Composition by Wilsted & Taylor,
Oakland, California.

LIBRARY OF CONGRESS
CATALOGING-IN-PUBLICATION DATA

Reddell, Rayford Clayton.
    Growing fragrant plants/Rayford Clayton Reddell
and Robert Galyean
        p.   cm.
    ISBN 0-06-016073-X: $35.95
    1. Aromatic plants.   2. Gardens, Fragrant.
    I. Galyean, Robert.   II. Title.
SB301.R43   1989
635.9'68—dc19   89-45059
                                        CIP

The photograph appearing on page 167 was taken
by Rose Hodges.

89 90 91 92 93   10 9 8 7 6 5 4 3 2 1

This book is dedicated to the memory of Bill Derveniotes,
without whom we probably couldn't have written it,
as he would have been the first to tell you.
Besides casting an ever-critical eye over each word we wrote,
he was adamant about fragrance, whether or not aromas pleased his fine nose.
Mostly, however, while preoccupied with fragrance,
we never had to fret that our precious roses were in any
but the most capable of hands.

Contents

Preface

When I bought Garden Valley Ranch in Petaluma, California, forty-three miles north of San Francisco, the only fragrant plants I intended to grow were roses. Although the twelve hundred bushes I planted occupied only a speck of my nine acres, ministering to their needs was as much as I could handle just then. When I had any time at all to wonder about how I would use the rest of the nine acres, I supposed, if my venture were successful, that it would eventually be taken up by more rosebushes.

After I had sold rose blooms at the San Francisco wholesale flower market for three years, I knew that I was onto something worth expanding, but still all I thought of were roses. Also, I knew that the ranch needed a full-time foreman.

Robert Galyean had lived in San Francisco for ten years—long enough to get his fill of city life. He yearned to move to the country, and rose farming sounded like just the ticket. We increased the rose field to four thousand bushes, and Robert moved up to Petaluma to coddle them year round.

After a year of pampering the queen of flowers, Robert mastered the skills necessary to grow champion roses. Four thousand rosebushes were no longer enough; he wanted more responsibility. Put in more roses? No, we were growing more than enough roses for San Francisco florists, and we didn't want to glut the local market.

Robert agreed to meet me in San Francisco one evening to have dinner and to mull over our next step. That afternoon I went to a local variety store to buy a birthday card for a friend. While waiting to pay for it, I spotted a display of potpourri near the cash register. It looked thoroughly unappealing through its clear wrapping, but I picked it up anyway to have a whiff. Phoo, it smelled even worse than it looked. The salesperson saw me wince and was visibly surprised to hear me say, "I'd like this too." My nose was twitching for something better.

Could the answer involve fragrance? Just as I had learned that people prefer large roses to small ones and pastels to reds, it was equally clear that they liked fragrant blossoms better than scentless ones. What about leftover rose petals? Everyone seemed to want them for one reason or another. People even bought those our wholesaler was forced to dump when the market was slow or when we were caught in those inevitable flushes of bloom.

That night at dinner I suggested to Robert that we go further than just drying rose petals. "We'll sniff out everything useful for good potpourri and grow as much as we can harvest," I announced. When Robert asked if I knew anything about drying materials or how potpourri was made, I had to own up to near ignorance. "But how hard can it be?" I wondered out loud. "This," I gestured at the sickeningly sweet, garish blend of dehydrated junk, "couldn't have been too hard."

The next day Robert called to say that he had stayed up half the night reading what various gardening reference books had to say about potpourri. "Rose petals are the real essentials," he said with relief. "After those, lavender and a whole slew of herbs make good materials for drying, and *they* hold their scent after drying!" As he spoke, I caught a faint whiff of the first batch of Garden Valley Ranch potpourri.

Once he got into the idea, Robert couldn't stop. In a week he had a list of more than one hundred fragrant possibilities, half of which I had only heard of and couldn't remember ever having seen, plants such as stewartia, elaeagnus, osmanthus, abelia, buddleia, wallflower, choisya, viburnum, and a fistful of herbs. His enthusiasm for heady flowers and foliage fired mine, and we decided simply to grow everything fragrant we could think of as long as it had a chance for survival in Petaluma and was useful one way or another in potpourri.

The following spring, after having staked out paths and outlined beds during the winter, we installed a one-acre garden that Stephen Suzman, a landscape designer, fashioned for us. We began planting in March and popped the last plant into its hole on Memorial Day. On weekends we enticed everyone we knew to come to the ranch to help out. Many came, but few returned. We dug and mounded nonstop, and had "fun" only when the sun set. During the week, Robert planted alone, trying diligently

It's true that *Digitalis* isn't fragrant, but by the time you wade through these scented violas, pinks, bearded irises, and roses, you'll be so drenched in perfume that you'll never wonder whether or not these foxgloves are also perfumed. Besides blending their aromas nicely, these plants complement one another with their varying shades of white.

to memorize the Latin names for everything he stuck in the ground.

We made mistakes—most of them because Petaluma staged an unprecedented winter the following year. Stephen had asked us to research previous temperature highs and lows for the Petaluma area. Everything we found out seemed to indicate that it was safe to plant Bouquet de Fleur citruses, because the thermometer didn't often dip below a temperature that would harm those sensitive bushes. Mother Nature, however, had something else in mind when she claimed our Bouquet de Fleur citruses and some other tender plants during an exceptionally cold December.

We tested flowers that were fragrant while fresh, but discovered they were scentless when dried (sweet peas, gardenias, daphnes, magnolias, clematises). Still others retained their scent, but turned an unappealing color (woodruffs, jasmines, citrus blossoms, and several of the herbs).

The standards we set for ourselves—insisting on plants that were fragrant both fresh and dried—needed lowering in no time. The first concession was the hardest: roses. While it's true that rose petals are the essence of most potpourris, none retains strong scent after drying.

Only essential oils revive faded aromas; don't let anyone persuade you otherwise.

Some of the rose varieties that are most useful for potpourri bloom with no detectable fragrance whatsoever. Olé, for instance, is a scentless, eye-blinking, Chinese lacquer red rose that dries to a lovely clear shade of darker red. Fragrant Cloud, on the contrary, is as fragrant as any rose I know when fresh, but its dried petals are not only devoid of smell, but turn a ghastly, washed-out shade of orange-red.

Other plants were useless while fresh, except for the beauty they lent the garden. Shade-loving sweet woodruffs, for example, produce perky, tiny, white blooms and handsome mid-green foliage that yield no fragrance at all. Essential fragrant oils aren't released until the cuttings are dried. Then sweet woodruff makes up for lost time with a scent that makes new-mown hay seem stale.

Final categorical exceptions were plants that are not fragrant when fresh or when dried, such as pansies. We've heard that there actually are some scented pansy varieties, but haven't been able to get our hands on seeds for them. If you've ever seen these gaily colored flowers dried, you know why we decided to cultivate them despite their lack of scent.

There are seven divisions of fragrant narcissuses, including the talcum-scented King Alfred daffodil shown here. A plus is that all family members multiply quickly. Narcissuses are also famed for repelling gophers. Although narcissus blossoms don't retain fragrance once they are dried, they make colorful additions to potpourri blends.

The fragrant garden had its flubs (citruses, daturas, and certain gardenias, magnolias, and daphnes), but triumphs (wisteria, buddleias, lilacs, lilies, wallflowers, and every single herb) overshadowed them. They're what this book is about—our successes (though we mention failures, too, in hopes that those plants will flourish for you). I personally bless the garden for giving me something new to write about. After finishing *Growing Good Roses*, my fingers itched to get back to a typewriter keyboard.

This book is really Robert's. I've only chronicled what I've witnessed. I, too, have increased my gardening knowledge immeasurably, but I haven't traveled Robert's horticultural mile (though I'm just as opinionated).

Although your gardening goals may not be as specific as ours, especially if you don't intend to make potpourri, you might just as well keep fragrance in mind while plotting your garden. After all, if you have a choice of two varieties— one fragrant, one scentless—wouldn't you prefer the fragrant one? That's what I thought. So would we.

CHAPTER I

Establishing Ground Rules

"What would you like your garden to smell like?" a fragrance expert asked when we first owned up to wanting a garden devoted to perfume. "Daturas," we answered, having just the night before sniffed ourselves silly on its intoxicating aroma in a Berkeley garden.

"Can't have them in Petaluma! It can freeze there every now and then," he snapped back.

"What else smells like daturas?" we asked, hoping something did.

"Gardenias, sort of," he offered.

"Gardenias! They don't smell *anything* like daturas," we objected, silently blessing him for hitting on something we knew.

"Both contain indole," rejoined our pro, firmly reseating us on our dunce stools (neither of us had the slightest idea what indole was, much less how it smelled). "Maybe you should read up on fragrance," our mentor tactfully suggested, handing us Roy Genders's *Scented Flora of the World*, our first bible on fragrance.

We pored over what Genders had to say, much of which might just as well have been written in Latin, such as the names of the plants whose heady aromas tempted us. We had never heard of three-quarters of the scented flora he described, so we took his word for how they smelled. We knew a thing or two about roses, though, and when we skipped ahead to read what he had to say about them, suddenly we felt qualified to object to some of his comparisons. We began to realize that what smells like one thing to one person, even an expert, smells different to someone else, but chamomile and apples? Those particular smellalikes tested our imagination. Yet much of what he said was right on the mark. The scent of sweet peas, for instance, does indeed favor that of wisteria. We agree that stocks and pinks share an *undertone* of clove, and that lilies of the valley smell somewhat like honeysuckle, even though they don't look anything alike.

In this chapter we set down some arbitrary lingo so that we can speak a common garden language. As Roy Genders does, we categorize fragrant flowers and scented leaves by their predominating essential oils, in hopes that such groupings will help later when we claim *this* smells like *that*. Then we suggest how to deal with plant names—when to refer to them as one commonly does, when to be proper. Finally, we offer help for avoiding and correcting inevitable mistakes.

We have tried to conform to the botanical listings in *Hortus Third*. In many cases we discuss varieties too new to be listed in *Hortus*. For some plants we have chosen to refer to species as they are most commonly marketed by nurseries, growers, and suppliers. In a few instances we take deliberate exception to *Hortus's* classification, as with marjoram and oregano, which we maintain deserve separate botanical status.

Climates we call *temperate* are those in which it never freezes at all. In *severe* climates lows range from 32° F to 20° F. In *cruel* climates the thermometer can be expected to regularly dip below 20° F.

Almost everyone will agree that fragrance is notable in the plants we discuss, either in the flowers or the leaves. There are exceptions about which even we disagree. One of us, for instance, can detect the unmistakable aroma of brown boronia (*Boronia megastigma*) at twenty paces; the other detects no fragrance even if he buries his nose in boronia blooms. We've omitted plants whose perfume most people can't smell, those so obscure that they can't easily be purchased, and those so perversely difficult to grow that we would only aggravate you by tempting you to try them anyway.

Distinguishing Among Fragrances

Most flower fragrances fall into one of ten rather broad groups, not all of which you're likely to be wild about. In addition to those, there are four groups of plants in which it is the leaves, not the flowers, that yield the sweet stuff. Rarely does a plant possess both pungent blossoms and leaves, although allspice, French marigolds, and several sages somehow pull off this difficult trick.

Some scents, like some people, refuse categorization: sweet alyssum, for example, smells like new-mown hay; and some flowers, particularly orchids, can smell one way by day and another at night, like a farm boy out on a date. Sweet woodruff isn't sweet or smelly at all, until it's dried. Despite the many exceptions, though, you'll find the groupings handy when choosing what to buy, grow, and smell. You may, for example, want to put at least a county between you and skunk cabbage and its peers.

Where does the smell, heavenly or otherwise, come from? Flowers harbor essential oils in the epidermal cells on the top of their petals

Without the inspiration of fine gardeners like Vita Sackville-West, we may never have become so bold as to combine scarlet tulips with sky blue forget-me-nots, much less consider accenting the tasteful combination with brilliant yellow. Most bulbs make fine container plants and happily coexist with shallow-rooted annuals.

and release them into the air in minute quantities. The warmer the air, the speedier the discharge. If you want to sniff a flower on a cool, breezy day, hold it close to your nose and gently breathe into it. The warmth of your breath will accelerate the release of the fragrant oil. (If it has been a while since you brushed your teeth or it you've just eaten garlic, you'll taint the experience.)

The thicker, more velvetlike the petals, the more oil they retain and the slower its release, which is why the flowers most praised for their commercial perfume, such as lily of the valley, orange blossom, and tuberose, all have thick, substantial petals.

Perfume by Color

The degree of fragrance in flowers can also be predicted in part by their coloring. Generally, the lighter the color, the stronger the scent. White flowers are the most heavily perfumed, followed by off white, pink, mauve, yellow, and purple. Blue, orange, or red flowers are highly pigmented and have little or no scent. In Sweet William, for instance, white varieties are powerfully fragrant; pink versions are mildly perfumed; and the reds are scentless.

As rules of this sort seem meant to be broken, exceptions abound, particularly in roses, with many modern whites having little or no detectable fragrance (Pascali, John F. Kennedy, Pristine), while many reds are powerfully perfumed (Mister Lincoln, Precious Platinum, and Dolly Parton).

The continued hybridization of flowers accelerates scent confusion. Racing to discover new colors, pollinators relegate scent to a back burner. In the late nineteenth century a French fragrance specialist stated that more than 60 percent of scented flowers were either white or pale yellow. Today many other color groups boast fragrance not because hybridizers were bent on retaining perfume, but because the ancestry of their cross-pollinations happened to include strongly scented varieties.

Flower Fragrance Groups

Scented blossoms are classed according to the predominating chemical substance of their essential oils.

1. Indoloid flowers are pale brown, sometimes blotched with purple. All are unpleasant, smelling like decayed meat or fish. Flowers containing indole bloom mostly in South Africa and southwestern Asia, although North America has the skunk cabbage (*Caralluma europaea*). You've probably just learned as much as you want to know about this group, unless you're interested in providing pollination chores for midges and dung flies, the only insects that will go near the indoloids.

2. Aminoid flowers are usually cream or dingy white and reek of ammonia. They contain trimethylamine, which is found in the

Tuberoses (left) may be the Big Bertha of fragrance, but they know no shame as far as horticulture is concerned, demanding copious drinks of water poured over hot, rich soil that drains perfectly. Then, however, sinfully fragrant, star-shaped blossoms make you forget what a pain tuberoses can be.

You may never notice that lily-flowered tulips are only lightly scented if you plant them with perfume-packed wallflowers like this mahogany variety (right). By so doing, you create not only a scented mix, but a smashing color combination as well.

early stages of putrefaction (it's also present in herring brine). The aminoids include pyracantha, privet, giant fennel, hemlock (do you suppose the last thing Socrates smelled was ammonia?), and hawthorn, the latter being less unpleasant than others in the group. Plants in the aminoid group should be grown at a distance from your home, so their unpleasant fragrances will not waft indoors after they pollinate.

3. The heavy group includes flowers with some amount of indole, but they're sweeter and not unpleasant unless inhaled at close quarters. Indole in these flowers is less concentrated because it's cut with benzylacetate and methyl anthranilate, which diffuse foul overtones. Nevertheless, if in your enthusiasm over a tuberose and plumeria lei after you've just set foot in Hawaii, you bury your nose in your garland, you'll detect the unmistakable hint of putrefaction. Flowers in the heavy group also include osmanthus, philadelphus, viburnum, lily of the valley, and honeysuckle.

4. Aromatic flowers contain eugenol, the essential oil found in plants scented with cinnamon, clove, vanilla, and balsam. A flavor of clove is unmistakable in stocks, carnations, and peonies. Vanilla is obvious in witch hazel, acacia, and sweet peas. Almond fragrance, a bittersweet scent, is present in heliotrope, flowering rush, and choisya.

5. Violet flowers contain ionone. This ketone is what gives violets and mignonettes their distinctive scent. As it fades, it takes on the less-charming smell of damp woodland moss or freshly cut cucumbers. Even insects tire of it, which is perhaps why violets are in the unique group of self-fertilizing flowers that require no help from pollinating insects.

6. Rose-scented flowers contain geraniol, an alcohol. Leaves of rose geraniums are laden with geraniol. Because of these concentrations, essential oils from rose geraniums are often substituted for attar of roses. The discerning nose, however, can discriminate between the delicate fragrance of true rose attar (usually from damask roses grown in Bulgaria) and that from the headier rose geranium.

7. Lemon scents really could be a division of the rose group, since citral, the primary agent of lemon-scented flowers and leaves, is what you get when geraniol is oxidized.

Lemon scent is pronounced in *Rosa bracteata*, a member of the China family of roses. Even modern roses such as White Lightnin' smell of lemon. Undertones of lemon are also found in fragrant water lilies, verbena, and in the elegant *Magnolia* x *Soulangiana*.

8. Fruit-scented flowers are those whose fragrances include an overtone associated with a specific fruit. Most will swear that *Philadelphus* smells more like oranges than oranges do themselves. Freesias are thought to smell like ripe plums, *Iris graminea* like apricots, and the Jap-

Azaleas are no longer considered botanically separate from rhododendrons, but rather a subspecies. Usually, only white and pale yellow varieties are known for their fragrance, but there are numerous exceptions.

anese rambler *Rosa Wichuraiana* like green apples. The robust *Rosa Soulieana* smells for all the world like ripe bananas.

9. Animal-scented flowers are close to the fruit-scented, but they have an additional compound of alcohol that produces a fatty acid. Some flowers smell only of fruit, others of animals as well. Flowers may give off a hint of vanilla when fresh, but end up smelling like tomcats when they're old or have just been pollinated. Evergreen shrubs and ground covers of the hypericum family can simultaneously smell of goats and ripe apples.

The herb valerian and the oxeye daisy contain valeric acid, also found in human perspiration. In a single sprig this might not be particularly objectionable, but a whole clump of valerian can smell like a postgame Super Bowl locker room if you get too close to it on a warm day—hardly what you want your visitors to smell when they're visiting your fragrant garden.

Musk is the commonest fragrance found in the animal-scented plants. It's most often associated with moss and musk roses, but is also present in *Muscari moschatum* (musk hyacinth) and the foliage of *Delphinium Brunonianum*. Some people find musk so pleasant that they buy perfumes that smell of it. Others consider it a bit too animalistic.

It's interesting to note that almost all flowers smelling of musk are native to Afghanistan and western China, where the musk deer also is found, probably munching them.

10. Honey-scented flowers are closely related to the animal-scented group, but they have the distinguishing sweet aroma of honey. Butterflies are irresistibly attracted to honey scents, which is why you'll find them covering your buddleia from just before it blooms to well after. Honeysuckles and several escallonias also smell of honey, as does sweet sultan.

When both the flowers and the leaves of a fragrant plant are scented, the leaves are the more heavily perfumed. Not only that, but their fragrance lasts longer and intensifies with age, usually increasing when dried. That's because moisture continues to evaporate from the leaf cells, concentrating the essential oils left behind. They remain inert, releasing themselves only when cells are broken, when the leaf is bruised or crushed. The opposite is true for flowers—as they age, they become less fragrant.

Whereas the essential oil composition can be complex in flowers, it's often quite simple in leaves, sometimes even a single substance. The strongly scented wintergreen (*Gaultheria procumbens*), for instance, owes its powerful fragrance to the presence of only methylsalicylate. Leaves of the rose geranium (*Pelargonium capitatum*) contain concentrations of geraniol, the treasured ingredient of attar of roses.

Scented-Leaf Groups

Numerous scented leaves fall under the same fragrance groupings as flowers. For instance,

Roses of the *rubrifolia* species have eye-blinking pink petals, white edges, and brilliant yellow stamens. Although blossoms are sweetly scented, the species is better known for its unusually colored foliage. Young growth starts out purplish red. As it matures, foliage turns increasingly purple until fall, when leaves decide they always wanted to be red after all.

rose geranium and several of the pelargoniums are in the *rose* group. Wintergreen and rue are included in the *aromatic* listings, and rhizomes of *Iris florentina* are members of the *violet* group: when dried and pulverized, they yield the violet-perfumed orris powder. The *lemon* group is seductively represented by balm, lemon verbena, and lemon thyme.

Other fragrant leaves contain chemical elements not found in flowers, hence the four separate leaf scents.

1. Camphor and eucalyptus scents are found in trees of the same name, also in chamomile, bay, lavender, and myrtle.

2. Mint fragrances contain menthol, detectable in every form of mint, some pelargoniums, and specific eucalyptus leaves.

3. Turpentine-scented plants have borneol acetate in their essential oil. It is most pronounced in rosemary.

4. Sulphur smells are found in roots as well as in the leaves of mustard, garlic, onion, and watercress. We think highly of them, not for their scents, but rather for their culinary values.

Names

Botanical names of plants and their families, such as Asclepiadaceae, Dipsacaceae, and Hamamelidaceae, can be next to impossible to pronounce and remember. Even when you finally get them right, they don't *sound* right, and a name you would swear you had committed to memory one day won't come to you the next for the world. Besides, to stand there in your muddy gardening boots and call fragrant sweet peas and stock *Lathyrus odoratus* and *Matthiola* may raise some eyebrows. When buying, however, trot out all the botanical verbiage you can wrap your tongue around. Otherwise, you'll end up with scentless soundalikes.

Another reason for learning proper names is that what is called by one common name in one place is called by another name elsewhere. For instance, what is periwinkle in England and myrtle on the American East Coast, is called vinca (also the proper name) in California. In addition, many common names are interchanged so freely that sometimes you'll have to use proper names even at the risk of seeming pretentious.

Never ask for "mock orange" at a nursery, no matter who told you it was the name of what you smelled and fell in love with in her garden. Only *Philadelphus* legitimately deserves this sobriquet, yet everything that smells remotely like citrus ends up being called mock orange.

Fortunately, the common and botanical names of some plants are the same—buddleia (*Buddleia*), freesia (*Freesia*), magnolia (*Magnolia*), and wisteria (*Wisteria*). Others, such as hyacinths (*Hyacinthus*), differ by a single letter. The botanical and proper names of many plants, however, have nothing whatsoever to do with each other. Wallflowers are properly called *Cheiranthus*, lilacs are *Syringa*, and pinks and carnations are *Dianthus*. Some common names hint at what the proper names might be. Bay, for instance, is often called laurel, helping you to remember the correct name of *Laurus*. But then you must also remember to tack on *nobilis* when you go shopping, for *Laurus nobilis* is the bay you want to scent your garden and flavor your cooking.

A friend of ours, who is a great cook, could have saved some time and money with this particular bit of advice. She told us that when a gusty rainstorm toppled a tree in her garden, she decided to put the space to practical use by planting a bay tree. She uses bay leaves often in her kitchen and always resented what she had to pay for tiny jars of them at the supermarket. Besides, she knew she could make her own bay wreaths in December if she had a tree of her own, thereby plumping out her Christmas-shopping coin purse. Off she trotted to her neighborhood nursery, expecting a simple transaction. Instead, she was surprised with a choice—California or French bay? Being loyal to her native state, she chose the California version. Too bad. When the leaves she plucked from her sapling didn't smell like much, even when she crumpled them in her hand, and didn't give a trace of flavoring to her recipes, she realized she had made a mistake and cursed herself for not bothering to ask which to buy. (Now she has swung to the other extreme and won't spend a dollar at a nursery without calling us first.)

Be careful too that you don't go overboard with your newfound lingo. As Alan Lacy advises in *Home Ground*:

"I suspect that for most people one of the darker joys of gardening is that once you get started it's not at all hard to find someone who knows a little bit less than you, and then it's very difficult to resist the urge to strut your stuff. Gardeners are natural-born show-offs, and once you learn the merest basics, stuff-strutting comes easy. A person who knows which end of a tulip bulb goes up and which goes down is possessed of information that a surprising number of people in America don't have. But, of course, we all must start somewhere when it comes to gardening; no one is born knowing the difference between a zinnia and a ragweed seedling."

CHAPTER II

Selecting Trees and Shrubs

You might believe that we begin with trees and shrubs because theirs is the longest chapter. Actually, we start here because trees and shrubs are the first plantings you should consider if you're installing a garden from scratch or if you're revamping what you already grow. Trees and shrubs dictate a garden's architecture; they are the focal points that provide dramatic backdrops for lesser plantings. Once a garden's boundaries are determined, it's easy to plan and plant around them.

A friend of ours bought a home on the San Francisco peninsula that was in need of remodeling. One of the reasons he purchased the fixer-upper was that it had a large, sunny, rear garden that he was eager to claim as his hobby. Because the house demanded attention first, he put his landscaping dreams on hold.

One sunny spring day, weary of carpentry and eagerly anticipating horticulture, he visited his local nursery. As it happened, magnolias were on special. Our friend wasn't certain of all the plants he would ultimately include in his garden, but of one thing he was sure: he *had* to have a magnolia tree to refresh those scented memories of his youth.

He told the nursery employee that he wanted a fragrant white variety with thick petals. The employee suggested *Magnolia grandiflora*, which sounded just like what our friend had in mind, especially the "grand" part. He rushed home, dug a hole smack dab in the middle of his rear yard, and planted his magnolia.

A year later, when he could finally turn his attention to serious gardening, a landscape consultant shocked our friend by telling him that the first alteration his garden would need was transplanting that magnolia.

"Are you crazy?" our friend asked. "That tree couldn't be happier anywhere other than where it's growing. Why, it's doubled in size since I planted it."

"That's just the problem," the consultant replied. "By the time it's done with its doublings, it will be more than fifty feet tall and branch out over the entire garden, meaning that you can grow only shade lovers. If you're set on keeping that tree, I'd suggest moving it right now to the back corner of your garden.

What's more, I'd check with your neighbor to learn how she will feel about magnolia branches extending over her property."

Our friend agonized over the magnolia uprooting for a month before he took out his shovel and set about to do what he was finally convinced was inevitable. (That magnolia tree, by the way, is indeed now more than fifty feet tall and spreads its branches over neighbors' yards in two directions, but everyone seems pleased with the fragrant spillovers.)

If you're considering dividing your garden into sections or "rooms," don't even worry about which plants will occupy those quarters until you select their delineating hedges. If you want a windbreak along your garden's perimeter, choose those plantings first, giving consideration to what stands a chance of flourishing beside or beneath them.

Later on, when we talk about annuals, herbs, bulbs, and other "temporary plants," you won't have to be so deliberate about deciding where they are to grow; mistakes are easily corrected, moved, or banished. For plantings listed in this chapter, however, give careful consideration not only to the size we tell you ours have become, but to how large they're likely to grow where you garden. Ask someone who already grows them. If you don't know anyone who does, check with a local agricultural agent or a reliable nursery.

For now, trust us by believing that you, just like our magnolia buddy, won't want to transplant any tree or shrub that tells you it wants to flourish where you planted it. No matter what else might tempt you later, plant your trees and shrubs before you dig another hole.

Abelia

Although there are almost thirty species of these evergreen, semievergreen, or deciduous shrubs, abelias are known mostly for their practicality. Abelias are among gardeners' staples: they grow easily; require no pruning, but respond well to it; prefer full sun, but will tolerate shade; have practically no diseases or predators; and several varieties bloom when little else is in flower.

This genus was named for Robert Abel when

In the Royal Horticultural Society's stately garden at Wisley, twenty miles outside of London, bushes of *Rhododendron luteum* (Pontic azalea) in full bloom are handsomely reflected in a stream, and their brilliant yellow is strongly contrasted with a foreground planting of rosy primulas.

he discovered the species *A. chinensis* in China in 1816. The deciduous shrub grows to five feet, and is covered in tiny, oblong, shiny leaves that are mahogany before they turn green. At summer's end the plant covers itself with rosy, sweetly scented flowers that look like miniature *Digitalis* (foxglove). Where fall is moderate, blooms last well into winter. Four other species are known for their fragrance.

A. floribunda is native to Mexico, so it's only half-hardy in most other climates, requiring placement near a sunny wall or other shelter. The four- to five-foot shrub remains compact and in late February bears mauve, tubular flowers that droop in fragrant clusters.

A. x *grandiflora*, also known as the "glossy" abelia because of its particularly shiny leaves, is the most widely grown and popular of the abelias. It's also the tallest, growing to five-foot heights, and half as wide. Lightly fragrant, blush pink blooms cover bushes from June through October.

A. serrata is perhaps the most strongly scented, and surely the showiest of the fragrant species, with light pink blooms splashed with orange—not a tasteful color combination. The three- to four-foot evergreen shrub is native to the Orient, and compact with oblong, serrated leaves.

A. triflora is native to the Himalayas and grows gracefully to five feet. White, vanilla-scented blossoms with pink, tubular throats appear in clusters in late June on axils of leaves and tips of branches.

Acacia

Authorities swear that there are as many as eight hundred species to this genus, although fewer than ten varieties are widely grown in Britain, and no more than twenty in the western and southern United States. Acacias are native to areas with temperate climates—Tasmania, South Africa, and the shores of the Mediterranean. Acacias grow most freely today in Australia and New Zealand, where they're also known as wattles. Because of their hardiness and tolerance to drought, acacias are used to bind hillsides, for landscaping near beaches, or, if densely planted, as windbreaks. Some noble Texan had the good taste to introduce *A. Farnesiana* to the Lone Star state, where it now grows like a native from Beaumont to Wichita Falls.

A. Baileyana is by far the most widely grown species in America, probably because of its unusual hardiness and rapid growth. Trees scramble to thirty feet tall with girths even greater. Leaves are feathery and bluish gray. Blooms, also known as mimosa when sold as cut flowers, are actually violet-scented clusters of fluffy, yellow stamens that festoon trees during January and February.

A. Dealbata is similar to *A. Baileyana*, only larger and more quickly established. In Aus-

You may decide to plant *Abelia* simply for its profound practical appeal; it thrives almost anywhere you place it and is happy left alone or shaped to your liking (after it has finished blooming, please). As a special bonus, several varieties, like the one at lower left—*A. chinensis*—bear sweetly scented blossoms from summer through fall.

As do other plants native to the Mediterranean, *Acacia* loves temperate climates. Where it grows contentedly, most species develop into drought-resistant trees that effectively bind hillsides. Wherever it flourishes, *Acacia* reliably harbingers spring with festoons of fluffy blossoms that are usually yellow (below, right). Several varieties are so strongly scented of violet that their blooms are distilled to fortify perfumes.

tralia *A. Dealbata* is known as the silver wattle because of its shiny, gray twigs and young branches. Its flowers, also yellow and intoxicatingly scented, are formed in six- to nine-inch panicles.

A. Farnesiana, also known as sweet acacia, was named after the Farnese Palace in Rome. It's the species praised for the production of cassia oil, used to fortify violet scents. The trees, which at maturity are shorter than the two varieties already mentioned, are deciduous and have thorny branches. Plantings perform best in alkaline soils where the thermometer never dips below 15° F. Blossoms are golden yellow and formed in tiny balls. A fully grown tree, though no taller than ten feet, can yield up to twenty pounds of blossoms each season.

Where *A. longifolia*, also known as Sydney golden wattle, grows well, it serves abundant uses. Since it usually becomes a billowy, overgrown shrub that grows at an amazing pace, it serves as a roadside planting to protect against dust and the lights of oncoming traffic. *A. longifolia* seems oblivious to the soil in which it's planted. It is such a good soil binder that it is planted near beaches, even those with strong prevailing winds, which simply make it thrive prostrate. Unlike the foliage of most other species, the foliage of *A. longifolia* is bright green, with leaves up to six inches long. Blossoms, two-inch, golden yellow spikes, are sweetly scented and cover all branches.

A. podalyriifolia, sometimes called the pearl acacia, is happier grown as a shrub than as a loose-headed tree. Foliage is soft gray and pleasant to feel. Blossoms borne in fluffy, light yellow balls appear earlier than do those of almost any other prevalent species—as early as November on southern California's temperate coast.

Acacias aren't long-lived (twenty to thirty years), but they're such quick growers that you can replace a toppled adult with a sapling that will grow to twenty feet in three years. You can also grow acacias quite easily from seeds (gather your own from varieties you know you like). Seeds may be germinated in soakable peat pots and, once established, set out where they are to grow.

With most varieties you have a choice of treating acacias either as shrubs or as trees; they'll do as they're told. If you prune out the lead shoot, plants develop as bushes; if you remove early side growth, acacias mature into trees.

If they're watered too often, almost all acacias establish prodigious root systems that stretch over the surface of the soil. If you want to keep your sidewalks from cracking open to acacias' invasive roots, water trees infrequently, but deeply, to encourage taproots that plunge themselves deep into the ground in search for water.

Berberis
Barberry

Although there are more than four hundred species in this evergreen and deciduous genus, most are praised not for their fragrance, but rather for more practical garden contributions. Some varieties are formidable as barriers and hedges because of their abundant thorns. Other species are planted to camouflage leggy plants such as rhododendrons and azaleas or just for their showy, colorful (sometimes marbelized) foliage. Although many varieties are scented, some don't really smell nice, just strong.

The most popular species by far, and the most readily available from local nurseries, is *B. verruculosa*, commonly called the warty barberry. Besides being evergreen, it's hardy to 0° F, and grows into a neatly tailored, elegant shrub. Left to its own devices, it gets to be four feet tall and almost as wide, though it responds well to compact pruning. Leaves are a glossy, dark green, white underneath. During fall and winter, random leaves turn red and colorfully accent their emerald bushes.

In early summer, barberry's arching stems are covered with lemon yellow flowers that are sweetly scented. In fall, large, blackish purple berries form where the flowers were.

Barberry bushes are particularly valued in climates said to be "hard," meaning that there are extremes in temperatures. Barberry prefers sun, but tolerates shade; it also demands nothing more than "average" garden soil and moderate irrigation.

Betula
Birch

The reason we can legitimately include birches is that a couple of species within this genus of graceful trees and shrubs are actually praised for their scent.

B. alba, more commonly known as white or silver birch because of its starkly flashy, outer, often-peeling bark, is native to Britain and perfectly at home in America (it's the most frequently planted deciduous tree in the western United States). Trees grow to more than sixty feet tall and retain their grace no matter what their girth, which often grows to half their height. Birches make sensational trees for landscaping, especially when you carefully consider the breadth of plants available to you for planting beneath *B. alba*'s languid limbs or just next to her weeping boughs. Few people, however, know of the scented attributes of the flaky white bark.

Since the bark contains a powerful resin, it has often been used for making beer. When distilled, the bark yields the essence of the scent commonly known as Russian Leather. Birchbark oil was also once used to medicate soap for the treatment of eczema.

You might plant *B. lenta* simply for its landscape value and attractive, serrated, heart-shaped leaves, or because when stems and leaves are crushed, they emit a pleasant, clean aroma. If you ever intend to try distilling essential oils, you'll want to consider planting an entire grove of *B. lenta* since it's the most highly praised source for the essence of wintergreen. *Gaulthe-*

ria procumbens, the fragrant ground cover, is more commonly distilled as a source of wintergreen, but when fanciers want the real stuff, with no afterhint of black pepper, they plant the birch source.

Whole trees are chopped to the ground during the summer, and all parts are diced and placed to steam in a vat. Although only the innermost of the three layers of bark is saturated with the valuable oil of wintergreen, every shred of wood is distilled, so as not to miss a single expensive drop.

Established trees of *B. lenta* grow to more than eighty feet tall, so don't carelessly dot your lawn with them. Depending on how low you let their limbs arch, or weep, however, you can plant a lot underneath them.

Almost all species of birches produce cat-

When it comes to landscaping, *Betula* has few rivals; not only do birch trees mature into graceful trees with billowing branches, but also a host of plants are delighted to grow beneath their languid limbs. If it's the really smelly stuff you're after, you'll find it in the papery, ever-peeling bark of birch trees rather than in the faintly scented stems or leaves.

kins—berrylike, inedible cones. Although the catkins of even the otherwise fragrant varieties don't smell, particularly because of their ideal size they make nice additions to potpourri blends.

All varieties of birches share a love for water and a preference for loamy rather than sandy soil and sun rather than shade. Birches also share a nasty habit of attracting aphids that drip honeydew, although you can nip this mess in the bud by spraying trees just as leaves begin to unfurl and again two weeks later. Even with these precautions, however, I wouldn't park my new car under a birch tree if I were you.

Boronia

Boronias are small evergreen shrubs from Australia that aren't long-lived (they actually *look* frail because of their wispy growth habits), but are easily started over from seeds or cuttings. The fragrance of some flowers is thought to combine citrus and vanilla; in other varieties, scent is harbored in foliage.

By far the most widely grown variety in both the United States and Britain is *Boronia megastigma*, or brown boronia. Native to Australia's Perth area, brown boronia doesn't often get taller than two feet, but its four-petaled, shell-like flowers (chocolate outside, sulfur inside) bloom when little else does—in February and March.

I believe that all gardeners fond of fragrant plants are cursed by one variety they can't smell. *Boronia megastigma* is mine. While others swoon over its supposed verbenalike scent, I sniff in vain until I'm in danger of hyperventilating. I know, however, that my friends aren't pulling my leg because in Europe blooms of brown boronia are distilled by perfumers for their costly essence.

Boronias like to grow in slightly acid, sandy soil and must be watered carefully—they can't go dry; neither can they sit in water. Plan to replace bushes every three years.

Buddleia

In *The Scented Garden*, Rosemary Verey writes: "Shrubs of the genus *Buddleia*, being mostly vigorous and hardy, are too easy and accommodating to receive the attention that they deserve." Those words are sweet music to the ears of overworked gardeners; self-reliant plants

Buddleia isn't called the butterfly bush for nothing. Butterflies can't seem to get enough of its lush honey scent—neither will you if you plant the right varieties. Be sure to grant *Buddleia* its eternal wish to start anew each year by cutting shrubs back severely before spring triggers fresh growth.

such as these give us extra time for those that need constant babying.

Buddleia was discovered in China in 1869 by a French missionary, Père Armand David. He lent his name to the species *Davidii*, but named the genus in honor of Rev. Adam Buddle, an early eighteenth-century botanist. Today there are more than one hundred species, though *B. Davidii* is still the most popular, with numerous varieties available in colors from white to deep violet-purple.

Buddleia shrubs are elegant and fast growing. If planted in a sandy loam in full sun, a plant you buy in a one-gallon container will easily grow to eight feet in one season. Foliage is gray-green and willowlike, with leaves up to nine inches long. Tiny flowers appear in crowded masses that form long conical sprays. All are sweetly aromatic, with honey being the prevalent scent. Lush, full blooms appear in early summer. There is often a second, though inferior, bloom in fall.

Buddleia is also known as the butterfly bush. You'll see why if you admit just a single plant to your garden—when buddleias first begin to release their honey musk in early summer, butterflies you never saw before will suddenly cruise your garden in packs. Monarchs and swallowtails will converge on the plants, adding striking color contrasts to a bush already in full bloom. Many people make a point of planting buddleias outside their windows so they can enjoy both their delicious scents, wafted indoors on soft summer breezes, and the sight of fat butterflies weighing down floriferous spikes.

Beware of gardeners who speak of pruning plants "to the ground." One cringes, hearing about how they hacked down their roses, magnolias, and wisteria—plants deserving more-moderate treatment. *B. Davidii*, however, must be lopped off at the ankles each spring before new growth appears. Believe us, we know: when we planted buddleias in the sunny border of our garden, we pruned only lightly; the first-year plants had delighted everyone with their prolific, irresistible blooms, and we wanted still more. A short way into the next season, we realized that we would pay for our greed when bushes shot to heights of more than ten feet and half that wide. To cap it off, blooms were skimpy.

Another species, *B. alternifolia*, can be trained into a handsome, weeping willowlike tree. You must identify the plant's leading shoot early on (it will be the noticeably thicker one) and cut out all others until the trunk reaches five feet. The shoots that develop above this height will form dense heads that by mid-summer are covered in lavender-spiked flowers with an aroma like heliotrope. Prune *B. alternifolia* immediately after it blooms, keeping eyes ever on the watch for maintaining the desired weeping-tree shape.

Finally, there's *B. Fallowiana*, perhaps the most fragrant of all varieties. Its foliage is so closely covered with fine hairs that the plant takes on a silvery cast, providing a complementary background for the pale, lavender-blue panicles of bloom.

Buxus
Box

We considered saying that as far as our noses are concerned, box isn't notably fragrant, but decided that we didn't care to deal with the thousands of gardeners who swear that box is fragrant. Actually, box is more pungent than scented, especially when wet. In *Adventures in My Garden*, Louise Beebe Wilder wrote: "The pungent smell of the leaves is to me highly refreshing and stimulating, but all do not like it. Near me is a cottage half surrounded by a fine Boxwood hedge but of it the woman who dwells therein said, 'It's gloomy and I don't like the smell all through the day and night.'" Other plant lovers swear that not only is box scented, its fragrance is hypnotic.

In truth, we believe that box's sharp smell is an acquired fragrance for gardeners, somewhat as the rather bitter endive is an acquired taste for lettuce fanciers. Once you identify the odor, however you characterize it, the smell of box is unmistakable. More important, once you see what box can do for the architecture of your garden, you'll plant it whether or not you like its fragrance, even if you can't smell it at all, for box is the quintessential hedge, edger, and topiary plant.

Buxus is a genus of more than seventy evergreen shrubs and small trees native to the British Isles, South Africa, and Southeast Asia. Most species are impressively hardy.

B. sempervirens, often called common or English boxwood, is among the tallest of the boxwoods, often reaching heights greater than fifteen feet, with an equal spread. If left unclipped, plants become billowing masses. When pruned, *B. sempervirens* will assume practically any shape that suits you. Foliage is dark green, oval, dense, and leathery. Should you prefer to edge your garden (or just a section of it) with golden rather than green foliage, plant *B. sempervirens* 'Aurea'.

Buxus sempervirens 'Suffruticosa', or dwarf boxwood (sometimes called Dutch box), is perhaps the most valued dwarf hedging in all the garden. Though slow growing to four or five feet, it's usually clipped even lower to form a neat perimeter to beds of colorful annuals and perennials. Foliage is small and dense.

One day a neighbor came to our garden for a visit at the same time a gardener from England had arranged for a tour. Our local friend was interested mostly in our roses, but agreed to inspect the fragrant garden as well. Shortly into the tour, it was clear that we should never have tried to group our two visitors. The American knew of few plants, which seemed to increasingly annoy our British friend.

When we approached the beds of geraniums that are bordered in 'Suffruticosa', our local friend asked, "Well, I know why you want these fragrant geraniums, but why in the world did you outline them with that nasty boxwood that stinks so?"

The English woman was visibly shocked and made up an excuse about needing to return to a part of the garden that we had already visited, "to get a closer look." After she regained her composure, she joined us again and tolerated our far-less-knowledgeable localite, though we knew that she hadn't forgiven the slap at *Buxus*.

Box is said to grow best in chalky soil. Although *Buxus* prefers sun, it will tolerate shade. Box has few pests other than mites and scales, both of which are easily controlled with occasional spraying.

Box has few peers when it comes to garden architecture; if you want to create "rooms" within your garden, as Harold Nicholson did for Vita Sackville-West in their magnificent garden at Sissinghurst (shown here), be certain to consider *Buxus*. Where fragrance is concerned, however, box draws mixed reviews. Some gardeners relish its pungent scent; a few find it hypnotic; others swear it's gloomy.

Calycanthus
Allspice

Calycanthus is a genus of deciduous shrubs and small trees native to eastern Australia and the United States. They prefer well-drained, acid soil and protection from cold winds. *Calycanthus* is ideally planted next to a wall, where it will not only be sheltered, but will have a backdrop against which to show off its blossoms. *Calycanthus* has an unusually extended blooming period, beginning in early summer and extending into fall, when the blossoms are replaced by small, pear-shaped fruit.

C. floridus is native to North America and grows in abundance from Virginia to Florida, but is commonly known as the Carolina allspice. Shrubs that can be trained into multi-stemmed trees grow to eight-foot heights and about half as wide. Oval leaves that have dark green topsides and downy, gray-green undersides grow all along spreading branches and, when crushed, smell strongly of camphor. Two-inch flowers that are actually masses of narrow sepals and petals are reddish brown. Everyone seems to agree that the blooms smell like ripe fruit, although experts can't seem to agree on the specific fruit. Some say apples, others pineapple, a few insist on strawberries. The bark of *C. floridus* smells strongly of cinnamon and is sometimes used as a substitute for it, hence the nickname allspice.

C. occidentalis, or spice bush, is a lesser-known member of the genus, probably because it's not as aromatic as its cousin, though its flowers are showier. Bushes that grow to twelve-foot heights are covered with wide, oval-shaped leaves that are bright green during the growing season, then turn yellow in fall. Two-inch, reddish brown blooms shaped like small water lilies cover branches from April to August. Experts agree that the wood and leaves are pleasantly scented when crushed, but that the blooms smell at best like an old wine barrel.

Caryopteris
Bluebeard

The reason that gardeners who are fond of fragrance always include *Caryopteris* in their gardens is not really its fragrance (though its leaves are powerfully scented even if its flowers aren't), but rather for its contribution of blue from late summer until frost.

Caryopteris is a genus of deciduous, shrubby plants that are native to northern China and Japan. Because bluebeard is so hardy, it rarely freezes to the ground except in the most harsh climates. Where winters are mild or where the plants are protected because of their garden location, gardeners cut shrubs back to the ground each spring anyway and treat the plants as perennials.

C. incana, common bluebeard in America, blue spiraea in Britain, grows taller than other genus members—to three or four feet—has narrow, gray-green leaves and clusters of lavender-blue flowers borne in clusters at the ends of shoots and leaf axils. Foliage is downy

Blossoms of most *Calycanthus* look futuristic, with oddly colored, brownish maroon petals and sepals. While few fragrance fanciers agree on the precise perfume of the blossoms, everyone concurs that the bark of *Calycanthus* is redolent of cinnamon. At summer's end, bushes adorn themselves with small fruits.

on the underside, and when bruised smells strongly of spearmint.

C. clandonensis, or blue mist, is similar to *C. incana* in all respects except size. It rarely grows more than two feet tall and no wider. Three-inch-long narrow leaves mound the entire bush. Most varieties have periwinkle blue flowers, but two forms—azure and heavenly blue—are deep blue.

Chionanthus
Fringe Tree

Chionanthus is a member of the olive family, with only two species. The lower-growing variety, *C. retusus*, is native to China, whereas the loftier *C. virginicus* is native to the eastern United States from Pennsylvania to Florida, but most prevalent in Texas. Although both varieties are hardy throughout the world, they don't blossom until they're established. There are male and female plants, although you probably will never know the difference unless you have both, in which case you'll notice that the females produce fruits that look like olives and that male trees produce larger flowers.

C. retusus, often called the Chinese fringe tree, usually grows more like a shrub than a tree, although if content, can tower to twenty feet. Leaves are two to four inches long and hairy on their undersides. Panicles of white, four-inch, fragrant flowers with fringed petals appear sometime between May and July.

In the eastern United States *C. virginicus* is known as the fringe tree; in Texas it's called the snowflower tree. Leaves and flowers of the *C. virginicus* are about twice the size of its cousin *C. retusus*, though the blossoms are not as pungently scented (as if to make up for less perfume, they appear earlier, during late April).

In Texas established trees of *C. virginicus* grow to more than thirty feet tall; in northern European gardens they reach less than half that height. Blooms of *C. virginicus*, like their cousin, are pure white and droop in racemes over the entire tree. Blossoms have a purple spot at the base of each of their four or five narrow, fringed petals.

Leaves of both varieties turn yellow in fall. *Chionanthus* is among the last of the deciduous plants to leaf out each spring.

Choisya
Mexican Orange

Although there are six members of this genus of the rue family, you'll probably see only one variety outside of Mexico, where all are native. Only *C. ternata*, hardy to $15°$ F, is in general cultivation.

C. ternata grows rapidly to six to eight feet and about as wide. Bushes look more dense than they really are because of the way the leaves are formed. Foliage is lustrous, yellowish green, and appears toward ends of branches in fans of three leaves each. Because the leaves are set on the extremities of branches, they camouflage the sparsity of foliage beneath.

Flowers also appear at ends of branches and look quite similar to small orange blossoms.

When bruised, foliage of most *Caryopteris* (left) smells delightfully of spearmint, but that's not why most gardeners plant bluebeard; rather they plant it for its extended contribution of blue to the garden—from periwinkle to azure. Then, too, *Caryopteris* is unusually hardy and can be cut to the ground each spring just before next year's shapely growth takes off.

When they bloom, mature trees of *Chionanthus* droop with fragrant racemes of fringed petals like those on the right; hence the nickname fringe tree. Foliage disappears in winter and is among the last to sprout each spring. You should be forewarned that in most places fringe trees mature into large shrubs rather than trees.

The white blooms are pungently scented and fill the air with orange-blossom perfume in April and intermittently throughout summer.

When bushes are in bloom, you have a good chance to kill two birds with one stone. If you cut flowering branches to your heart's content to bring the scent of orange indoors, at the same time you keep bushes shapely; left uncut, they'll become straggly. Pruning and thinning bushes throughout the blooming season will force replacement wood to sprout from inside the bushes.

Although *Choisya* has few pests or diseases (frost causes damage, which can be cut off), it's fussy about the soil in which it grows, resenting alkaline soils or water with high levels of salts. Thoughtful gardeners plant *Choisya* in identical soil mixtures to those they prepare for their rhododendrons.

In cool-summer locales, *Choisya* prefers full sun. Where summers are hot, light shade is appreciated. If the spot you chose to plant your *Choisya* is too shady, bushes will become straggly and refuse to bloom. Wherever *Choisya* is planted, drainage should be quick and thorough; otherwise, roots may rot. Water infrequently, but deeply.

Cistus is nicknamed rockrose because its blossoms resemble those of wild roses. *Cistus* is famed, however, for its resinous foliage, which, when bruised, smells strongly of wood, usually balsam. This species, *C. skanbergii*, has bright rose-pink flowers, downy spicy foliage, and stems that smell like cedar. To keep your *Cistus* plants happy, rarely water them and prune only dead wood.

Cistus
Rockrose

The evergreen, shrubby *Cistus* came to be called the rockrose because bushes produce single blooms that resemble wild rose blossoms. The flowers themselves are not scented; it's the resinous leaves that release a balsamic perfume, especially when bruised.

Cistus is a genus of about twenty species native to the Mediterranean and the Iberian Peninsula. Plants vary from low shrubs only one foot high to upright bushes to eight feet. Most are hardy to 15° F. The saucer-shaped flowers, usually with five petals, are papery thin and have conspicuous stamens. Blossoms of most varieties open in the morning and drop their petals at the end of each day (some last two to three days, never longer). Bushes are so laden with buds, however, that rockroses stay in bloom for two or three months if the weather is sunny.

C. x *hybridus*, or white rockrose, is perhaps the most widely grown variety in the United States. It makes a spreading bush two to five feet high and about as wide. Leaves are two inches long, gray-green, and crinkly. Pure

white flowers with yellow centers appear in early spring.

C. ladanifer is for some reason more popular in Britain than in America, though it's our personal favorite. Also known as the gum cistus or crimson-spot rockrose, this variety produces blossoms that are four inches across. The blooms are pure white except for a crimson blotch at the base of each petal. Leaves are long, narrow, dark green, and gummy to the touch. They release their balsamlike fragrance throughout the summer, especially in the morning.

C. skanbergii is also more popular among the English than with Americans. Bushes are covered with gray, downy foliage that is spicy with fragrance. Stems are thought to smell like cedar. Bright rose-pink flowers that never last longer than one day cover bushes during midsummer.

C. salviifolius, often marketed as *C. villosus* 'Prostratus' is also known as sageleaf rockrose. Bushes grow only two feet high, but have a spread to six feet across. Foliage is light gray-green, veined, and crinkled. Flowers that are white with yellow splotches at the base of their petals bloom profusely in late spring. *C. salviifolius* is praised as a ground cover.

Rockroses are sun lovers, tolerant of poor soil, fast growing, and drought resistant. In California they are widely planted in fire-hazard areas. Where naturalized, bushes will tolerate anything from cold, salt-laden ocean winds to dry desert heat.

Since *Cistus* hybrids don't breed true from seeds, they should be propagated from three- to four-inch cuttings from half-ripened wood in July and August. After they have rooted, plants should be potted up, since they resent transplanting.

We made a terrible mistake with our rockroses the first year we cultivated them by assuming that they would respond to pruning. They don't, and few of them recovered. We have since learned to remove only dead and frost-damaged wood and to encourage bushy growth by pinching tips of new shoots to thicken growth beneath.

Citrus

It is with a certain resentment that we include this entry, since we've had almost total failure with citruses. For fragrance fanciers who garden where Jack Frost never visits, however, citruses are musts. Or, if you're fortunate enough to have an orangery and the staff to maintain it, be advised that citruses make good container plants and winter-over well in greenhouses.

Shortly after he finished designing our fragrant garden, Stephen Suzman had a party to show off the plans for his inspired creation. He had also just begun buying plants that were shortly to be installed in focal points. Among the first species purchased were Bouquet de Fleur citruses that were intended to grow in two matching beds, along with jasmines, gardenias, and wallflowers.

If you live where the thermometer dips much below 30° F, you may not be able to grow citrus at all, except in pots and movable boxes—not much of a compromise, since many citruses have an affinity for container culture. If you garden in a more temperate climate, however, you can bring to blossom one of the most intensely fragrant of all flowers (be sure not to pick them if you want fruits to follow).

Before deciding to give citrus a try, read *Citrus, How to Select, Grow and Enjoy* by Richard Ray and Lance Walheim.

A couple of days before the party, Stephen called to ask if he might use indoors one of our twelve potted Bouquet de Fleur citruses to scent his house. We happily agreed, looking forward to sniffing for ourselves. On the evening of the party, we didn't need the nose of a bloodhound to track down the lusty orange scent: that one plant filled the entire house with a sensuous, heady perfume.

From reading the preface, you know that our beloved citruses lasted only one year; an unusually cold snap the following winter knocked flat our even dozen Bouquet de Fleur plants.

The next season we stubbornly replanted, this time choosing Meyer Lemon, said to be highly frost tolerant. Same story as for the earlier citruses, only this time, there were four crippled survivors. Two citrus fiascos were enough; the following year we planted dwarf apple trees that now grow as contentedly as do our roses—their first cousins.

Still determined to grow *some* citruses, we have managed to squeeze in a few blood oranges and kumquats (the hardiest of the citrus clan) in particularly protected spots. When danger of frost is forecast, covering these few plantings doesn't seem like an unreasonable chore.

Perfume distillers grow citruses in abundance, for no chemical substitute found to date can compare with the natural essence of citrus. If you want your citruses to fruit, of course, limit your smelling to flowers on the plants. If you pick blossoms, no fruit will follow.

Clethra

Although *Clethra* is a sizable genus, only two species are in general cultivation, the rest being too tender for all but the most temperate climates. The plant is named after the Greek *Klethra*, or alder tree, which its leaves resemble.

C. alnifolia is native to the eastern United States and commonly known as summersweet, sweet pepperbush, or mignonette tree. The deciduous shrub grows to a height of ten feet with thin, strong branches that arrange themselves vertically. Scented leaves that don't appear until late spring are dark green, two to four inches long, and toothed along the edges. In late summer the tips of branches droop with four- to six-inch-long racemes of sweetly scented, creamy white flowers. Many gardeners plant *C. alnifolia* close to where they grow their rhododendrons, since they like the same soil and light. Plants respond well to clipping and make attractive informal hedges.

C. arborea, or lily-of-the-valley tree, is evergreen and native to Madeira. The graceful tree grows at a moderate rate to twenty feet and is densely clothed with narrow, shiny, dark green leaves. In late summer or early fall pure white, urn-shaped flowers appear that resemble lily of the valley, even to the scent. Trees like to grow in peaty soil and are sensitive to cold; although if damaged, the plant will grow again from old wood, even from its roots if frostbitten to the ground.

Check carefully the varieties of hawthorn you choose— they don't all smell good, or at least not after they lose their fresh balsamic fragrance. On the plus side are handsome spiny trees with smashing winter berries.

Crataegus
Hawthorn

The fact that we have included hawthorn in this book is not necessarily an endorsement. Its varieties aren't always fragrant, and those that are often smell bad rather than good. That's because their essential oils contain trimethylamine, which gives them a fishy overtone. The blooms aren't always unpleasant though; in their early stages they emit an agreeable balsamic, in some cases almondlike, fragrance. Blossoms start smelling tacky after they've been around a while or when midges have just pollinated them. In any case plant hawthorn at a distance from your home to prevent unpleasant aromas from wafting indoors.

Hawthorns do have their pluses: first, their lovely, spiny, upright growth. Their stems have decorative, long, widely spaced thorns and attractive pinnate leaves. Whether or not you like the scent of their flowers, the blooms are pretty in their formation of terminal cymes. Finally, trees produce heavy clumps of haws, their berries (in some cases edible). Fruits last well into winter, shriveling but not losing color. Blooms are white, pink, or red, the latter having the least scent. Berries may be yellow, orange, or any of several shades of red. Hawthorns make stunning street trees with their distinguished, conical shapes to twenty-five feet. Leaves of all hawthorn varieties turn some autumn color before they drop.

Hawthorn is first cousin to the rose, so it's not without needs. Like its demanding relatives, it likes full sun, lots of water and nutrients, good drainage, and protection against insects, who love its succulent growth just as much as they do that of roses. Some varieties are more disease resistant than others, particularly *C. Phaenopyrum*, which has handsome open limbs and white flowers followed by bright red berries.

Daphne

If you ask gardeners devoted to scented plants to name the most persnickety plant they grow, many will say daphne. But if you ask these same perfume fanciers to choose their favorite, most seductive scent, they may say daphne again. Daphne makes backyard gardeners seem schizophrenic. One moment they tell you that they've *had* it with some daphne or another; the next time you see them they insist that you stop by for a whiff of the very same variety that they had just vowed to banish from their gardens. Why do we tolerate such duplicity?

I think it's the scent. For while all of us addicted to perfume gather things we like to sniff while walking through a scented garden, we'll always find room in our clutches for a sprig of daphne. Daphne's fragrance is irresistible because its blossoms harbor many distinct scents all at once. Lemon is there, to be sure, but so is honey and roasted nutmeg. Then there's per-

Each fall hawthorn trees turn an autumnal shade, drop their leaves, and form hawks—yellow, orange, or red berries (some edible, others poisonous). Although the fruits may shrivel as winter progresses, they retain brilliant colors.

fume *power*. Daphne is so strongly fragrant that a mere sprig of the more-intoxicating varieties can scent a whole room. If you bury your nose in daphne rosettes, you'll be bowled over by their bawdy perfume.

Although there are more than four hundred evergreen and deciduous daphnes to choose among, we've grown only five—the same ones you're likely to try, because they're the most readily available varieties: *D.* x *Burkwoodii*, *D. Cneorum*, *D. Mezereum*, *D. odora*, and *D.* x *Burkwoodii* 'Somerset'.

If you live where winters are cruel, you may have to content yourself with *D. Mezereum*, the only truly hardy variety. If so, you should steel yourself for *D. Mezereum*'s habits. Plants grow best from seeds that take at least two years to germinate, after which they put on only a foot of growth in a *decade*! No garden spot seems to accelerate *D. Mezereum*'s growth, but if it's not planted in deep, cool soil, it won't even budge. At its happiest, *D. Mezereum* grows no taller than four feet, and its bush is gawky with leaves that look fragile.

When they finally appear, however, its blooms are a welcome sight. Nothing much else is blooming from the New Year through March; and even if something were, you'd probably not notice its fragrance anyway after getting a whiff of *D. Mezereum*'s tiny, purple-pink flowers with bright orange stamens. There is a deeper colored form, *D. Mezereum* 'rubra', and a white variety, *D. Mezereum* 'Alba'. In all forms poisonous berries follow the blooms.

Something else you must know if you decide to plant *D. Mezereum* is that it resents being cut, especially when in bloom—just when you yearn to take your shears to it. Think of *D. Mezereum* as your contribution to the winter garden and traipse outside when the impulse to revel in its aroma overwhelms you.

D. Cneorum might also do for those of you who dwell where winters are harsh. It is native to southern Europe, where it's praised as a top-notch alpine plant. Known also as the garland flower, *D. Cneorum* bears sweetly scented, rose-pink blossoms in terminal clusters each May and again in August. Since it is evergreen, *D. Cneorum* looks like an agreeable garden plant even when it's not in bloom.

A fine British horticulturist, Albert Burkwood, tried his hand at hybridizing daphne and hit the jackpot when he crossed *D. Cneorum* with *D. caucasica*, a deciduous shrub from the Caucasus. One promising offspring would have been reward enough, but Burkwood delivered two lovely sisters. The first, *D.* x *Burkwoodii*, produces clusters of fragrant, white flowers around the tips of branches on a three- to four-foot plant. Though often planted as an edging, *D.* x *Burkwoodii* also mixes well in an informal border of shrubs. Still, although considerably less temperamental than most of her cousins and quite pretty on her own, I'm afraid *D.* x *Burkwoodii* is almost homely next to her ravishing sister, *D.* x *Burkwoodii* 'Somerset'.

More robust than her sister, 'Somerset' gets at least a foot and a half taller and proportionately more plump. Her disposition is nicer too.

When we planted our fragrant garden, we included everything we knew to be scented and many more plants that we hadn't actually smelled but that were tempting, according to what we had read or heard. A few proved to be flops, most performed tolerably well, but a few outdid themselves. 'Somerset' tops the list of overachievers. I remember the early March day

If you're the least bit serious about fragrance, you have no choice but to grow daphne, even though its temperament is bound to irk you (daphne seems bred with a mind all its own). When you finally see eye to eye with certain varieties, however, you can produce blossoms with irresistible scents—intoxicating blends of honey, lemon, and spice. *D.* x *Burkwoodii* 'Somerset' is our favorite.

we planted two bushes of 'Somerset'. The plants seemed healthy enough, although the foliage was an off-color, grayish green and looked moody. "Just another daphne showing how finicky it is," we said as we gave the bushes a loving nudge into their new, permanent, we hoped, holes.

Late that May the plants produced scads of clusters of pinkish white, intensely fragrant blossoms. 'Somerset' was pronounced an instant hit, and we looked forward to the next year's crop, even though we didn't really have any idea what a treat was in store for us.

In spring of the following year, both bushes were cloaked in new growth, with buds everywhere you looked. Whereas the first spring's bloom had been restricted to clusters of flowers at stem ends, this time there wasn't a leaf in sight. While we grow many plants that cover themselves with their flushes of bloom—old garden roses, wisterias, clematises, viburnums—in all cases *some* foliage or plant framework is visible. But we could see nothing but bloom on 'Somerset' and had to think hard to remember what the plant looked like before the floral shower. And the fragrance! If you stood somewhere between the two bushes on a warm evening that late May, you were in danger of swooning.

Our two magnificent bushes of 'Somerset' are planted in the sunny border of our garden, with Irish yew planted all along the north edge and with a few jutting south to form compartments. One day Robert was leading a group of gardeners around his scented plot. When one woman rounded a yew finger and came face-to-face with her first wide-open 'Somerset', she stopped so abruptly that she actually skidded on the pea-gravel path.

"What's *that?*" she blurted.

"Daphne 'Somerset'," Robert replied coolly, pretending that it looked that way most of the time.

"What did you *do* to it?" the gardener pleaded, as if begging for a secret growing tip.

"Not much, really," Robert admitted. "It's hard to treat plants much differently from their neighbors when they're planted as close as these in this border. We try to mulch in extra leaf mold and always make certain that the irrigation emitters right next to it aren't clogged."

It was clear that the enthusiast hadn't yet heard what she wanted to learn. "No, I mean how did you get it to *bloom* like that—all at once!" she exclaimed impatiently.

Robert confessed that he couldn't take credit for that. 'Somerset' simply puts on its magnificent show all at once. The performance is in three acts. Act One, really a prologue, begins when buds appear at every nook and cranny along all visible wood. The drama becomes heavy in Act Two, when blooms open fully for three weeks. Act Three is short, no longer than ten days of quick aftermath. There is sometimes a modest second blooming in August, with flowers just as sweetly scented, but not displayed nearly so spectacularly.

And now to the fussiest of all. *D. odora* is so highly prized by gardeners where winters are temperate that they are bound and determined to have it, no matter how many times they must stubbornly replant. Bushes that you caress into adjacent identical holes grow as though they're in different time zones. After talking with numerous gardeners with similar "I can't *imagine* what caused that daphne to die" stories, I've decided that there *is* no answer. It's as though *D.*

Daphne odora looks finicky, don't you think? There's only one conceivable reason why we gardeners devoted to fragrance insist on growing it—the flowers of *D. odora* harbor the quintessential daphne fragrance. A clutch of only a few fresh, turgid blossoms handily perfumes an entire room.

odora were hybridized with some evil, recessive gene that causes a percentage of offspring to suddenly self-destruct.

The reason we fragrance freaks stumble over our garden tools to keep *D. odora* in our gardens is its seductive perfume, the quintessential daphne fragrance. Why else should we tolerate such an ungrateful plant? Blossoms are pink to deep rose on the outside, with creamy throats. They flower in nosegay clusters on the tips of branches on neat bushes that usually get to be about four feet tall and a bit wider. Foliage is narrow, but thick and glossy. There is a pure white variety, *D. odora* 'Alba', and *D. odora* 'Rose Queen' blooms larger flowers.

Of the five bushes of *D. odora* we originally planted in our garden, three still flourish. First to die was the one that came to rest in a perfectly prepared hole in a prime garden spot. The second went belly-up right next to one that contentedly doubled its size in three years.

Besides everything else, *D. odora* is no better than half-hardy. Where it is grown in Europe, it's restricted to sheltered spots like those in front of a wall facing south. I know gardeners so determined to have *D. odora* that they plant it in large containers fitted onto casters, which allow them to rush out and drag the whole plant inside when there's danger of a freeze. On the other extreme, I've seen bushes of daphne more than ten feet tall and almost as wide that freeze to some degree every winter.

While daphne prospers in full sun in cool summer climates, it prefers shelter where summers are hot or where the noonday sun reflects from walls or walkways. Whether the heat is direct or reflected, daphne's roots should be kept cool, an objective best achieved by anchoring them in humus-laden soil deeply enriched with leaf mold. A scattering of lime rubble or a liberal amount of mortar where roots are to anchor themselves helps too.

Just to keep us confused, some daphnes fancy shade rather than sunlight. *D. Laureola*, the spurge-laurel, thrives in shade all over Britain. *D. pontica* not only prefers dense shade, it likes poor drainage too. *D. retusa* complicates daphne cultivation even more by preferring no lime at all in the soil in which it grows.

Although we'd love to have some yellow daphne, we've steered clear of them because of what we've read about their habits. *D. aurantiaca* is reputed to be one of the loveliest daphnes in cultivation. Its evergreen bushes reach three feet and are covered in fragrant, golden yellow flowers each March. Alas, bushes are tender and rare in cultivation except in central China, where they are native. *D. Giraldii*

is far more hardy and even germinates well, but the blooms, although typical of daphne form, have no notable fragrance. We have no intentions of pampering some scentless daphne.

Daphne resents being transplanted or growing on roots other than its own, so plants should be set out as small as your patience will bear. It grows at glacial speed, but sluggish growth beats the pain of seeing an adolescent wither and die for no apparent reason. If your patience makes Job seem rash, you might try planting daphne from seed. Just remember that some varieties take more than two years to germinate. I can't imagine having a garden with so much spare room that I could allow some areas to remain bare for two years after seeding them. In that amount of time, I'd surely find an annual that suited me for that spot and settle for instant reward.

Daphne must be watered regularly, but never too much at a time, and drainage must be quick and thorough. Daphne roots like water, but they rot if they sit in it. Other than root rot, daphne is vulnerable to infestation by aphids. (I'm also told that it is stunted by cucumber mosaic virus.) Fertilizers aren't essential, but occasional top dressings of peat moss and sand accelerate root development. Pruning isn't recommended at all, for once bushes get large enough to need shaping, you'll keep them trim enough by snitching their fragrant blooms for the house (even though almost every reference you check tells you not to).

If our garden had to be cut in half for some reason or other and I was told that I could grow only two of the five daphne varieties we now cultivate, I'd abandon *D. Mezereum* and *D. Cneorum* in a flash. The former is too poky to suit me, and the latter is puny compared to *D.* x *Burkwoodii* and 'Somerset', although it resembles them. Next, I'd reluctantly hand over my *D.* x *Burkwoodii*. Although she's a beauty, her sibling is a stunner.

I'd really be in a pickle trying to choose between 'Somerset' and *D. odora*. Were I to base my decision only on fragrance, or course, I'd choose *D. odora*. For sheer beauty, 'Somerset' would be a shoo-in. In fact, that's it—if I could grow only one daphne, it would be 'Somerset'. It might not be as powerfully perfumed as its cousin, but it smells mighty nice, and wait until you see it burst into full bloom!

Davidia involucrata
Handkerchief Tree

If you're ever looking for a single tree to dramatically dot your lovely lawn, consider planting *D. involucrata*. The handkerchief tree is to trees in May what the poinsettia is to shrubs in December. Each spring small greenish yellow flowers with red anthers appear on long stalks. The blooms are nothing to write home about, but what follows is worth considerable praise: pairs of bracts of unequal size (the larger up to seven inches) hang from the tree, making the entire plant look like a resting place for creamy white doves.

Besides being called the Chinese dove tree, *D. involucrata* is also known as the ghost tree. The reason it is more commonly called the handkerchief tree is that when covered with creamy bracts, the tree looks like a conical clothesline for freshly laundered linen handkerchiefs.

After the bracts appear, the show continues with the formation of fruits not unlike walnuts that hang on well into winter. Even after the deciduous nature of this genus of a single species causes the tree to drop everything, it's still a pretty sight because of its lovely shape.

Nothing said so far has anything to do with fragrance. The smelly stuff is captured entirely within the tree's eye-catching, vivid green foliage. When crushed, leaves give off a pungent, incenselike scent.

Even though handkerchief trees make the perfect exclamation-mark accents for lawns, they're also beautifully at home in the foreground of darker-leaved, flowerless trees, particularly conifers. Except for the green of lime trees, nothing else seems as brilliantly green as the foliage of *D. involucrata*.

Handkerchief trees are generally considered to be hardy, but in cruel winter climates, it's wise to plant trees where they'll receive some form of warming shelter. They appreciate some amount of shade and require only moderate water. If content where they grow, handkerchief trees (especially in California) gracefully tower to more than forty feet.

Elaeagnus

There are forty-five species of these practical shrubs. They are particularly useful if you need to landscape over poor soil, since they thrive in barren land, even if sea winds blow over them. But you don't need desolate conditions to grow the species well; bushes also thrive in fertile terrains.

Some varieties get to be small trees, but most grow between six and eight feet tall and make graceful bushes. Almost all species have pretty green or golden leaves with silvery undersides.

Don't plant *Elaeagnus* for its flowers. Blooms are powerfully fragrant, but you must know precisely where to search to see them at all, even if your nose keeps telling you that you're on the right track. Blooms appear at leaf axils, almost entirely camouflaged by foliage.

E. commutata, also known as the Missouri silver tree, is the North American native. It's deciduous, dropping its leaves with the first hard frost. Small, pale yellow, scented flowers appear in concealed spots in early summer, followed by bright silver berries.

E. glabra is evergreen and makes a luxurious

Davidia isn't famed for its flowers, which are small and insignificant, but rather for what follows the bloom—pairs of creamy white bracts, then fruits about the size of walnuts. When a tree is in its full glory with pale foliage, it looks like a drying rack for fresh laundry. The handkerchief tree's fragrance is harbored in its foliage—bright green leaves that when crushed smell like incense.

hedge with its long, tapering leaves on smooth stems. Tiny, white, pungent flowers appear coyly in early autumn.

E. macrophylla is our favorite. Shiny, evergreen leaves with silvery scales underneath give bushes a cool look even during summer's peak. White flowers that smell something like daphne last throughout autumn.

The deciduous *E. multiflora* has two distinctions unique to the genus: flowers smell like lilac and are followed by orange edible berries.

Last Christmas we made wreaths from plants we were going to have to cut back anyway—rosemary, poplar suckers, myrtle, and several herbs. When we began running out of plant materials for wreath frameworks, we cast covetous eyes toward our *Elaeagnus*. Its bushes could certainly afford to give up some growth, but we wondered if its foliage would suit the purpose, since leaves are spaced widely apart. They worked perfectly—in fact, the wide space between the leaves proved to be an advantage. With the stems massed over one another, the leaves on some filled gaps on others, and the dark grayish green foliage complemented everything we tied on top.

Eucalyptus

Although eucalyptuses occur naturally only in Australia, Tasmania, and New Zealand, they're cropping up everywhere because of hybridizers' determination to breed hardiness into the genus. To date, there are more than six hundred species, hybrids, and varieties. No other tree rivals the eucalyptus in variation of size at maturity, from shrubs less than 10 feet to the tallest broad-leaved tree ever recorded—373 feet.

Eucalyptuses made their California debut in 1856, after which they were planted so widely for windbreaks, shade, firewood, and in places where nothing else would survive, that you can now travel hundreds of California miles without ever losing sight of some eucalyptus variety. There are several reasons why eucalyptuses caught on so well. First, they are pretty trees with stunning foliage and, once established, bear attractive, fragrant blossoms. Second, eucalyptuses are tolerant of most soils and many climates—from hillsides to deserts. Finally, eucalyptuses are fast growers—to fifteen feet per year during early growth of some species.

If you're in search of bushes with large flowers, don't choose *Elaeagnus*. If it's fragrance you seek, however, please consider one of the powerfully perfumed species, like this one—*E. umbellata*; the autumn olive is as showy as *Elaeagnus* gets. Some gardeners believe that certain *Elaeagnus* species smell as nice as daphne; others say lilac.

Eucalyptus foliage is consistently notable, but differs vastly as plants mature. On seedlings and saplings, foliage is soft, randomly shaped, and more gray than green. As trees mature, foliage becomes uniform, long, tapered, and greener.

Even more remarkable than its foliage is the bark of the eucalyptus. The smooth outer bark of most varieties is deciduous and, once trees are four to five years old, peels off each winter to expose creamy bark underneath that darkens into intricate, mottled patterns.

Prolific flowering doesn't commence for most varieties until they are about five years old. Even then they take their time maturing—what first appear as buds on leaf axils open a year later into one-inch tufts of stamens with petals that are no more than fragrant filaments.

Not only the blossoms of eucalyptuses are fragrant. In fact, leaves and twigs are even more redolent of eucalyptus oil. The essence is reputed as useful for diseases of the lungs. Undiluted, the power of the fragrance is overwhelming. When cut, we know it as the essence of Noxzema. While most varieties are praised for their medicinal scent, others smell strongly of peppermint, spearmint, or citrus.

Eucalyptuses have their drawbacks, mostly the messiness. Besides leaves that fall throughout the year, mostly in winter, bark flakes off. As though that weren't enough, trees drip resinous oils, binding together all their droppings.

By far the most commonly grown variety in the western United States is *E. Globulus*, or blue gum ("blue" from the color of the foliage, "gum" from the balsamic gum that exudes from the tree trunk). *E. Globulus*, although fragrant throughout, isn't for anyone who lives in a city or anywhere else where it can't be given lots of room to scramble as many as one hundred feet, with masses of leaves that regularly drop to the ground, preventing anything else from growing just beneath the spreading tree.

E. Gunnii is becoming increasingly popular because it doesn't grow as tall as other varieties (usually to thirty feet) and because it's among the hardiest of varieties. Also known as cider gum, *E. Gunnii* tolerates temperatures down to 5° F.

While visiting a botanical garden in Hawaii, we saw for ourselves the variety we'd most like to grow. *E. citriodora*, also known as lemon-

If you decide to plant *Eucalyptus*, you have some selecting in store (there are more than six hundred choices). *E. Dalrympleana* (below, left) has the most vividly colored bark of any variety. Other species, like those below on the right, mature into graceful trees that have fragrant leaves, peeling bark, and, in time, perfumed blossoms.

scented gum, is a lovely tree that graces almost any landscape, assuming you have the room for it to thrust its slender trunk to one hundred feet and assuming that you don't live someplace where temperatures dip below 24° F. Although its bark isn't as dramatic as its cousin E. Dalrympleana (the most vividly colored bark of any eucalyptus variety), it does shed its tan bark to turn powder pink. All parts smell strongly of lemon-scented gum.

Eucalyptus trees that are properly planted where they like to grow will thrive with moderate watering and practically no fertilizing, other than the addition of iron when leaves turn a telltale yellow.

Eucalyptuses growing in the United States knew no pests until 1984. During that year, the eucalyptus longhorn beetle somehow found its way to American shores. Since no natural predators came along, these beetles have become a serious problem, leaving their devastating oval holes in trunks and branches.

Eucryphia

Although there are five or six species (all of them fragrant) in this genus native to South America, Australia, and Tasmania, you'll probably see only two varieties for sale—the rest are just too tender to suit no-nonsense gardeners. Even the few species you manage to find will need extra wintering-over precautions. With

the help of some rather cushy straw matting, our few *Eucryphia* bushes have survived a couple of winters that some citruses couldn't handle.

If you don't have to worry about freezing temperatures or if you're willing to provide a little extra winter shelter, try *Eucryphia*, particularly if you like honey-scented, white flowers with yellow, pink, or red anthers.

Both the most strongly scented and the most readily available species, *E. lucida*, grows differently throughout the world. In Britain it's called a dwarf (up to ten feet) tree. In the eastern United States, where *E. lucida* also grows to ten-foot heights, it is called a shrub because its girth is usually more than half its height. In California, growing to more than thirty feet almost as though it were a native, *E. lucida* is called a slender evergreen tree. In America *Eucryphia* boasts large, fragrant, white blossoms in summer; in England the show takes place closer to fall.

Wherever it grows, *E. lucida* is smothered in densely leaved, dark green, oblong foliage. The large, white blossoms are borne on short stems from leaf axils.

E. x nymansensis is more tender than its sister, but it also grows faster—to more than fifteen feet, with half as much spread. Foliage that doesn't all look alike is lustrous, green, and abundant.

Although *Eucryphia* species are said to grow

If you're bored with colorless Februarys, consider adding forsythia to your garden— few flowering shrubs bloom earlier or with more-vividly colored blossoms (usually yellow, like those below, left). Only two species are noted for their fragrance.

Forsythias are favored shore plants. You'll understand why if you ever see them planted above a pond, the way they are below, right.

in neutral soil, ours have performed best in acid soil—that just adjacent to our rhododendron and azalea dell. Pruning isn't necessary, just pinching occasional lead shoots to encourage bushiness is sufficient. If you can keep them over winter, *Eucryphia* species are generally pest and disease free.

Forsythia

If you, like us, appreciate early signs of spring, give forsythia a spot in your garden; no other deciduous flowering shrub is more grateful for February's meager sun than forsythia, and except for witch hazel nothing blooms earlier. The genus *Forsythia* was named in honor of William Forsyth, the celebrated English botanist and former superintendent of the Royal Gardens. Most members of the seven species have yellow flowers, but only two are fragrant.

F. Giraldiana is the more popular of the scented species, probably because it's the hardier grower—to ten feet, with almost as much girth. The foliage that appears after the vanilla-perfumed, light yellow blossoms have dropped is a rich green, tinted bronze. *F. ovata* grows more slowly than its sister, rarely to more than five feet tall, but its pure gold blossoms are just as sweetly scented.

Forsythias are easy to grow, tolerant of light shade and almost any soil. Because they look so nice reflected in water, forsythias are favored plantings for bank covers. When forsythias bloom, no foliage is in sight, and the plants literally transform their naked branches into cascades of four-petaled, tubular flowers. After the glamorous show is over, bushes settle down with handsome lush foliage that looks good next to any plant. Prune forsythia immediately after it blooms by cutting to the ground old and weak wood—up to a third of the bush.

Franklinia

It's a mystery why this genus of a single deciduous species isn't more prevalent, since it's one of the world's most beautiful trees and grows easily from seed. Before it was indiscriminately cleared from riverbanks along with timber, *F. Alatamaha* was discovered in Georgia in 1765 by a botanist who named his find for Benjamin Franklin.

F. Alatamaha slowly grows to more than twenty feet tall, retaining its elegant shape all the while. The slender trunk is reddish tan and faintly striped. Spoon-shaped leaves up to six inches long are bright green during the growing season, then turn crimson in fall. Chalice-like, white blossoms appear in late summer. As do other members of the tea family, such as magnolias and gardenias, franklinias smell strongly of vanilla. Blooms may last well into fall. Franklinias like to grow in the same garden spots rhododendrons like.

Trees of *Franklinia* are slow growers, but eventually reach twenty feet and are consistently elegant, regardless of their height. Leaves are long, shaped like spoons, and turn crimson in fall. In late summer, just when foliage begins to redden, white, vanilla-scented blossoms appear and persist until winter.

Gardenia

Hardly anyone, gardener or not, is ambivalent toward gardenias. For some, gardenia's luscious scent is *it* where fragrance is concerned. For others, it's vulgar. For southerners, especially those with warm brick walls, gardenias are a must; properly placed, they're practically carefree. Gardeners in chillier climates, however, must adore gardenias sufficiently to go to the trouble of overwintering them under glass. In southwest Louisiana and southeast Texas, near the Gulf of Mexico, gardenias grow wild in cemeteries from potted plants that rooted after being left there. In Provence, French devotees *keep* their gardenias in large terra-cotta pots and bring them indoors during winter. The only fact upon which all these gardeners agree is that, whatever they think of it, nothing else smells quite like the gardenia.

Although there are more than 250 species of these tender evergreen shrubs (occasionally small trees), only one species is in general cultivation—*G. jasminoides* (also known as cape jasmine), with forms ranging in height from less than one foot to more than ten feet and in growth habits ranging from ground cover to gargantuan bush.

Except in China, where it grows native, *G. jasminoides* isn't modest in its needs. The soil in which it is planted must simultaneously drain quickly and retain moisture (best answered by incorporating lots of peat moss during cultivation. As with rhododendrons and azaleas, gardenias should be planted "high" or in raised beds, and their roots shouldn't be crowded or placed where they'll have to compete for nutrients. Finally, gardenias should be fed every three weeks with an acid plant food, and regularly sprayed for aphids. Even with all this pampering, flower buds refuse to set unless the minimum temperature is at least 60° F (even then, buds will drop if temperatures vary too widely).

Gardenia foliage is glossy, dark green, and arranged in whorls of three leaves. Heavily scented, waxlike blossoms, whether single or double, are white and up to four inches across.

When we planted *G. jasminoides* in our garden, we chose 'Mystery', mainly because it's the most floriferous form for our area, but also because its rangy growth habits respond well to shapely pruning. Although touted to be hardy to 20° F, our plants appear to be rudely shocked by every hard frost that comes along. They do bloom nicely toward the end of summer, sometimes continuing into fall, but we're certain that they would blossom more spectacularly if our summers were warmer. When they do bloom, however, we're swayed toward that camp of perfume fanciers who wouldn't dream of a garden without gardenias. Blooms shouldn't be cut with stems too long and shouldn't be fingered at all (body oils discolor petals). Finally, blossoms are best floated in a bowl, with the bloom held well above the water's surface.

We also tried *G. jasminoides* 'radicans' because it's a superb ground cover for areas that you won't really walk on. Although this form of jasmine spreads two to three feet, it never gets more than one foot tall. Dark green leaves randomly streaked with white provide a handsome background for one-inch gardenia blooms that look like miniature carbon copies of their larger relatives.

We know a fashionable woman who, just like Bette Davis in *Now Voyager*, wouldn't dream of attending a socially important event without a solitary gardenia pinned somewhere on her apparel. When no gardenias bloom in her own garden, she unhesitatingly pays a small fortune to purchase them out of season; they're her trademark. When someone intimates that gardenias are too powerfully scented, she counters with, "That's because you try to smell too many of them at once—one blossom is perfection."

Halesia
Snowdrop Tree

Native to North America, *H. carolina* is nicknamed snowdrop tree because its fragrant, milky white flowers actually resemble hanging snowdrops. *H. carolina* blooms in May, just when foliage begins to appear. Leaves grow to be four inches long, oval, and toothed. In the fall they turn yellow and look good with the small brown fruits that hang on well into winter. If you want a snowdrop tree, you must prune young *H. carolina* to a single stem. Otherwise, plants become large shrubs.

Halesia grows best in well-irrigated, deep soil that is rich in humus—the same garden conditions as for rhododendrons. In fact, snowdrop trees are favored overhead plantings for azalea and rhododendron dells, especially when they grow tall enough to look up into when they're in bloom.

Because they're both deciduous and members of the storax family, *Halesia* is often confused with *Styrax japonicus*, the Japanese snowbell. If you prefer your snow flowers on a tree rather than on a bush, the Japanese would suggest that you plant their *Styrax* instead of *Halesia* because plants seem to naturally develop into graceful trees.

Snowbell trees bloom in June after foliage has developed, and the fragrant blossoms hang from branches, whereas their leaves contrastingly point upward. Like its cousin, *Halesia*, *Styrax* prefers rich, well-drained soil and plenty of water.

Hamamelis
Witch Hazel

Witch hazel is something of an acquired smell. When you first see its flowers, you'll probably think that they're some sort of disfigured foliage and doubt whether they harbor any fragrance. If you bother to lean over to sniff them, your nose will change your mind, for the scent of witch hazel is incenselike, almost addictive.

Hamamelis is a genus of six species native to Japan, China, or the United States. Most are shrubs, though some get to be trees. All varieties have curiously twisted, scented flowers that bloom when almost nothing else does—in the dead of winter. Blossoms usually appear on leafless stems. The leaves appear later and make their contribution to the plant's beauty by turning some autumn color before they drop.

H. japonica grows in several forms, all neat, bushy, and shapely. The variety *arborea* (tree-like) reaches twenty feet and taller in its native Japan. Though it's only half that tall in America, its yellow, curvaceous petals with red calyxes are also sweetly scented. 'Moonlight', another yellow-with-a-red-base form, has blossoms even more powerfully fragrant.

The Chinese variety, *H. mollis*, is a large bush which begins blooming in December and keeps on going, sometimes through April, producing golden flowers all along its stems. All its forms are fragrant.

Two notable species are native to the United States. *H. vernalis*, also known as the Ozark witch hazel and perfectly suited for moist soils, produces pungent copper blooms to salute each new year. *H. virginiana* is the variety used for astringents that are popular for facials and in barbershops. Its blooms are smaller than those of all other varieties, but are sweetly perfumed nonetheless. *H. virginiana* is the only species of witch hazel that prefers shade to sun.

Idesia polycarpa

It's amazing that this lovely tree doesn't have a host of nicknames, since hardly anybody remembers its botanical name. Anyone who has ever grown *I. polycarpa*, however, can testify that it's among the loveliest of all shade trees.

When you first see *Hamamelis* in bloom, you're likely to think it odd; flowers have curiously twisted petals that don't look as though they would harbor pleasant aroma. In fact, however, the scent of *Hamamelis* is so pungent that some fragrance freaks fear falling under the spell of witch hazel's incenselike delicious perfume.

True, it's deciduous, but you don't need shade in the winter anyway. It's also a wonder that there are so many of these trees growing throughout the world since it wasn't discovered until 1866.

Native to Japan and China, where trees can grow taller than fifty feet, *I. polycarpa* is one of the most graceful trees in cultivation. Leaves are heart shaped, exceptionally large (at least six inches and up to ten inches long), bright green, and supported on crimson stalks.

Early summer flowers consist of large drooping panicles (sometimes more than a foot long) of sweetly scented, greenish yellow blossoms with orange anthers. While both male and female trees bloom, only the females set fruit—forming berries the size of peas that turn from green to red.

Ilex
Holly

You might believe that we've blundered by including this entry because no one thinks of holly as fragrant, but one species actually is, though that probably won't be the reason you include it in your garden. Holly is best known for its shiny decorative leaves and the bright festive berries it sports at year's end.

There are more than three hundred known species in the *Ilex* genus, native to Europe, North and South America, Africa, Asia, and Australia. Growth habits vary from dwarf shrubs to trees that tower more than fifty feet tall. Leaves may be solid or variegated green or yellow, large or small, toothed or smooth, with red, orange, yellow, white, or black berries.

The species that boasts fragrance among its attributes is *I. Aquifolium*, also known as English or Christmas holly. *I. Aquifolium* is native to the British Isles and northern Europe. Each May bushes produce minute, sweetly scented flowers on tiny stalks. Male, female, or bisexual plants are pollinated by insects in search of nectar at the base of blooms' creamy white petals. Although you, too, will like the way they smell, confine your appreciation to flowers left on the bush; if you pick them, no berries will follow.

If you decide to plant *I. Aquifolium*, you have a host of forms to choose from—some have leaves with centers or edges in silver or gold; some foliage is strongly toothed, while others are smooth and flat; some produce brilliant red berries, while others are dark to maroon. You must also decide how large you want your holly to get—some grow to be only short pyramidal bushes, others weep, and still others grow staunchly upright.

The white wood of *I. Aquifolium* is highly praised among woodworkers, since it is finely grained and takes a hard polish.

Laburnum
Goldenchain Tree

If you've ever been to the Chelsea Flower Show, you've been treated to a lovely, late-May, London sight—*Laburnum* trees in their glory— bursts of yellow as bright as sunlight in all

You'll probably plant holly for its shiny foliage and decorative berries and forgive most species for their scentlessness. If you're adamant about fragrance, however, *Ilex Aquifolium* is quite sweetly scented, and it boasts a host of forms— varieties with toothed edges, brilliant red or maroon berries, and gilded with silver or gold.

those densely planted little parks where vivid colors are a welcome surprise. If you're fond of fragrance, you have a double treat, since the vanilla-scented blossoms of *Laburnum* heavily perfume the air.

Laburnum is a genus of three species of deciduous trees and small shrubs, all native to Europe. The bark is dark green and shiny while its foliage is bright green and, like clover, divided into three leaflets.

L. alpinum is also known as Scotch laburnum since it was first discovered in the Highlands of Scotland, where it grows to thirty feet. Although its pendulant blossoms are thin compared to other species, it blooms later (an advantage if you'd prefer bursts of yellow in July rather than in spring). There is a form known as *L. alpinum pendulum*, with gracefully weeping branches.

L. anagyroides, also known as *L. vulgare* or common goldenchain, doesn't grow as tall as *L. alpinum* (rarely to more than twenty-five feet), nor are its blossoms as powerfully scented or as long, but it's an early bloomer, usually by May. Leaves of this variety are lance shaped and have downy undersides. There is also a 'Pendulum' form, for those of you who are fond of trees that weep. Our favorite laburnum is actually a cross between the two species just mentioned. *L. Watereri* also known as *L. Vossii*, grows to a size somewhere between that of its parents. It is the most fragrant of the lot, and its drooping, golden yellow racemes are the largest and longest (almost two feet on mature trees).

All laburnums are tolerant of some degree of shade and grow well in poor soil, even that with limestone. Few pests, other than mites and snails, bother laburnums, and pruning is rarely required except to keep out sucker growth and to shape as desired. You should, however, give any laburnum you plant as much protection from the wind as possible since they all hate it.

After laburnums bloom, they set poisonous, pealike seeds in long pods. Because the blooms are to be followed by deadly seeds, bees don't visit the plants. It's a good idea to remove seedpods after they've developed, not so much because they're poisonous, but because a heavy crop is a drain on the tree's strength.

We once saw a display of *L. Vossii* at a flower show in England. Trees had been grown in large containers, trucked in after they were in full bloom, and tied over a series of arches. Every American we saw who passed by this miraculous sight said the same thing: "I didn't know there were *yellow* wisterias!" Laburnum blooms are similar to those of wisteria, and the fragrance is almost identical—small wonder, since they both, like freesias, are members of the Leguminosae (pea) family.

Unless someone has already told you that *Laburnum* is nicknamed goldenchain tree, you're likely to call it yellow wisteria. The drooping racemes of *Laburnum* not only resemble those of wisteria (except for their golden color), but they also smell rather like them.

Laurus nobilis
Bay

Native to southern Europe, where it can reach fifty-foot heights, *L. nobilis*, also known as Grecian laurel or sweet bay, is a must-have for gardeners who also cook, for its leaves are the traditional bay of cuisine. The Roman name *laurus* is derived from *laudis*, meaning to praise. *L. nobilis* was fashioned to adorn the heads of those held in highest esteem; its leaves were woven into wreaths for distinguished poets, hence Poet Laureate. The highly praised fragrance of bay was thought to drive away pestilence, so much so that Emperor Claudius, in a calculated effort to avoid the plague, moved his court to Laurentium because of the dense plantings there of *L. nobilis*. The British wasted no time in securing seedlings of *L. nobilis*, and by the Elizabethan period, bay leaves were liberally strewn over the floors of manor houses to sweeten their air, and steeped in hot-water baths to soothe aching limbs.

Although *L. nobilis* blooms and sets scented fruit, its evergreen foliage is what dependably harbors the essence of bay's sweet fragrance.

Leaves are leathery, dark green, oval, and up to four inches long. Inconspicuous, small, yellow flowers appear in early summer and are followed by black or deep purple, fleshy berries.

L. nobilis likes to mature into a dense, broad-based, tapering cone. With the help of fingers for pinching out lateral shoots, thereby encouraging bushy growth, and shears for clipping to desired shapes, bays make fine topiary, standards, sculptured hedges, and splendid formal container plants.

While *L. nobilis* seems indifferent to the soil in which it's planted, it is quite particular about water as it's developing—lots of it, with perfect drainage. Black scale has been our bay's singular disease, and that was easy to control with a couple of sprayings.

L. nobilis does have a sister, *L. benzoin*, which is native to North America, where it grows rampant in damp woodland areas from Canada to Florida. Although shorter than *L. nobilis* (to ten feet) and deciduous, *L. benzoin* has fragrant leaves and bark that is praised for the distillation of wintergreen.

Commonly confused with *L. nobilis* is *Umbellularia californica*, California laurel, or pep-

Many gardeners don't think of clipping *Laurus*, but, in fact, bays make splendid hedges. Whether you allow plants to mound or to tower into trees, or you shape them as topiary, if you're particular about sniffing as well as cooking, be sure to choose *L. nobilis*—the true fragrant bay of cuisine.

perwood. A native to the western United States, *U. californica* thrives throughout Oregon and California, where it often serves as a poor flavor substitute for *L. nobilis* in the kitchen and as a second-rate decorative tree for landscaping the garden. Although it can develop into a massive tree more than eighty feet tall and even wider, pepperwood more commonly grows as a billowy shrub, especially near windy areas. Foliage is lighter and more yellow than that of Grecian laurel.

In the fall of our garden's second year, we began making fragrant culinary wreaths for the holidays. While thyme, rosemary, sage, and a host of less-common herbs made good additions to the wreaths, nothing was more generally satisfactory or more pleasing to the eye than *L. nobilis*. Friends to whom we gave the wreaths told us that they cooked with their bay leaves throughout the next year and that they never lost their pungency.

Now Robert makes culinary wreaths throughout the year because bay, their staple, doesn't mind a haircut twice each summer. Regular clipping also insures compact growth in the desired direction.

Liquidambar
Sweet Gum

The Spanish botanist Hernandez, writing about a tree in the early seventeenth century, described the gum it exuded through its bark as "liquid amber," and so named a genus. Resins in the wood and bark of *Liquidambar* yield storax, a staple in perfumeries for adding balsamic traces to fragrances. When flowers are macerated for extraction of their scents, storax is added to make the odors more permanent, to complement them, or to imitate vanilla.

Liquidambar is deciduous, dropping five-lobed, maplelike leaves after they have turned some brilliant fall color. A slight balsamic fragrance is detectable in the foliage when it drops, especially when the leaves are crushed.

Although there are six species, including *orientalis*, which is really a slow-growing bush, the most beautiful is *Styraciflura*, also known as American sweet gum. It grows gracefully to 120 feet (even taller in the eastern United States, where it is native) retaining a natural cone shape. Trees branch to the ground, but can be pruned up for ease of foot traffic.

It would be perfectly reasonable to plant liquidambar simply for its ease of growing and splashy fall colors. If you insist on fragrance, however, you can have that too—liquidambar's maplelike leaves, when crumpled, emit balsamic perfume.

The needs of *Liquidambar* are few, other than neutral or slightly acidic soil and careful staking, especially when young. Fall coloring is most vivid if trees are in full sun. Although all varieties turn from some shade of green to autumn colors, particularly striking ones are 'Burgundy', a deep purple-red; 'Festival', a blotched yellow, peach, and orange-red; and 'Palo Alto', which first turns orange-red, then bright red.

Magnolia

Not only are we both from the south, but we both had grandmothers with the largest magnolia trees in town. We were often sent scurrying barefoot up these trees to pluck blossoms from precarious limbs that wouldn't hold anything heavier than a seventy-pound boy. Neither of us understood the importance of the task then. We do now; magnolia blossoms are among the most divinely scented of flowers.

Magnolias have three convenient groupings, determined by when they bloom. Group I flowers first, as early as February and as late as May (some have repeat fall bloom). Magnolias in group I are deciduous, with blossoms preceding foliage. The stark framework of their leafless trees provides quite a dramatic setting for showy blooms.

M. denudata has large, globular, white flowers suffused with purple. *M. denudata*'s fragrance is sweetly seductive, and plants bloom at an early age.

M. quinquepeta is distinguished by erect, bell-shaped blooms that are snow white inside and crimson outside. *M. quinquepeta* grows slowly to a height of less than twelve feet.

M. x *Soulangiana* isn't as strongly scented as other varieties, but its delicate fragrance is irresistibly sophisticated—sweet, but with a def-

Magnolia x *Soulangiana* is among the least powerfully perfumed of the magnolias, and it has plenty of fragrance. Magnolias grow in all sizes—from shrubs with intricately patterned limbs to trees towering to one hundred feet. Almost, but not all, are elegantly scented.

inite lemon afterscent. Blooms are basically white, with purple at their bases, shaded in between. There's a variety with pure white flowers and another with grape purple blossoms.

M. stellata, the star magnolia, is one of the first varieties to bloom. Flowers are off white, star shaped, and have twelve to sixteen sweetly perfumed, narrow petals. Established plants are something between a bush and a twiggy tree. *M. stellata* doesn't take up a lot of room, and it flowers at an early age, with blooms covering the entire plant.

Group II members blossom mostly in early summer and include some of the more unusual varieties of the magnolia family.

M. acuminata, known as the cucumber tree, is valued less for its delicately perfumed green and yellow blooms than for being an ideal shade tree (its leaves are a foot long). *M. acuminata* is among the hardiest of the *Magnolia* genus.

M. hypoleuca is native to Japan, where it reaches 100-foot heights. Dark green leaves provide a flattering background for large, heavily fragrant, goblet-shaped blooms of light yellow with scarlet stamens.

M. macrophylla looks like a tropical tree because its leaves get to be three feet long and one foot wide. Blooms are white with purple bases and appear only on mature plants. Trees have white bark and won't tolerate severe winters.

M. sinensis comes from China and grows to a height of less than fifteen feet. Blooms are pure white with scarlet stamens and have a fragrance akin to lilies.

Group III includes most of the evergreen varieties—those that reach magnolia's greatest heights and have the longest bloom cycles. Most flowers appear in late summer, but begin in spring and extend through fall.

M. grandiflora, the laurel magnolia, is native to the southern United States, probably Florida. It can reach one hundred feet, with a spread half its height. Blooms are large, creamy white, and powerfully perfumed. Although it is generally hardy, some forms tolerate more cold than others.

M. virginiana is semievergreen and less lofty than *M. grandiflora*, reaching only fifteen feet. *M. virginiana* is also known as swamp laurel and swamp sassafras becuase it flourishes on swampy ground. Its cuppy flowers start out white and end up apricot three weeks later when the petals fall. Some people think the fragrance of *M. virginiana* is like that of lily of the valley, only stronger.

Magnolias like to grow in full sun with their roots plunged in rich, well-drained, slightly acid soil. Never crowd magnolias; they look best with nothing around them, or at most a shallow-rooted ground cover. In fact, soil around the base of magnolia trees shouldn't become compacted from foot traffic. You might try a well-defined water basin or an obvious, thick mulch to keep pedestrians away.

If wind is a problem, plant magnolias near, but not against, a wall or background. This will also help show off their blooms and intricately patterned limbs.

Most magnolias, such as the variety on the left, have blossoms shaped like tulips. Others, such as *Magnolia stellata*, on the right, have blooms formed like stars. Although many varieties mature slowly, magnolias bloom at an early age.

Malus
Ornamental Crabapple

For a long time, horticulturists just couldn't decide what to call these plants—did they belong with pears or apples? It was finally proclaimed that they were different enough from everything else to deserve a genus of their own. Today's orchard apple owes its very existence to *Malus*—so highly praised during medieval times that Shakespeare himself often spoke of the custom of adding roasted crabs to punch and ale at Christmastime. It was also thought to make a tasty conserve.

Malus species are not the crabapples valued for making jellies; those are simply called crabapples and sold among apple varieties. Gardeners devoted to fragrance plant *Malus* for its showy fragrant flowers; they buy their crabapples at the supermarket.

There are now more than thirty-five species of ornamental crabapples in commerce. Most varieties develop into trees anywhere between six and thirty feet tall, although several, particularly the fragrant ones, become almost as wide. All are deciduous and bloom red, pink, or white flowers. A few are still valued for producing edible fruit. Leaves are oval, often fuzzy, and some color between dark green and purple.

Because new varieties are being introduced faster than one can keep track of them and since only a few have any notable fragrance, be sure you sniff the *Malus* that you consider buying. We grow three.

M. coronaria matures into a tall, dense, round mound. Sweetly scented flowers appear in late spring. There is a variety named 'Charlottae', whose flowers are pink, double, and two inches across.

M. hupehensis grows even wider than it does tall (to twenty feet). Branches are rigid and grow at 45-degree angles from a central trunk. In early May deep pink buds cover all parts of the plant. Powerfully fragrant flowers open light pink and fade to white. The sparse fruit that follows isn't considered ornamental.

M. Sargentii, also called Sargent crabapple, slowly grows its zigzag branches into a dense shrub, usually no more than fifteen feet high or across. In late spring small, white, fragrant flowers cover the entire plant, followed by tiny, red fruits that last well into fall.

If you also grow roses, you won't be frightened of aphids, spider mites, mildew, and rust since you'll have already been forced to eradicate them. Otherwise, be forewarned that *Malus* species may attract every pest and disease that plague roses, particularly if you grow them in the northwestern United States. Nearly everywhere else *Malus* species are considered to be ideal flowering trees, for they're long-lived; tolerant of wet, acid, alkaline, or rocky soil; take heat; require little or no pruning; and can be trained into espaliers.

Michelia Figo
Banana Shrub

Michelia species are closely related to magnolias, but have flowers all along, rather than only at the tips of, their branches. Although there are more than fifty species of these evergreen trees and shrubs native to tropical Asia and the Himalayas, only one is in general cultivation in America—*M. Figo*, sometimes called *M. fuscata*, commonly, banana shrub.

M. Figo grows slowly, usually to six or eight feet, though a contented adult planted in a prime spot may tower to fifteen feet. Three-inch-long, medium green, glossy leaves densely cover the plant.

Blooms first appear as early as March, continue heavily until May, and periodically throughout summer. Flowers resemble their magnolia cousins, but they're smaller—one to one and a half inches wide. The basic color of the blossoms is creamy yellow, shading toward brownish purple. Flowers have a fruity fragrance unmistakably similar to ripe bananas.

M. Figo likes to grow in rich, well-drained soil. Fragrance reaches its peak when plants are grown in sunny garden locations protected from the wind. Banana shrubs adapt well to containers and can be trained to espalier. Many people would grow nothing other than *M. Figo* under their bedroom windows.

You won't always agree with fragrance fanciers who rave about a bloom that to their noses smells like some specific fruit, but you won't quibble over *Michelia Figo*, with its small, creamy, mostly yellow blossoms that smell exactly like ripe bananas.

Myrtus
Myrtle

Although myrtle is endemic to subtropical America, it's so closely associated with the Mediterranean that it's either also native there or so naturalized that it might as well be. In both ancient Greece and Rome, myrtle represented love, good will, and, especially, virginity. The most-fragrant varieties supposedly came from Egypt, where plants exuded gum resembling myrrh, which is how the genus got its name. Oil of myrtle was esteemed for its medicinal values and was thought to effectively combat bronchitis. It was also rumored that myrtle oil passed so quickly through the body that it could make urine smell like violets in fifteen minutes (if true, oil of myrtus should provide a pleasant antidote for asparagus eaters).

There are more than sixteen species of myrtle, from shrubs to small trees, but the most popular among fragrance freaks is also the most prevalent, *M. communis*. It has glossy, dark, evergreen leaves similar to those of box. Small, pure white flowers with dark yellow stamens that appear in midsummer make sweet additions to salads.

Myrtle is scented throughout, releasing its fragrance whenever blossoms, leaves, or stems are bruised. After flowering, shrubs bear bluish black berries that are edible when fresh and flavorful when dried.

Because its foliage goes smack down to the ground when plants are kept clipped and shaped, myrtle makes a superb hedge. Haircuts should be given regularly to keep plants from becoming leggy. Old plantings left unclipped grow to be huge. With moderate trimming, bushes get to be five to six feet high and four to five feet wide. If you can't afford that much space, buy the dwarf, slow-growing, compact form. Myrtle makes a neat, low-growing, formal border.

M. communis 'Variegata' has leaves edged in white. It's available in full or dwarf size. *Lophomyrtus obcordata* includes a variety with purple leaves. *Amomyrtus Luma* is the species for

At Filoli's picture-perfect garden in Woodside, California, the most strongly scented of all myrtle—*Myrtus communis*—is cultivated as a hedge because its foliage grows smack down to the ground. Many gourmets fancy myrtle blossoms in their salads; others prefer the edible fruits that follow. All parts of myrtles are fragrant—stems, leaves, and blossoms.

those in search of towering heights and impenetrable barriers. It's native to Chile, where it grows to be twenty-five feet tall. Though it rarely reaches that height in colder climates, it's praised there, too, because of its hardiness.

Myrtle adapts easily within spaces you select for it to grow. Although it prefers sun, it will tolerate moderate amounts of shade. It won't budge, however, where drainage is poor.

Be precise when buying myrtle. If you follow our advice and select *M. communis*, insist on exactly that. Even experienced nurserypeople somehow believe the term refers to what's "common" for them, much of which has no trace of scent.

Osmanthus

If you like the looks of holly shrubs or trees, but can't forgive them for not being fragrant (except for the solitary *Ilex Aquifolium*), osmanthus might be just the plant for you. Although osmanthus blooms are inconspicuous, they certainly are powerfully fragrant (you can smell them before seeing them). Like holly, osmanthus has leathery, evergreen foliage, grows well both in sun and medium shade, and tolerates a variety of soils.

Osmanthus and holly so resemble each other when they are out of flower or berry that gardeners have coined an acronym to help them remember the difference between them. It is: "oo-ha"—osmanthus-opposite, holly-alternate—a short cut to recalling that the leaves of osmanthus are always directly opposite one another, while those of holly alternate.

Although eight species make up this handsome genus, three are very popular both in America and Britain, probably because they all have nicknames and include the most-fragrant varieties. They grow to varying heights.

Although it's the shortest, *O. Delavayi*, or Delavay osmanthus, has the largest flowers of the entire genus. Native to China, *O. Delavayi* was discovered by and named for a Jesuit missionary, Abbé Delavay. The shrub grows slowly, but gracefully, to six feet, arching its branches with oval, one-inch-long, tooth-edged, dark green leaves. *O. Delavayi* looks nice grown on a retaining wall over which it can drape its graceful branches —a particularly fragrant place to walk under between March and May, when the plant is clustered in blooms.

Next in height and speed of growth is *O. fragrans*, which grows at a moderate rate to ten feet, taller as it ages. The sweet olive, as *O. fragrans* is also called, will grow as it's told—if lead shoots are allowed to develop, a tree will mature; if lead shoots are pinched, bushy growth will follow. Sweet olive can also be espaliered, planted as a hedge, or grown in a container. Leaves are long (to four inches), glossy, midgreen, and may be smooth or toothed. The flowers that appear mostly in spring and early summer are tiny, white, and smell like ripe

Should you want to fool visitors to your garden into believing that you grow fragrant holly, plant *Osmanthus*, which closely resembles holly but smells much better. Three species are commonly cultivated for their uncommon scents.

apricots. Young plants appreciate shade while they're maturing, but grow happily in full sun once they're established.

O. heterophyllus, also known as *O. Aquifolium* and holly-leaf osmanthus, grows upright to eight feet (some forms eventually reaching twenty feet) and, of all varieties, looks the most like holly. *O. heterophyllus* has several forms: *O. heterophyllus* has dark green leaves; *O. heterophyllus* 'Purpureus' has purple-tinted foliage; *O. heterophyllus* 'Rotundifolius' has small, round leaves with few spines; and *O. heterophyllus* 'Variegatus' has densely set leaves that are edged creamy white. Most forms produce white, quarter-inch-long, fragrant, tubular flowers during fall and early winter.

Osmanthus may be propagated from cuttings of half-ripened wood or by layering branches to root in the ground. Pruning isn't generally necessary other than to keep bushes trim or to shape them if they're grown as a hedge. Osmanthus is generally free from pests and diseases.

Philadelphus
Mock Orange

Lots of plants are incorrectly called mock orange, usually because their blooms smell like oranges. *Philadelphus* species are the true mock orange, not because they smell of citrus, though most do, but rather because their blossoms *look* like orange blossoms. While not all of the seventy-five species in this genus are fragrant, those that are handily make up for their scentless sisters.

Before Linnaeus came along to start making some sense of the botanical mishmash that preceded his efforts, mock orange and lilac, because they had hollow stems, were both called *Syringa*, from *syrinx*, Greek for panpipe. Although some gardeners still confuse them, only lilac is properly called *Syringa*.

Philadelphus species number among those plants that you simply *must* smell before you plant them in your garden, for we're not speaking of mild fragrance here; we're talking heavy-duty perfume. While many people praise mock orange's heady aroma, others will walk out of their way to avoid it. The scent from the more strongly fragrant varieties will stay with you long after you sniff it, as though it has saturated your olfactory system. Some people like the aroma in the garden, but can't bear it in the house—a bouquet cut on a warm summer evening can heavily perfume a large room, as can other members of the *heavy* fragrance group—tuberose, osmanthus, lily of the valley, and honeysuckle. *Philadelphus* can give you a headache if you smell it over a period of time.

Philadelphus species are deciduous and vigorously grow into fountainous, five- to ten-foot bushes with midgreen foliage. Most bloom in early summer.

P. coronarius, sweet or European mock or-

Philadelphus happens to smell like oranges, but that's not why it's nicknamed mock orange; it's because the blooms resemble those of citrus blossoms. Be certain that you're prepared for the heady scent before you plant mock orange—it can be overpowering, especially in large doses.

ange, is an early bloomer and a strong grower—quickly to as tall as ten feet. These creamy white flowers, borne in clusters, smell strongly of orange.

P. x *Lemoinei* is a hybrid with a host of forms, most growing to at least six feet, all fragrant. This species is distinguished from others because its blossoms cover an entire plant when it's in profuse bloom. Dr. J. Horace McFarland, the famous rose grower, wrote about a *P. Lemoinei* hybrid named 'Belle Etoile', a variety which forms a "spreading shrub with graceful arching branches thickly set with enormous single flowers, with a lavender blotch at the base of each petal, the odor of which is that of gardenia and is so pronounced as to completely dominate a considerable area in its vicinity."

P. x *virginalis* is another hybrid with several forms. Blossoms of this variety are snow white and double.

Philadelphus species will thrive in almost any garden soil as long as it's well drained. They prefer full sun, but will grow in partial shade. Old wood should be thinned out just after the plant has bloomed to make room for the new wood on which next year's crop will blossom. Mock oranges are generally trouble free.

Pieris

When you wonder what to plant around your leggy rhododendrons and azaleas, consider *Pieris*—a handsome, evergreen, underappreciated genus of ten species. In the United States, *P. japonica* is commonly known as lily-of-the-valley shrub; in Britain *P. mariana* (native to Maryland) is identically nicknamed. To complicate matters even further, in both countries *Pieris* is often referred to by its earlier name, *Andromeda*, honoring the charming daughter of Ethiopia's King Cepheus.

All members of the *Pieris* genus have fragrant white blooms (a few species also come in pink and light red, but they have little or no perfume). Although the blossoms of most species end up white, they start out with a greenish cast. The individual flowers are urn shaped and, while forming into panicles, look like tiny strings of beads. Most varieties open their blossoms between February and April, long before most other spring bushes come into bloom. *Pieris* is a member of the Ericaceae—heather—family, and its blooms are deliciously scented of honey, vanilla, or both.

Another reason for choosing *Pieris* species as a border to your rhododendron dell is that they like the very same growing conditions—shady, acid soil that drains quickly, but at the same time retains moisture. Although most bushes hover at around three feet, some species will tower to more than ten feet, especially if their soil drains well enough to prevent a buildup of salts.

Pieris is generally trouble free from insects and diseases and requires no special pruning other than removing spent blooms (you'll want some indoors long before they start to fade).

Pinus
Pine

Pinus is a genus of coniferous, evergreen, resinous plants. Although they vary from semi-prostrate shrubs to trees that tower more than 250 feet high, most pines grow to become moderate to tall trees.

Pine leaves are actually needles in groups of two, three, or five, bound together at their bases with a woody sheath. Pinecones, the fruits of the trees, may be long, broad, squat, shaped like a banana, or the size of a pineapple.

During England's Tudor period, pinecones were floated in vats to flavor wine and ale, and hung on clotheslines inside the house to sweeten the air. Pinecones were also placed in linen and clothes drawers to refresh the scent of the laundered contents.

Pine trees have long been valued for their bark, from which pitch, tar, and turpentine are extracted. Because these resinous secretions were also used for fueling torches, *P. sylvestris* acquired the common name of Scots pine, originally Scots fir, from the Anglo-Saxon *fyre* (fire).

Because there are more than one hundred species in the *Pinus* genus, no nursery you visit will carry them all. At best, they'll have a reasonable selection of perhaps a dozen varieties. (For rare species, visit a nursery that specializes in bonsai.) The five species we mention are among the most commonly available.

P. nigra, or Austrian black pine, is a particularly hardy pine. Although it's a slow grower and rarely reaches heights taller than forty feet, it makes a formidable windbreak. Dark green needles are set in twos and threes. Cones are three inches long, oval, and light brown.

P. Pinaster is also known as the cluster pine because its handsome purple-brown cones, each up to seven inches long, form in clusters of as many as a dozen each. *P. Pinaster* grows rapidly to as tall as ninety feet and is hardy to 0° F. Because they readily adapt themselves to sandy soil and ocean exposure, many *P. Pinaster* trees are planted in San Francisco's Golden Gate Park to bind sand dunes.

P. pinea, also known as the Italian stone pine, is native to the rocky Mediterranean coast and the Italian hill towns. Growing at a moderate rate to more than sixty feet tall, *P. pinea* takes on different appearances as it ages. When young, it's nothing more than a bushy stub. During middle age, its trunk thickens, and the top of the tree begins to look like an umbrella. When fully mature, the Italian stone pine takes on a striking, dramatic look as its top becomes flattened. Gray-green needles are up to eight inches long. Six-inch, brown, oval cones with edible kernels look as though they've been polished.

P. radiata, or Monterey pine, is a fast grower (as much as six feet a year when young) along the California coast, where it is native. If Monterey pines are planted in deep soil (if soil is shallow, they'll topple in the wind) where temperatures don't dip below 15° F, they'll tower to one hundred feet and produce masses of lopsided, clustered cones that last well on or off the tree. Needles that grow in twos and threes are bright green.

In the United States, *P. Strobus* is known also as eastern white pine, whereas in Britain it's sometimes called the Weymouth pine because a Lord Weymouth introduced it to the English in 1705. Whatever it's commonly called, *P. Strobus* is a handsome tree with soft needles that are often striped with silver and smooth, curved, powerfully resinous cones that measure up to eight inches long.

Pittosporum

While several wonderful plants native to Australia and New Zealand have never become popular in America, *Pittosporum* certainly has. Particularly in the western United States, pittosporums are considered a gardener's staple, because the plants are so dependable and consistently attractive.

Pittosporums grow into large bushes or small trees. All species are evergreen; most are borderline hardy. Once established, a pittosporum will respond well to clipping or, all on its own, mature into an interesting outline. Although there are many species within the *Pittosporum* genus, including some praised mostly for their fruit, the three we grow are esteemed for their fragrant purple or white flowers.

P. tenuifolium is grown by those who want to snip its pale green, wavy, glossy leaves for flower arranging, particularly by gardeners who also want a fragrant hedge that they can clip as though it were privet. Stems look like polished ebony, and the foliage of some forms is edged with silver and red. Deliciously scented, dark purple flowers bloom from leaf axils each May.

P. Tobira, which makes a dense shrub or a moderate-size tree, is by far the most prevalent of the species. With leaves a darker green than any of its relatives, each spring *P. Tobira* has

If you're fond of fragrance, when shopping for *Pittosporum*, make certain you don't buy a species known instead for its fruits. *P. Tobira* will satisfy the piggiest of noses with irresistible wafts of orange—bumblebees love it too.

clusters of creamy white, orange-scented flowers at branch tips. Because individual plants look gawky with their crooked stems, they are usually set in masses so that they camouflage one another's rangy growth habits.

In Britain *P. undulatum* is also called Victorian box; in Australia it's unfortunately confused with mock orange (*Philadelphus*) because its fruits resemble small oranges. The flowers that precede the fruit may be either white or purple; either color produces strongly fragrant blossoms, especially in the evening, when they are pollinated by night moths. With judicious pruning, *P. undulatum* may be trained as a hedge. Left on its own, it will develop into a handsome, multitrunked, dome-shaped tree.

Pittosporums would prefer to grow in full sun, but they will accept half shade. Although they can eventually become drought resistant, at least while they're developing, pittosporums prefer plenty of water; they also like to be fertilized once or twice a year. Watch for aphids and scale and spray as soon as you see them.

Prunus

This enormous genus embraces the spring-flowering fruit trees, closely related to their bearing cousins, the "stone fruits" (almonds, cherries, nectarines, peaches, plums, and prunes). The ornamental *Prunus* species are divided into evergreen and deciduous classes.

Hidcote was among the first of the great English gardens we visited. After we had toured the formal garden, we walked to the rear of the property to see an ash grove that we had read about. On the way there, we walked through Major Lawrence Johnston's informal woodland garden. At the moment we first entered one of the semienclosed dells, we both caught a whiff of something powerfully fragrant that we couldn't identify. Looking around to see where it could be coming from, we spotted only some rhododendrons and azaleas in bloom, and we knew they couldn't be perfuming the air because they were the wrong color (dark reds and pinks—never fragrant).

Prunus is a formidable genus embracing fruit-bearing trees as well as ornamental shrubs, some of which can be trained into perfect umbrellas. The deciduous varieties include the Japanese flowering cherry.

Since there was no one around to ask about the delicious scent, we continued our walk, admiring the ashes. When we returned, there was a group of English gardeners in the fragrant dell, and we spotted a woman who looked as though she could help us. When we told her that we could smell something that we couldn't see, she knew right away.

"Oh, that's *P. Laurocerasus*," she assured us, pointing to the densely planted, sunny perimeter at the edge of the grove. "You have to lift the leaves to see the flowers at all."

Known in America as English laurel and in Britain as common laurel, *P. Laurocerasus* is often grown as a clipped hedge; otherwise, it will quickly grow into a greedy tall tree that's difficult to plant around or under. Evergreen foliage is midgreen to dark green with leaves from three to seven inches long. Each May, small, dull, white flowers form in clusters all over the plant; they remain concealed to the eye, but not to the nose. Small, black, berrylike fruits follow the blossoms.

At Garden Valley Ranch we've planted *P. lusitanica*, or Portugal laurel, because it grows more slowly and is easier to shape than English laurel. Portugal laurels can so easily be trained to a single trunk that they're often planted as formal street trees. Foliage that fully covers the plant is myrtlelike and has serrated edges. Blossoms are easier to spot for this variety because they droop in racemes beyond leaf edges. Red-to-purple fruit follows.

Of the deciduous varieties, we've planted only *P. serrulata*, the Japanese flowering cherry. Although it's easy to understand why ornamental fruit trees are so highly praised (they have particularly nice shapes and put on quite a springtime show), it's also easy to resent their not bearing fruit. Although our trees of *P. serrulata* are densely covered with frothy pink blossoms each spring, the fruit trees in our orchard are also in bloom. Even though fruit trees might not be as sweetly scented as their ornamental cousins, they *do* smell, and, of course, they bear.

Several varieties of **Prunus** bloom only at stem tips, others beneath leaf axils, and some droop with weighty racemes of sinfully fragrant blossoms. *P. lusitanica*, the Portugal laurel, is hard to beat for heady perfume.

Rhododendron

Rhododendron is a genus of more than eight hundred species with more than ten thousand named varieties. Even though only one fifth of those are commercially available, it's difficult to say which varieties will perform best for you. Where we live, for instance, in San Francisco's Bay Area, the rhododendrons that grow to staggering heights in foggy Golden Gate Park only hover at the ground in the comparatively sultry East Bay. For a comprehensive account of this massive genus, we refer you to *Rhododendron of the World* by David G. Leach.

Azaleas were once considered to be different enough from rhododendrons to deserve a classification all their own. Now they no longer enjoy separate botanical status and are instead listed as a subseries of *Rhododendron*.

In spite of the immense diversification within the genus, rhododendrons have certain common needs. They all hate wind, prefer acid soil, and require more air at their root zones than does any other garden plant. They also demand moisture, meaning that the soil in which they're planted must drain thoroughly, but at the same time remain damp. Only soils rich in

organic matter (ground bark, leaf mold, peat moss, or sawdust) can meet these dual needs. In most gardens this translates into planting rhododendrons in raised beds.

Soil beneath rhododendrons should be regularly mulched rather than cultivated. These plants are surface rooters and each year need copious amounts of mulch such as pine needles, leaves, and wood by-products. Sun tolerance differs by variety; most accept some sun in cool climates; all like the filtered shade of tall trees. A good feature of both azaleas and rhododendrons is that you can plant (or transplant) them in flower, meaning you can preview (and sniff) seedlings or mature plants before buying.

While we grow a few azaleas, mostly *R. Exbury* or *R. occidentale* hybrids, we avoid many of the large-flowered varieties because they're so frost tender. Besides, rhododendrons are more fragrant than azaleas, and we prefer their pale colors.

We allotted our rhododendrons a spot all their own—a raised bank just beside a grove of native California willow trees that dapple shade over everything beneath them. We planted four hybrids (mostly from the *Maddenii* series) and two species rhododendrons.

Although there are exceptions, most rhododendrons known for their fragrance are either white or pale yellow. Rhododendrons are good plants to purchase when they're in bloom, not just because you can satisfy yourself over how they look and smell, but also because they transplant easily when in mature flower.

'Forsteranum'—an upright, compact grower with large, white, fragrant blossoms that have a striking yellow flare.

'Fragrantissimum'—a variety with a spicy fragrance that makes up for its leggy growth. Blossoms that are large and funnel shaped start out pink in bud and end up white in bloom.

'Lady Alice Fitzwilliams'—a good addition to any rhododendron dell, since she has a neat, compact form. Pink buds, white flowers.

'Martha Wright'—produces masses of creamy white, fragrant blossoms with yellow centers.

R. calophyllum (probably the same as *R. odoriferum*) blooms large, white, redolent flowers (tinged green inside, blushed rose outside) on a compact plant.

R. taronense is a straggly grower, but it has lovely, dark green leaves and deliciously scented, white flowers.

Except when espaliered or grown against a tree, rhododendrons look best when massed. Those varieties shamed for their leggy growth can be interspersed with those praised for their compactness. Besides, it makes good garden sense to lump together those plants that crave the very same growing conditions.

Although we've seen some showy rhododendron plantings throughout the world, the most impressive were those at Stourhead, England. The varieties were sunk into County Kent soil in 1786, and many are now more than eighty feet tall. Although only a handful are fragrant, that fact doesn't dim the show.

Robinia
False Acacia, Black Locust

During the sixteenth century, a nurseryman to the King of France obtained seeds from an unnamed member of the Leguminosae family. It was such an instant hit that the genus *Robinia* was named in honor of its finder, Jean Robin.

Although native to North America, more specifically, to the eastern United States and Canada, *Robinia* now grows throughout the world, where it is praised for quick, disease-free growth and for the vanilla-scented racemes of pealike flowers.

R. Pseudoacacia is the most prevalent species of the genus. Trees have deeply furrowed, brown bark and gray-green, feathery leaves on sparsely branched limbs. Each May and June fragrant, creamy white blossoms hang in clusters up to seven inches long.

All rhododendrons appreciate the filtered shade of tall trees, making them a favorite among landscapers. Be sure to give bushes plenty of mulch, and don't cultivate the soil at ground level; rhododendrons are shallow rooted.

Locust trees now grow native in California's gold country because early settlers brought seeds with them from the East. Since they're now so common, *Robinia* is too often overlooked as a worthy garden addition, especially where its brittle limbs can be protected from the wind. Stay on the watch for aggressive roots that often sucker.

Romneya
Matilija Poppy

When we planted a row of Lombardy poplars all along our garden's western border to absorb the gusts from a westerly prevailing wind, other gardeners kept saying: "They'll sure break the wind, but you'll never get anything to grow beneath them—nothing ever grows under poplars." But we swore we would find *something* that would. How dare they tell us that so much space had to remain barren? Someone finally suggested a rugged little shrub called *Romneya*, mentioning that it grows where little else does. Boy does it ever!

Bushes of *Romneya* are so tough and independent that in California, where they're native and known as tree poppies, they're used to bind hillsides and to choke weeds along roadsides. *Romneya* never notices the soil it's growing in; even pure sand and fine gravel will do. Bushes don't need water during summer, so they can be planted where you haven't had time to install irrigation lines.

Two species, *R. Coulteri* and *R. trichocalyx*, are virtually indistinguishable, although *tri-chocalyx* is said to be more hardy (you'll usually find *Coulteri* more readily available, and we assure you it's plenty tough). The plants of both species grow to be eight feet tall, with three- to four-inch, gray-green leaves that are hairy and serrated at their edges.

Considering the ironclad bushes they grow from, *Romneya* blooms are miraculously delicate, with five or six crinkled, white petals surrounding a bulging cluster of golden yellow stamens. Their fragrance is light, but exotic, like some of the softer-scented lilies. The blooms don't last well when cut from their bushes, but they'll open in a vase from tight buds. They also appear at a welcome time—after spring's floriferous show, but before summer's flush.

When you choose sites for *Romneya*, be sure first that they are permanent, for it despises being moved. Second, look around to see if there's room for it to spread, for it surely will. Third, because *Romneya*'s invasive roots will strangle nearby weaklings, avoid placing it next to less-vigorous plants.

Romneya is a perennial for those in love with their loppers. After flowering, bushes should be cut to six inches above the ground. New shoots will appear after spring rains, and off they'll go once more.

Skimmia

Skimmias are evergreen shrubs that are as valued for their fruits as they are for their sweetly scented flowers. Although they are no

Black locust trees are so common along California's Gold Coast that many people assume they're native. In fact, *Robinia* trees flourish because seeds were brought west by settlers who were already addicted to the false acacia's sweet perfume. Black locusts need protection from wind, and, like acacias, mature into graceful trees with prodigious roots.

more than half-hardy to freezes, skimmias make terrific city plants since they are undaunted by polluted air.

S. japonica, native to Japan, is the most commonly sold variety in the United States. It grows slowly into a dome, never to more than five feet tall, but just as wide. Leaves are bright green, oval, mostly at the tips of branches, and aromatic when crushed. Blooms that appear in clusters in April are creamy white and sweetly fragrant (*S. japonica* 'Fragrans' is said to smell exactly like lily of the valley).

If you plant both male and female plants, the females will set fruit after their blooms have been pollinated; in fact, many people are after the fruits because they're showy and persist on the bushes well into winter.

Skimmias must grow in shade; not too much, or plants become lanky, but not too little, or leaves turn yellow. Soil should be slightly acid, easily accomplished by adding peat moss at planting time. Skimmias are troubled by spider mites and thrips.

Stewartia

Most species of *Stewartia* are native to China and Japan, though a couple were discovered in North America. Although rather rare in the United States, gardeners who grow stewartias praise them without limit for their never-ending contributions to the garden. In winter, while dormant, stewartias are valued for their graceful branches. In summer strongly scented blooms that look like single camellias cover the plants. But many people grow stewartias for their autumn show—leaves that turn from green to orange, red, and even deep purple.

We grow only one variety, *S. Pseudocamellia*, also known as Japanese stewartia. Although it's still only a shrub, we've been told that it could climb to sixty feet. Already, however, it's producing creamy white flowers with orange anthers each late summer and bronzy purple foliage each fall. Stewartias are slow growing, but thrive best in moist, acid soil. They appreciate shade in warm climates.

Romneya species are terrific choices for fair-weather gardeners—plants aren't fussy about soil and require little or no irrigation during summer. In spite of these hell-bent-for-survival traits, blooms of *Romneya* are fragile and exotically perfumed. Choose planting sites carefully; Matilija poppies will choke out weak neighbors, and they detest being transplanted.

Syringa
Lilac

It's hard for us to build expertise on growing lilacs. Although recent winters in Petaluma have included freezes, we can't always count on them, and lilacs benefit from an occasional hard freeze. Fortunately, there are a few varieties that do well without plummeting temperatures.

Syringa is a genus of something more than thirty species of deciduous shrubs and small trees. Well-grown varieties of some species reach twenty feet, with almost as much spread. Plants may take three years to establish themselves and start flowering, but once they do they're prolific bloomers. The blossoms come at a good time, too, in late spring, when early bloomers have faded away and summer flowers are still buds.

The most common lilac of all, *S. vulgaris*, continues to be the most favored among lilac fanciers. Its colors include pinkish lavender, blue-lavender, and white—the traditional hues. Modern varieties embrace all shades of red, including bluer tones and one that is almost black. Recent introductions sometimes aren't fragrant though, so be sure you've had a chance to sniff the flowers of the variety you purchase. Some forms have double blooms, although single ones are often showier.

S. vulgaris does have one annoying habit—it spawns rampant sucker growth. There's a way around the problem, by budding it onto privet (*Ligustrum ovalifolium*). Rootstock of privet stays underground as it's supposed to do.

Lilac appreciates an alkaline soil. If yours is on the acid side, bury some lime around the drip lines (that circumference under bushes where water would drip if the plant were soaking wet) of the bushes.

Be especially careful when pruning lilac. Next year's buds form in pairs where leaves join stems. When removing spent blooms, watch out for these treasured formations, since they're often just underneath the bloom you're removing. An overly nonchalant pruner can lop off next year's blooms.

When plants become aged and gnarled, they must be thinned. Cut old limbs flush to the ground to encourage new shoots. Otherwise, trim and shape for desired growth patterns in September or October. You can start by removing weak branches and those that cross over the center of growth.

While some noses will wrinkle, rather than sniff, at certain entries in this book, no one seems to quarrel with lilac's fragrance. It's consistently clean and fresh—never overpowering, but never in doubt either.

Viburnum

Viburnum is a genus of more than two hundred species of deciduous and evergreen shrubs, divided into groups depending upon when they flower or set fruit. One group is made up of those species which bloom on barren wood; another blossoms at the same time its foliage appears; and the third group is cultivated for showy autumn foliage or fruits, which follow a scentless bloom.

We've never met a fragrance fancier who doesn't care for the fresh, clean scent of lilac—never overpowering but always noticeable. Before you take pruners to your lilac bushes, be certain you know where and when to trim; otherwise, you're likely to inadvertently clip off next year's blossoms.

Recent introductions of lilac hybrids include red and dark purple, but the more traditional lilac color and white are still favorites (also the most fragrant).

Seven deciduous species are famed for their spicy, rich fragrance: *V. bitchiuense*, *V.* x *bodnantense*, *V.* x *Burkwoodii*, *V.* x *carlcephalum*, *V. Carlesii*, *V. Farreri* (also known as *V. fragrans*), and *V.* x *Juddii*. These seven varieties share a few basics: they all grow to between six and ten feet tall (some varieties grow even taller, especially those plants growing in prime garden spots that warrant lofty heights); they have blossoms that start out as pink and end up white; and they become leggy if you're not careful (begin shaping or espaliering them into shape while they're young).

If you give viburnums rich soil and plenty of water, they'll flourish in either full or part sun (though most evergreens look better when given protection in hot areas). Because they so readily adapt themselves to various climates, viburnums grow all over the world.

When we debated all possibilities for plants around a magnolia grove, we mentioned to a local nurseryman that we'd like to grow the snowball bush and asked if any forms were fragrant.

"No, you have to give up fragrance for *those* showy flowers," our misinformed horticulturist told us. "Snowballs just don't smell." So, we bought *V. Opulus* and coached ourselves not to vainly sniff their dramatic, heady blossoms. We've since learned that one *Viburnum* species, *V.* x *carlcephalum*, is indeed fragrant and every bit as showy as its scentless sister.

We also grow one evergreen species, *V. Tinus*, because we needed a border around our white garden that not only blossomed white, but could be clipped as well. Although he isn't anywhere nearly so fragrant as his cousins in the intensely perfumed deciduous clan, *V. Tinus* does have a soft scent and an unusually extended period of bloom (more than half the year where we grow it). Its foliage also extends smack down to the ground. Be sure to plant bushes with their crowns above ground level; otherwise, they'll rot.

Like roses, viburnums are susceptible to aphids, spider mites, and thrips. The evergreen varieties sometimes mildew.

Although most viburnums are fragrant, if you're after rich perfume, be certain to consider the deciduous varieties famed for their spicy aroma. Blossoms of most species start out pink and end up white; some varieties make neat hedges.

This variety, *Viburnum Tinus*, is only lightly scented, but it's evergreen and in bloom for more than half the year.

CHAPTER III

Filling in with Vines and Trailers

After you've placed your trees and delineated your shrubs, you may notice gaps that need filling in with vigorous climbers such as honeysuckle that will either separate sections of your garden or hide others from view. You may even buy property that has naked fences, arbors, or pergolas that you can't stand to see barren and decide to mask them forever with jasmine or wisteria. Or you may simply yearn to experiment with splashes of sweet peas or moonflowers to learn how you like vertical garden accents—nothing for keeps, only a trial for one growing season. In any case, before you entice yourself with these fragrant entries, make sure you have *something* for them to climb over. No plant mentioned in this chapter will flourish without supporting props.

Consider also whether the vines you crave need to be cloaked in foliage all year long. If they must, select only evergreens. If you can live with bare limbs during the dormant season, you have more options.

Calonyction aculeatum
Moonflower

Moonflowers aren't thought of as highly in the United States as they are in Greece (where they're native), probably because in America they've been lumped with *Ipomoea*, and no one thinks of morning glory as fragrant. Perhaps another reason why moonflowers remain undervalued is that *C. aculeatum* is tender and winters-over only in temperate climates (although those in the know realize that, from seeds, moonflowers grow to thirty feet in a single season).

Each spring *C. aculeatum* twines its way to staggering heights with closely spaced, luxurious, long, heart-shaped leaves. From July through October, waxy, white trumpets that measure six inches long and across cover vines and fill the evening air with lush perfume.

Clematis

Clematises have never been as popular in America as they are in Britain, though they're catching up. In England one rarely sees an otherwise-useless, dead tree that hasn't been put to good use by providing a stump for clematis to quickly gobble up. Derived from the Greek word *klema*—vine branch—clematises cling to anything that their tendrils can grab.

Though not unreasonably demanding, clematises insist on a few basics. First, they must have something to grow on right away—arbors, fences, pergolas, trees, trellises, or walls—and they prefer to be tied and staked as soon as they're planted. Second, clematises like to grow in rich, well-drained soil that is slightly acidic (if your soil is neutral, add bone meal; if there's already too much acid, add lime). Although clematises grow toward full sun, their roots must be kept cool either by planting them in the shade of what they are to scramble over or by growing a shallow-rooted ground cover on top of their roots. Finally, clematises are among the few plants that like being sunk; the tops of their root balls should be set at least two inches underground.

Prune clematises depending on when they bloom. Varieties that blossom only in summer and on new wood like to be trimmed in fall. Those that flower only in spring on last year's wood need shaping just after their bloom is finished. Varieties that blossom both in spring (on old wood) and again in summer (on new wood) need light pruning after both blooms.

Before you plant a wisteria, make certain you want it for keeps and that you don't mind if its vines devour what they twine over (as you can see, this wisteria has no intention of turning loose that drainpipe, and it's beginning to peek around walls). Next, choose a scented variety in one of several shades of lavender-blue, lilac, pink, or white. Then sit back in anticipation of drooping blooms that reek of exotic vanilla.

If your garden has a dead tree that you don't care to remove but would like to hide, consider planting a clematis vine at its base—many varieties will gobble it right up. Several clematises produce blooms so strongly perfumed that you can handle the fragrance of no more than three or four blossoms at one time.

When we first planted our fragrant garden, we had to plan around a long finger of native California willows that had been planted years before near the garden's western perimeter. In and among the willows were some dead oak trees. The whole stretch looked so straggly and unappealing that we seriously considered bulldozing everything and starting over. Thankfully, some more-experienced gardeners who know of Petaluma's relentless wind talked us out of it.

"Clean up the willows and leave those dead trees right where they stand," they advised, "and plant clematises and climbing roses to fill in unsightly spots." What good advice; thank goodness, we took it! We've since planted trees to take the place of the dwindling willows (they're short-lived). Someday the willows will probably dissipate themselves entirely, and we'll remove their spindly roots, but we'll never touch those dead oaks or the clematises that now engulf them.

Since we were after quick action, the varieties we planted are veritable tree eaters.

Because it is reputed as the most vigorous of all *Clematis* species (quickly to twenty feet or taller), we planted *C. montana*, just like the ones that Vita Sackville-West used at the base of her tower at Sissinghurst. We knew that we didn't have to worry about an unprecedented freeze in northern California because *C. montana* is also known for its hardiness. *C. montana* blooms only in the spring of each year, but what a spectacle! Two-inch flowers that resemble anemones start out white in bud and end up pink in bloom. Blossoms form a shimmering cascade that completely hides foliage.

Gardeners have quibbled for years over precisely how *C. montana* smells. Some say macaroons, others boiling toffee. To our noses, as to Louise Beebe Wilder's, it smells most like vanilla blended with bitter almond. No matter what you believe it smells *like*, be forewarned that the fragrance of *C. montana* is so strong that many people can handle the heady perfume of no more than three or four blossoms floated in a bowl.

Since it grows almost as fast as *C. montana* and blooms in late summer or early fall, we planted *C. paniculata* (often called *C. dioscoreifolia*). This variety sports blossoms that are only an inch wide, but it showers its plants with them from head to foot. The fragrance is not unlike that of *Daphne*.

Because we wanted an evergreen variety to relieve the monotony of winter's deciduous stretches, we planted *C. Armandii*. We had read that it grows with gusto, but ours hovered at ground level long after the deciduous varieties had taken off. Once it started growing, however, it made up for lost time and scrambled to over thirty feet tall in less than three years.

'Nelly Moser' may not be one of the more notably scented clematises, but its bold color combinations make up for any lack of perfume. Although shading will differ, basic colors are mauve and fuchsia—a terrific combination in the right spot.

The leaves of *C. Armandii* are up to five inches long and are grouped in threes. White, fragrant blossoms that eventually fade to pink also appear in sets of three, as clusters at the tip of every branch.

Finally, we planted 'Duchess of Edinburgh' because we had seen it flourishing in Bois de Boulogne in Paris, and we wanted some double, white, fragrant blossoms of our own. Besides, local gardeners had tipped us off with the welcome news that the Duchess, if properly respected, blooms twice a year.

A friend of ours has managed apartments in the same five-story San Francisco Victorian for more than fifty years. Although she can't remember exactly when, not long after she moved in, she planted clematises at the bottoms of four wide light wells "that seemed to get just enough sun to make plants crane their necks for it." According to our friend, the clematises took an eternity to get above the second floor, but once they did, they quickly climbed to the roof. The plants now look like elderly wisterias, with huge, gnarled trunks. For more than a month in late spring, timid tenants in fear of the bawdy clematises don't dare open their bathroom or kitchen windows. Fragrance troopers *keep* their windows wide open, swearing that they never overdose on the intoxicating perfume, even in the evening, when fragrance reaches its peak.

Jasminum
Jasmine

The fragrance of jasmine has been acclaimed since perfume was first concocted. Jasmine was among the earliest fragrances to be captured in enfleurage (embedding blossoms in fat in order to extract and preserve their essential oils). Before pomades were available, women in the East used to roll oiled jasmine blossoms into their hair to sweeten it. Today jasmine is a mainstay in perfumery, potpourri, and the tea industry.

If you're confused between *Trachelospermum* and *Jasminum*, join the rest of us; unfortunately both are commonly called jasmine. In fact, they're not even related. *Trachelospermum*, or star jasmine, is a member of the Apocynaceae—periwinkle—family, whereas *Jasminum* is a member of the Oleaceae—olive—family. Even so, the two jasmines are uncommonly similar—they both vine or can be trained as shrubs, and both produce white or yellow, intensely fragrant flowers.

Although there are a few hardy varieties of *Jasminum*, most are tender. Then, too, not all jasmines are fragrant; unfortunately some of the most strongly perfumed varieties are the most sensitive to cold. For those in temperate climates or for you who are willing to go to certain efforts for winter protection, there are more than two hundred species of *Jasminum* from which to choose.

Although native to India, *J. grandiflorum*, often called Spanish jasmine, has naturalized itself all over Florida. Spanish jasmine is semi-evergreen, with glossy leaves and rather large flowers, for a jasmine (to an inch and a half across). The white, powerfully fragrant blossoms appear throughout summer.

J. humile, or Italian jasmine, grows either as a shrub or as a vine. In either case deliciously scented, bright yellow, starlike, half-inch blossoms appear in late summer and persist into early fall.

J. nitidum demands long stretches of warm weather to bloom well. Where it's happy, however, angel-wing jasmine, as *J. nitidum* is also called, produces unique blossoms that are shaped like tiny, white pinwheels. Because it responds well to pruning and since its growth is aimless anyway, *J. nitidum* makes a good container plant or a shrubby ground cover.

J. officinale, native to Persia and often called common white jasmine, is similar to *J. grandiflorum*, but it grows taller (to thirty feet) and has smaller blossoms, pungently scented nonetheless. Flowers that look like small funnels mass themselves into elegant sprays.

Don't plant *Clematis montana* casually—it's a house-eater. If you can provide vines with adequate support, however, you'll be rewarded with billowing masses of some of the most strongly scented flowers you'll ever smell. *C. montana* blooms only once each year, but it's a spectacle when it does. Individual blossoms resemble those of anemones; the overall effect is mind-blowing.

Some of the most seductively perfumed jasmines are frost tender. (If possible, grant them the warmth of a southern exposure, as in the photograph below, left.) Also, stay on the prowl for rampant growth; where content, jasmines can scramble taller than twenty feet before you know it.

When you grow your own sweet peas (below, right), you'll have such abundant blossoms that you can afford to cut them with luxurious vines and foliage still attached. There's a trick to coaxing long stems, but no secret to abundant blooms—just keep vines picked clean of blossoms.

J. polyanthum is native to India and doesn't care for cold weather. Where it gets plenty of warmth, however, the evergreen vine quickly scrambles to more than twenty feet. Rose-colored buds open into creamy white and pink, fragrant blossoms.

Even though we were warned that *J. polyanthum* is reputed for its sensitivity to cold, we planted it anyway, over an arbor at the entrance to the fragrant garden. It looked so hardy after the first summer that we imagined it was impervious to cold. We were proven wrong when an early winter frost crumpled our ten-foot vines to the ground. Stubbornly, we replanted, vowing to give the plants some winter protection the next season. The vines that are now more than twenty feet look as though they actually could withstand winter's bite, but we wrap them just in case, taking no chance of losing that intoxicating fragrance.

Finally, even though it's really an evergreen shrub rather than a vine, *J. Sambac* is one of the most praised of all the jasmines. In Hawaii the plant is called pikake, and its blossoms are a favorite for leis. In the Orient *J. Sambac* is the variety of jasmine preferred for teas.

Getting around climatic limitations is the biggest problem for growing *Jasminum*. Once you're over that hurdle, jasmines are fairly disease free, and the only insects that attack their tender growth are aphids. Jasmines like a reasonable supply of water, and they must have their growth regularly pinched back and shaped into place.

Lathyrus odoratus
Sweet Pea

The perfume of sweet peas is universally popular among those who enjoy aromatic flowers. Some people crave it because they think it marries citrus and rose. Others insist they detect an intimation of vanilla. Whatever its scent, those who love sweet peas start smiling from yards away when they see you're bringing them a bouquet of long-stemmed, intensely fragrant, frilly blooms.

Because the English so obviously cherish the sweetly scented annual, most people believe that the sweet pea originated in Britain. In fact, it was discovered in the midseventeenth century by a monk out on a ramble in Sicily. The English didn't get their hands on it until early in the following century. Even then, development was slow, mainly because it is difficult to start sweet pea seeds outdoors in the cruel British climate; greenhouses were necessary for good germination. (That's still true today— sweet peas perform best if started in a gentle heat early in the year and moved in April to where they are to begin flowering in June.)

The first recipient of the Sicilian find was a schoolmaster at Enfield Grammar School in Middlesex who had a greenhouse and a passion for trying new flowers. Neither he nor his early successors were avid hybridizers, though, and only a few variations were produced—among them a deep pink-and-white variety called 'Painted Lady', which had the same strong,

sweet aroma of its tiny maroon predecessors. In fact, at first not much at all happened with this Italian newcomer. John Keats was so taken with the flower that he called it sweet pea, and horticulturists raved that the plant was a wonderful addition to the garden, but still few gardeners took much notice of it.

Finally, in 1870, some of the seeds fell into the hands of a man who realized the sweet pea's full potential. The Gloucestershire gardener was so convinced of its commercial value that he abandoned his career in order to work full-time cross-fertilizing sweet peas in his Shropshire backyard. His single-mindedness paid off, for thirty years later he had hybridized half of the 264 new sweet pea varieties introduced in the Bicentenary Sweet Pea Exhibition.

By the beginning of the nineteenth century, the English were insatiable in their pusuit of new sweet pea varieties. Wavy petals appeared, flowers grew larger, new colors burst forth. As fragrance was thought to be far less important than hue, varieties of sweet pea with no detectable bouquet abound today. But many others, thankfully, are magnificently aromatic, and some of the strongly perfumed early varieties remain the most popular.

Sweet peas are members of the Leguminosae family, and of a genus of more than one hundred species. Only one, however, is perfumed—*Lathyrus odoratus*. This fragrant version comes in many hues, including red, salmon, pink, lavender, and white. After ordering catalogs from sweet pea specialists, ask only for those varieties called "heavily perfumed" or "strongly scented." You'll seldom smell a thing from those that are called "lightly aromatic."

Lists of sweet pea varieties, even those known for their deliciously fresh scent, seem endless. A sampling of those bound to suit you, in an array of colors, is given here:

'Crimson Excelsior'—huge, crimson red
'Geranium Pink'—bright, midpink
'Picadilly'—salmon to rose red
'Leamington'—lilac-lavender
'Noel Sutton'—rich, midblue
'Elizabeth Taylor'—outstanding, clear mauve
'Creme Beauty'—off white
'Royal Wedding'—pure white

You can also get mixtures of colors in one packet, usually called Old-Fashioned Mix. They're always fragrant and include an array of those colors just mentioned.

There are also knee-high varieties for those of you who can't have vines taller than four feet. They, too, are powerfully fragrant and bloom on long stems.

Sunset magazine suggests a planting technique that we like. It's also welcome news to those who don't like to do a lot of ground preparation, as it means digging a six-inch-wide trench in which all soil amendments are added. Some think a trench of one foot is deep enough, but try going deeper, to eighteen inches. The extra six inches won't be a lot of work and will pay off nicely toward summer's end, when mature vines need an extra little boost from their root development to reach the top of wherever you've trained them.

Get rid of one-third of the soil you remove—unless it's not very good garden soil, in which case get rid of all of it and use a packaged all-purpose soil mix. One-third of the refill mixture should be peat moss or sawdust. Some all-purpose garden fertilizer should be added, such as 20-10-10, applied at the manufacturer's suggested rate. If you use this method at planting time, all you have to do is use liquid fertilizer for the rest of the growing season.

Many people believe that all sweet peas are fragrant. In fact, only one species—*Lathyrus odoratus*—is scented. Even though you know the correct name, when ordering varieties, ask for those pronounced "heavily perfumed"; those labeled "lightly fragrant" are bound to disappoint you.

Sweet peas can be started directly within the trench when, as they say, "the ground can be worked," meaning that you can stand to be outdoors to garden and that weather forecasters aren't predicting another frost.

You can get a jump on the season by starting seeds in cold frames or greenhouses, planting them in starting pods. One more hint: soak seeds overnight before planting them. To increase germination rate, nick each seed with a sharp knife, just enough to break the skin, before soaking it. A few drops of liquid fertilizer in the soaking water won't hurt either.

As if sweet peas weren't wonderful enough on their own, they better their mark by improving the soil they're planted in. They do what is known as "fixing" nitrogen in the soil by depositing growth hormones that benefit later plantings.

To get the longest possible stems, you must follow a technique perfected in the early 1900s by an English gardener. He found that by identifying the main stem of a sweet pea early on and removing any wasted side growth, stems grew to eighteen inches or longer and produced multiple flowers.

The only trick to producing lots of blooms should be welcome news—harvest the flowers regularly. If you don't, vines "go to seed" and stop blooming in order to concentrate instead on reproducing themselves. During midsummer, you should be picking blooms every other day, perhaps daily during a hot spell. The plants won't mind, and your diligence will keep them in bloom.

Sweet peas are most satisfactory when fresh. They will dry thoroughly if you use the methods described in the chapter on preserving, and they retain their colors well. Although they end up like tiny bits of scentless crepe paper, try drying them anyway. You may be the only one who knows those vivid bits of colors in your potpourri blend are sweet peas, but seeing them may be just enough to help you conjure up memories of their delicious scent.

Lonicera
Honeysuckle

It was a toss-up whether to include honeysuckles here or along with trees and shrubs. Although there are some sensational varieties of *Lonicera* that grow into bushes rather than as climbers, we've chosen to include them all in this chapter because we, as do most gardeners, think of honeysuckles as vines.

The most frequently planted varieties of trailing *Lonicera* are not for the faint of heart or nose. Honeysuckles make their homes in the unseemliest of garden spots and, once established, scramble to blossom their hearts out with sweetly seductive, tubular flowers. In California there are hundreds of shopping malls surrounded with chain-link fences entirely covered with honeysuckle that, particularly on calm evenings, perfume whole parking lots. *Lonicera* has gobbled up miles of barbed-wire fences across America and, thriving along with weeds, perfumes many a country lane. At Garden Valley Ranch we planted voracious honeysuckles to conceal a well and its storage tanks; we dare you to find them.

By far the most popular of the rampant vining varieties is *L. japonica*, or Japanese honeysuckle. With dark, evergreen, somewhat hairy leaves, *L. japonica* climbs to heights well over 15 feet or easily covers a 150-square-foot area. Lushly scented, creamy white flowers tinged with pink and purple appear all over the vines from late spring through summer. There's a form with leaves veined yellow and another with purple flowers that have yellow throats.

L. Heckrottii, gold flame or coral honeysuckle, is semideciduous and not as vigorous a grower as *L. japonica*, but it has attractive blue-green leaves and blooms from spring to frost. Flowers that first appear as coral buds open into yellow-throated trumpets.

Be careful when selecting honeysuckle; many varieties are neither for the faint of heart nor the faint of nose—they camouflage chain-link fences and weight the air with sultry perfume. Most gardeners believe that all honeysuckles are either yellow or white, but some are hot pink, even red.

There are almost two hundred other species in the *Lonicera* genus, many of which either don't climb or aren't fragrant. Look carefully at plants that you consider buying, and make sure you can smell perfume from their blossoms. Ask also about growth habits, for honeysuckles are difficult to eradicate once they're established, so much so that they're widely planted to arrest soil erosion.

Be forewarned that honeysuckles need severe pruning every now and then to keep their undergrowth from becoming a tangled mess or a fire hazard. However, if you have an ugly fence, stump, or wall at the rear of your garden that you'd like to blot permanently from sight without a fuss, honeysuckle may just fill the bill.

Rosa
Climbing Rose

Although roses now scramble all over the United States and Britain, at one time each country had only one native climbing rose. *R. arvensis*, native to the United Kingdom, is an ugly rose that is lax in its growing habits; rather than standing upright as a bush, it trails and collapses into a mound. The blooms of *R. arvensis* aren't much either—pale, single blossoms that smell only faintly of musk. *R. setigera*, also known as the prairie rose, the climber native to the United States, is undesirable, too, for although it may reach nine feet, it will never be vigorous, and its deep pink flowers appear infrequently.

Rosarians the world over knew that the finest climbers grew in China; it was simply a matter of getting in with shears and out with cuttings. The Chinese were exceptionally suspicious of foreign explorers and refused to allow them to travel freely in their country. Until the nineteenth century, plant collectors could visit only the Fa Tee Nursery near Canton and the Chu River.

In 1803 William Kerr visited China with the majestic blessings of the Royal Horticultural Society; his endorsement paid off when he found a vigorous climber with double, white blossoms that smelled strongly of violets. The rose was named *R. Banksiae* 'Alba plena', in honor of Lady Banks, the wife of the president of the Royal Horticultural Society.

Even though restrictions on travel were still severe in the midnineteenth century, Robert

Although one usually thinks of honeysuckle as a vine, in fact, several *Lonicera* species mature into bushes or billowing shrubs. *L. syringantha*, for instance, produces lavender blossoms on a graceful, albeit deciduous, bush.

Fortune, a passionate English plant collector, found a way to roam about as no one ever had before. He shaved his head (except for a pigtail) and dressed as the Chinese did. Although he returned with three climbers unknown to the Western world, the most famous is *R. odorata 'Pseudindica'*, better known as Fortune's Double Yellow or Gold of Ophir. In the preface to my book on modern roses, M. F. K. Fisher tells of a rosy childhood memory, explaining that when the flush toilet came to southern California, settlers didn't remove the outhouses from their yards, they simply planted Gold of Ophir roses to gobble them up.

Early in the twentieth century, plant collectors were allowed to travel without harsh restrictions, and all hell broke loose in the hybridizing world. Climbing roses were soon no longer spindly and short; they were voracious, climbing to more than fifty feet. Climbing varieties were bred into all major rose families, leading to a wide array of scents. When worthy modern hybrid tea roses were introduced, they, too, were crossed with their climbing ancestors. The rest is history, well told in *Climbing Roses* by Christopher Warner.

As I admit in everything I write about roses, I favor modern hybrids because of their repeat bloom. Old roses, for the most part, have only one blooming cycle each year. I admit that it's stunning, but by August I've forgotten exactly what it was like, and I pine for more blossoms. Even with modern climbing roses, it's an uphill battle, since no climbing rose reblooms as faithfully as bushes do.

There are three modern climbing roses that enjoy high ratings by the American Rose Society. America, introduced in 1976 in honor of the bicentennial, is the only climbing rose yet to win an All-America award. Its coral color might not be for everyone, but its clean fragrance is. Royal Sunset is a strongly fragrant apricot climber that repeats its bloom about as quickly as does any variety. Then there's Altissimo—a house eater that will grow as a climber, pillar, mountainous shrub, or any billowy way you train it. Altissimo has dark red, seven-petaled, fragrant blooms with bright yellow stamens.

Besides roses that were hybridized as climbers, many varieties that first grew as conventional bushes have spontaneously mutated a

Madame Isaac Pereire, a member of the Bourbon family, can be shaped into a fountainous shrub, but it is happiest grown as a climber or pillar. However you ultimately train it, you'll be blessed with scads of sinfully fragrant blooms that swirl and quarter their magenta petals. If you want to dry whole blossoms for additions to potpourri blends, Bourbon roses are ideal. Early summer's bloom is prolific, autumn's is modest, with a smattering in between.

sport that climbs. Fortunately, several outstanding modern roses have accomplished this feat: Angel Face, Dainty Bess, Double Delight, and Queen Elizabeth, to name just a few fragrant varieties. Some roses that first grew as bushes actually grow better as climbers. Sutter's Gold, for instance, has intensely fragrant, yellow-and-red blossoms whether it grows upright or as a vine, but the climbing version is by far the more vigorous.

Roses don't climb in the usual sense, because they have no tendrils for attaching themselves to what they're growing on. Climbers must be trained, shaped properly, over whatever they grow on.

If you consider planting climbers, commit this to memory. They must always be trained to arch their canes with tips pointing downward. This shaping technique causes sap to travel the full length of canes and encourages blooms on stems all the way along. Besides, trained this way, they're pretty on a trellis or fence even when not in bloom.

Trachelospermum
Star Jasmine

No evergreen climbing plant is more often praised for its fragrance than is the star jasmine. Italians are so fond of it that you'll spot jasmines climbing and twining their way over Tuscan walls and sniff the heady sweet perfume on many a summer evening from Venice to Sicily.

Although the *Trachelospermum* genus includes more than ten species, *T. jasminoides* is by far the most frequently grown. Also known as cape jasmine, *T. jasminoides* starts out slowly, but once established quickly scrambles to more than twenty feet in any direction you choose to train its aimless self-clinging tendrils. New foliage is shiny and light green, but matures into lustrous, dark green, three-inch leaves. Intensely sweet, white flowers up to an inch across that look as though they're made of wax bloom profusely in clusters on short side branches.

If you want to train jasmine as a vine, you must begin coaching early by providing support as soon as you plant. Cording or wire is necessary to coax plants in the direction you wish them to grow. Once they get the idea, plants will obligingly scramble over large fences, posts, trellises, or walls. (If you want shrubs or ground cover, you must pinch back the lead shoots of baby plants to encourage bushiness.)

Jasmines like lots of water and no weeds to compete with their springtime feeding. Older plants should be cut back by one-third each year to prevent woody inner growth. Jasmines are not strangers to mites and mealybugs.

T. asiaticum is similar to *T. jasminoides*, but doesn't grow quite as large (vines to fifteen feet)

Rosa Soulieana (below, left) is a robust climber. Each spring, plants are covered from head to toe with blossoms that many people believe smell like ripe bananas.

The French like to swag everything, even the roses in the lovely garden in the core of Bois de Boulogne in Paris (below, right). By the end of summer, these roses will provide splashes of color along ropes, split rails, and even over ten-foot tripods. If you want your climbing roses to bloom repeatedly the way your bushes do, select carefully the varieties you plant. Some hybrids have only one magnificent spring bloom; others have a modest repeat in fall, but some bloom all season long.

and has smaller and darker leaves, and its blossoms are more yellow than white. *T. majus* is for those of you who live in harsh winter climates. Leaves are long, and the plant will quickly camouflage an entire wall, but flowers aren't as sweetly scented as others of the genus.

When you consider that star jasmine wasn't introduced to the botanical world until 1846, you begin to appreciate how popular it has become. Then again, if you're one of those people who enjoy an intoxicating perfume during a sultry, summer saunter, you wonder why *Trachelospermum* isn't even more popular.

Wisteria

Next to climbing roses, the wisteria is the most popular deciduous vine in the world. This is thanks to a hardiness that enables it to survive all but the cruelest of winters, great adaptability (it can be grown as a vine, tree, shrub, or bank cover), showy blooms, and luscious fragrance.

The scented varieties are natives of China, Japan, or the United States. Those from the Far East were first brought to the Western world from China in the early nineteenth century and introduced as *Glycine sinensis*, commonly called the grape-flower plant. It was later renamed *Wistaria* (then *Wisteria*) in honor of the American botanist Charles Wistar.

Wisterias are members of the Leguminosae family, as are sweet peas, which have a similar vanilla fragrance. The pealike blooms droop in clusters called racemes. Some varieties open their flowers slowly along their racemes; others pop all at once. Colors include purple, lilac, lilac-blue, pink, and white, with all shadings in between. Early bloomers show off in April; later varieties flower well into June.

Wisteria is a genus of ten species, four of which are known for their fragrance and availability.

W. floribunda is native to Japan. Most varieties of this species, which reach heights of up to thirty feet, produce ten- to twelve-inch, violet-blue racemes. One form, 'Macrobotrys', produces powerfully fragrant lilac-and-blue flowers along racemes that often reach three feet in length. Another, 'Rosea', has a distinctive pink coloring with purple at the wing (base) of each flower.

W. macrostachya is the U.S. native. It's vigorous, with lilac-colored racemes crowded softly along the middle to upper reaches of its curvaceous vines. Compared to its Oriental cousins, it is delicately scented, which may be a drawback to those of you interested in perfume power.

W. sinensis, the Chinese variety, has strongly aromatic, clear mauve flowers on a vine that can fill a 100-foot tree. 'Alba', a white form thought to be the first wisteria introduced to the West, is even more heavily perfumed. *Sinensis* foliage is bronzy green when young.

W. venusta is also a native of Japan. Its flowers aren't as perfumed or as long as other varieties, but they're fatter. They're pure white with a yellow blotch at their bases. Fuzzy down often covers the stems and parts of the leaves. The form 'Violacea' is violet-purple.

Before you commit yourself to a wisteria plant, be certain of three things:

1. You want it for keeps. Once it has established its massive root system, wisteria is almost impossible to eradicate.

2. You can provide strong supports for it to vine and trail over. When in full foliage near season's end, mature plants put on weight like a hungry tomcat set loose in a tropical fish store.

3. You are willing to train its aimless growth. Especially when young, these plants seem to know neither where you want them to go nor how to attach themselves. Wisteria vines must be tied strongly, but loosely enough to accommodate their rapid girth expansion.

With a little help from you, robust varieties will quickly climb two stories up the side of your house, fill spaces within exterior chimneys, or march along any roof line. Wisterias are the perfect plants for pergolas, arbors, and trellises. When in bloom, they'll provide a dense screen between you and your neighbors, and an even thicker one when foliage follows. The screen will disappear, of course, when their deciduous habit forces them to shed those leaves almost overnight. However, by winter you will probably be spending less time outdoors anyway, except when you are pruning.

Although wisterias aren't particularly fussy over soil, the dirt should drain well so that frequent irrigation doesn't leave roots sitting in water. They appreciate feeding, particularly with 0-10-10 at season's end. Remember that dormancy is broken with the appearance of blooms. That's quite a show to expect from a plant with only a smattering of foliage to help provide sustenance. Give them some food to digest as vines go into hibernation.

Plants that have been in your garden for only one year should be pruned only lightly, or not at all if you can live with their aimless habits for another season. During this time, their growth above ground is providing food for a well-developed root system.

After a year, you must begin pruning if you're going to have any say at all in the shape the mature vine will assume. If you're training it up a post with a trellis or arbor above, try to identify the main stem and cut out all others, especially suckers that abound at the base. Usually you'll have no problem identifying the primary stem—it will be longer and noticeably thicker than the others. Sometimes it's a close call between two. If your framework will support both, leave them. If it might not, make a decision and remove one, or the whole thing may topple down. Also, cut out the weak side shoots you find growing all along the vine's length—they'll never get any stronger, always deferring to the development of their superiors.

Although you'll love the show your vines provide outdoors, you'll be dying to cut some blooms for the house. Unless you use some of the vials like those used for orchids, or weighted containers with narrow channels within them, you'll find the blooms are difficult to handle. Pick some anyway and use them as best you can. You'll have so many on the vines that no one will ever miss the few you snitch for your living room.

During each growing season, vines of wisteria produce seed-pods, many of which literally explode during summer or lazily drop to the ground in winter. Some, however, persist until spring and dangle at the same time blooms do.

CHAPTER IV

Identifying Strongly Scented Roses

This book, the one before, and indeed Garden Valley Ranch itself, owe their existence to roses—the queen of flowers and our mainstay. So we're hardly unbiased where roses are concerned. Rather than assault you with the many reasons that you, too, should grow roses, we'll simply mention that no other flower blooms more faithfully than do roses and that there are varieties with blossoms in every color but blue. In this chapter we'll dispel some myths and mention roses famed for their perfume.

Rosy Myths

Some gardeners steer clear of roses because "they're too much trouble." If you query those who perpetuate this exaggeration, you'll learn that, for them, trouble is synonymous with spraying. While it's true that roses like more-than-average water and food, so do other pet garden plants. No, spraying is surely the bugaboo, for as impenetrable as roses appear, they're subject to untold fungi, diseases, and insects. While hybridizers are determined to breed roses that are more disease resistant than any before, no rosebush is yet so hardy that it doesn't demand periodic spraying. The good news is that spraying today isn't nearly so onerous a task as it once was. Thanks to companies such as Ortho, there are now liquid sprays in one easy-to-use formula that effectively conquer common rose diseases and insecticides with extended protective powers.

When I started growing garden roses, I was advised to plant both old varieties and modern hybrids. "Decide for yourself which you prefer," my mentor advised. What my consulting rosarian didn't mention was that most gardeners finally opt for one of the two camps and that the two rarely see eye-to-eye.

What separates old from new? Most agree that it's the year 1867, when the silvery pink La France was hybridized by Guillot Fils. Nineteenth-century hybridizers wanted new forms, more specifically, blossoms with high, pointed centers. La France was the first variety that promised to fulfill their dreams, but its supply of pollen was stretched thin as hybridizers scrambled to parent crosses.

Rose breeders were shameless in their rush to introduce new varieties, and they had their sights firmly fixed on only two elements: form and color. They didn't care what the bushes that their new babies grew on looked like, how disease resistant they were, nor even whether or not their blooms were fragrant. Although they succeeded in getting new colors, they also got just what they deserved: scentless blossoms.

By the beginning of the twentieth century, there were enough new varieties around that a new name was needed to separate old from new. Those who preferred the older varieties began calling them "garden" roses, labeling their offspring merely "modern."

I prefer modern roses purely for their manageable bushes and faithful reblooming cycles. Gardeners who insist on sticking with old garden roses claim they do so because old varieties are better for landscaping (I agree), more disease resistant (I do not agree), and more fragrant than their modern offspring (Bull!).

Anyone who says that you will not find richness and diversity of fragrance in modern roses hasn't stuck his or her nose into some modern varieties I can name—Fragrant Cloud, for instance. Hybridized by Germany's Tantau in 1963, Fragrant Cloud satisfies the piggiest of perfume fanciers. We attend an annual rose

The garden at my residence in San Francisco, where all this madness began, is wall-to-wall roses. I've managed to squeeze in more than one hundred bushes by including tree roses, climbers, and miniatures. You have to sidle through sideways, but if you carry a cutting basket with you, you'll fill it to overflowing anytime from May to November.

Pink Peace is one of the few roses that close their petals each night. It's also powerfully fragrant, and the blooms are enormous once they open in the morning. Foliage is a noncommittal green that looks prone to disease but isn't. Pink Peace is a reliable bloomer, and it looks good with other roses in spite of its hot pink color.

Margaret Merril (below, left) has been causing quite a stir in Europe, but has only recently found its way to American shores. Chances are it will be received with open arms, for it's floriferous, disease resistant, and particularly fragrant for a white rose.

I've never met anyone who doesn't like Just Joey (below, right)—the something-for-everyone rose. If you like stunning form, Just Joey has it in spades. If fragrance is your thing, you have some sniffing to do if you expect to find a substitute. And if you're into size, Just Joey is a must. The bush remains smaller than you think it should, but the blooms just won't quit.

show that has a special class for the most fragrant rose, judged by a sightless person. Any rose bloom, old or new, can be entered. We wish we had kept track, but we're certain that either Fragrant Cloud or Mister Lincoln (1980) has won more than half of the time.

As far as a range of scents is concerned, modern roses have that too. Many people believe that White Lightnin' (1980) smells of citrus and *Rosa Soulieana* (1896) like ripe bananas. Although those addicted to the perfume of roses might not be able to come up with smellalikes for their pet varieties, they swear that they don't smell like one another.

One rose myth that won't bother any of you except those who intend to make potpourri is that roses retain their aroma once dried. They don't. The lustiest of varieties hold on to but a hint of their perfume once they're dehydrated. Essential oils are a must for refreshing lost scents.

The biggest of all rose myths is that all varieties are fragrant. They're not. Peace, for instance, the world's most famous rose, has no distinctive scent, nor do countless other varieties, both old and modern.

As with other flowers whose scents are personal, roses smell differently, depending on who's doing the sniffing. Many people, for instance, swear that Tropicana isn't just fragrant, but that its blossoms smell specifically like

raspberries. Sniff though I might, to me Tropicana smells no better than plastic. To the contrary, I'm mad about the fragrance of Precious Platinum, while others claim it has only a mild scent. If you can, smell for yourself. If you can't, here are both modern and old garden roses famed for their perfume.

Modern Roses

The easiest way to group modern roses is by color. The American Rose Society (ARS) lists seventeen official color classes. For our purposes only seven are important—white, yellow, orange, pink, red, mauve, and blends—the other ten are either shades of these colors, or a color such as russet, which doesn't deserve a separate class.

Just as I suggested in *Growing Good Roses*, I believe that your rose-shopping bible should be the ARS *Handbook for Selecting Roses*—a yearly publication that costs only one dollar, but is worth hundreds. In that handbook roses currently being marketed are rated on a scale of one to ten as to performance both in the garden and in exhibition. Although the rating system is flawed because only a minority of rosarians take the time to vote each year and because too many ballot casters also exhibit, I don't know of a more reliable source (other than word of mouth or a smell for yourself) for learning which rose varieties to buy. If you're a newcomer to roses,

stick with varieties rated 8.0 and higher (8.0 is the lowest rating a rose can have and still be considered "excellent"). Save roses with lesser ratings, especially those 5.9 and lower—"of questionable value"—for later, after you've mastered the care of truly great roses. Advocating fragrant roses that mostly enjoy ratings above 8.0 by the voting members of the ARS (some are rated only slightly lower), I offer some suggestions, by color.

Among highly rated white roses is Pristine, my pick for *the* rose of the seventies. While the fragrance of Pristine won't overwhelm you (it's mild at its strongest), the performance of its bush is incomparable—strong, upright, floriferous, and reasonably disease resistant. Sheer Bliss, an offspring of Pristine and too new to be conclusively rated, may not be as vigorous a grower as her ancestor, but she's considerably more fragrant.

There are three white floribundas worthy of consideration. If you live in a warm climate, choose Evening Star, which requires heat to open it to perfection. Those who reside where it's cool might select Ivory Fashion—a variety light in petalage that opens prematurely where it's hot. Whatever your climate, there's always Iceberg, thought by many to be the best rose in the world.

For my money two other white roses, more fragrant than any yet mentioned, are worthy of

a spot in your garden. One is underrated by the ARS; the other has only recently been imported and isn't yet rated. White Lightnin', an All-America selection in 1980, has pungent, lemony fragrance. Unfortunately, it was registered as a grandiflora rather than as a floribunda (which is what it really is) and has suffered ever since. Exhibitors don't like it because the bush rarely blooms in classic grandiflora style—sprays with blossoms opened to the same degree. Instead, White Lightnin' thinks it's a floribunda and blooms with flowers in various stages, all on one stem. If you're interested in fragrance rather than competition, however, who cares?

Although Margaret Merril, an icy white stunner, was introduced in Britain in 1977, it still hasn't been commercially available in the United States long enough for rating by the ARS. Those of us who got wind of its heady fragrance and couldn't care less about its eventual rating already grow Margaret Merril. Its bush is tough, with leathery foliage and nicely formed blooms.

Yellow isn't a leading color among fragrant roses. In fact, Sunsprite is the only pure yellow variety currently listed among highly rated roses. Sunsprite *is* fragrant—pungent, in fact. I wouldn't suggest growing it, however, for the most annoying of habits—it prematurely drops its petals. Sure, the petals are fragrant

Even though it has been around since 1969, for my money, Angel Face is still about the best of today's mauve roses. Its blossoms are intensely fragrant and have ruffled petals surrounding a mass of golden stamens. Like most floribundas, Angel Face has clusters of blooms on each stem on a bush that grows low to the ground.

even when they fall one by one, but wouldn't you rather have them massed into a blossom still atop a stem? So would I, which is why I choose Gold Medal as the best of today's fragrant yellow roses. Although passed over as an All-America selection, and still languishing with only a 7.8 rating, Gold Medal is a terrific rose, particularly if you can allot space to a tall, vigorous grower.

Orange roses aren't notably fragrant. Among hybrid teas, there is only Folklore, which may not only disappoint you with fragrance, but attack you with its gargantuan growth (though it does make an impenetrable, living hedge). Among floribundas, however, there are some fine roses. From West Germany and the House of Kordes, there is Anabell—a prolific floribunda with glossy, leathery foliage. Delbard of France won an All-America rose for his orange floribunda, First Edition. Although it, too, is only lightly fragrant, its bush is a trooper with shiny abundant foliage. Finally, from New Zealand via Ireland, there's Sam McGreedy's sensational Tony Jacklin—sprays of eye-blinking, sweetly fragrant, perfectly formed, small, orange roses.

Fragrance picks up with pink roses. Duet rules the hybrid-tea class, with a workhorse of a bush. Cherish is a terrific, but low-growing, floribunda; and Queen Elizabeth is not only the first grandiflora, it's still the best.

Unfortunately the smelliest of the pinks are rated below 8.0 (still "good," just not "excellent") in the eyes of the ARS voters. Perfume Delight, for instance, is as powerfully scented as almost any modern rose. Its bush is a problem, having less vigor than you'd like, and a bit stingy compared to other fine modern roses, but what fragrance! Some of the same can be said of Pink Peace, mainly that it, too, has overwhelming perfume. And it's free blooming, albeit with dull green, disease-prone foliage.

Fewer red roses are actually fragrant than you might suspect. Olé, for instance, is a Chinese lacquer red rose that looks like it *should* be fragrant, but isn't. Similarly, Olympiad, the dazzling All-America hybrid tea named for the 1984 Olympic Games, hasn't a whiff of fragrance in its entire glorious blossom.

Fortunately some highly rated red roses *are* fragrant, most notably Mister Lincoln. Probably the favorite red rose worldwide, Mister Lincoln is robust with perfume from its almost black bud to its cherry red, fully open blossom.

Chrysler Imperial still hangs around, though I can't imagine why, except for its memorable name. I admit that Chrysler Imperial certainly is fragrant, but I hate that its bush is certain to mildew.

Fragrant Cloud is officially classified as orange-red, a color not everyone likes. No one,

If someone complains that modern roses don't smell as sweet as old garden varieties, suggest that he or she take a whiff of Fragrant Cloud—it's as richly perfumed as any rose, ever. Hybridized in Germany by Tantau, Fragrant Cloud is known in Europe as Duftwolke or Nuage Parfumé.

however, quibbles about Fragrant Cloud's perfume, which is ravishing. In Europe Fragrant Cloud is marketed as Duftwolke and Nuage Parfumé.

Among floribundas, Europeana is a good choice even though you won't swoon over its perfume. Europeana is sweetly, but lightly, scented. As a performer, however, it's unrivaled in its class.

Almost all modern, mauve roses are fragrant. That's because Sterling Silver, the first true mauve hybrid tea and somehow related to all modern roses, is powerfully perfumed. It's also a lousy rosebush, rated far below the cutoff for roses "of questionable value." Sterling Silver's grandchildren are another matter.

Foremost is Angel Face, a prolific floribunda packed with perfume. Angel Face is a true floribunda and grows low to the ground on a vigorous bush.

Paradise, a hybrid tea with an unlikely color combination—mauve and raspberry—is sweetly scented. Blooms are knockouts, but, alas, they grow on bushes that don't like to be sprayed, but are subject to disease.

Finally, there are roses labeled as blends because there is no one predominant color. Granada, for instance, is classed as a red blend; it also happens to be robust with perfume. Double Delight is a daring combination of red and white that is sinfully fragrant. Just Joey, technically an orange blend, is simply the largest, robustly fragrant, apricot rose you've ever seen; and my favorite rose, Color Magic, combines every shade of pink you can imagine into one jam-packed-with-perfume blossom.

Old Roses

Old garden roses are best divided by family—Alba, Bourbon, Boursault, Centifolia, China, Damask, Gallica, Hybrid Musk, Hybrid Perpetual, Noisette, Polyanth, Portland,

Rosarians despise being asked to name their favorite rose, for it means choosing among a list of can't-do-withouts. When I could hedge no longer, I named Color Magic my favorite. It has everything I want in a modern rose—rich colors, delicious fragrance, and dinner-plate-size blooms.

No one is certain precisely when Rosa Mundi made her debut, only that it was some time prior to 1800. Actually, it could have been almost anytime, since Rosa Mundi is a sport of *Rosa gallica officinalis*, the apothecary rose, which was at its heyday during medieval times. Although it blooms only once a year, Rosa Mundi does it in high style, with sensuously fragrant, white blossoms streaked red and pink.

Rugosa, Species, and Tea. There are fragrant members in every clan. Before you plant an old garden rose in your garden, be certain of its blooming habits. The majority of old varieties bloom only once each year—sometime during spring or early summer. Their floral shows are fabulous, but that's it—once. Other old roses, especially members of the Hybrid Perpetual and Bourbon families, bloom repeatedly (with their biggest flushes in spring).

R. damascena is perhaps the most famous of all fragrant shrub roses. The damask rose lent its name to Damascus, and, purely because of its perfume, crusaders carried seedlings to England. By the time Shakespeare began to write, *R. damascena* flourished throughout Britain, and the bard often mentioned scents as "sweet as Damask roses." Even though *R. damascena* flowers but once each year, it is still the favorite rose grown for extraction of attar of roses in Bulgaria, Turkey, and India.

R. damascena bifera, commonly known as the autumn damask, may not be quite as sweetly scented as its mother, but it does repeat its spring bloom, in fall. Crossings of *R. damascena bifera* with *R. gallica* produced the Portland family, from which came hybrid perpetuals and eventually the hybrid tea.

R. gallica is considered the oldest of all roses. *R. gallica officinalis*, also known as the apothecary rose, was widely grown during medieval times because it was thought to possess medicinal qualities. Today the apothecary rose is grown for its intensely fragrant, light red blooms followed by small, red, edible hips.

If you like the smell of musk (and can also accommodate a climber that scrambles more than twenty feet), you should consider *R. moschata*, the musk rose. Its flowers, with an indisputable scent of musk, are compared in color to the cream of Jersey cows. *R. moschata* reached Britain during the reign of Henry VIII

and has flourished ever since, not just for its musky perfume, but also because it reblooms in fall.

If rebloomers are what you insist upon, be sure to investigate the Bourbon family. We grow three bourbon roses in a 300-foot hedge because they are intensely fragrant, dry well as whole blossoms, and grow into enormous bushes that bloom madly in spring, modestly in fall, and intermittently in between. Mme. Isaac Pereire has huge, cup-shaped, crimson pink blossoms that smell like raspberries. Mme. Ernest Calvat is actually a sport of Mme. Isaac Pereire and has similar growing habits. Its blooms are also large, fragrant, and globular, but they're clear pink. Variegata Di Bologna rounds out our perfumed bourbon collection, with blossoms that are magnolia white, striped with crimson.

Representing the Centifolia family is Fantin-Latour, named for the French painter who re-ligiously included roses in his paintings. Fantin-Latour has more than one hundred pet-als, in deliciously fragrant shades of pink. Highly scented roses of the Hybrid Perpetual family are Ferdinand Pichard, with its lettuce green foliage and double flowers striped red, pink, and white; and Paul Neyron, the classic cabbage rose with hundreds of pink, tight, fra-grant petals that quarter and swirl themselves over blooms larger than eight inches across. The Alba family boasts Maiden's Blush, with oodles of once-per-year-only, pale pink blos-soms that darken toward the center. Among the "old" hybrid teas is Reichprasident von Hin-denburg, which looks like a peony, but smells like a rose.

These varieties don't even scratch the surface of the considerable array of fragrant old garden roses. For a fine pictorial reference of many more (arranged by families), have a look at *My World of Old Roses* by Trevor Griffiths.

Although John Champney, a rice farmer in Charleston, South Carolina, actually discov-ered the Noisette rose, credit is given to the Noisette brothers, who, with the help of Empress Josephine, made them the rage of France. Although Noisettes began as shades of buff, hybri-dizers weren't content until they were also saffron yellow.

CHAPTER V

Procuring Useful Herbs

Herbs are more strongly steeped in history than flowers are, probably because their lore was faithfully recorded in herbals—books on plant medicine. Long before they were valued for their aroma or culinary value, herbs were praised for their medicinal qualities. Pomander balls and herbal bags weren't devised just for their pleasant scent, but, more important, to ward off the stench of garbage, sewage, and disease. Cooks once employed herbs not so much to spice their recipes as to conceal that their meats were going bad.

With the advent of refrigeration, herbs regained appreciation for their more-subtle values—culinary flavoring and perfume simply for the sake of perfume. Even though most gardeners now grow them for the kitchen, herbs are still valued for their treatment of every ailment from the common cold to depression.

If you want to explore fragrance and don't already grow herbs, consider giving them a place all their own in your garden. Your herb patch needn't have rich soil; it won't even require much water. As you'll learn, many herbs prefer poor soil and little irrigation in order to fully develop their flavor and aroma. Those herbs that like nutrients and regular irrigation can be interspersed among other garden plants that like the same growing conditions.

Achillea
Yarrow

Yarrow's generic name, *Achillea*, comes from the belief that soldiers who fought with Achilles during the Trojan War used yarrow to heal their wounds. During the twelfth century, knights wouldn't stray from home without a supply of yarrow in their herbal first-aid kits. In France yarrow is known as the *herbe aux charpentiers* because it was said to heal wounds from carpenter's tools. Today yarrow has almost no medicinal value and is virtually useless in the kitchen, except as a poor substitute for hops in homemade beer. Even so, yarrow still flourishes because it grows so easily and blooms for so long each year.

A. Millefolium, native to Britain, where it grows wild in pastures, is also called common yarrow. Broad flower heads smell like musk, feathery leaves like feverfew. Flowers bloom all summer long, mostly in some shade of white or yellow.

There are several other species of yarrow: *A. ageratifolia*, the Greek yarrow that is low growing and blooms white; *A. Clavennae*, which has silky, silvery gray leaves; *A. filipendulina*, which grows to five-foot heights and has deep green, fernlike leaves; and *A. tomentosa*, or woolly yarrow, which looks like a deep green, hairy mat.

Gardeners who swear by companion planting like to include yarrow with their other medicinal herbs because it's said to repel ants, Japanese beetles, and flies; it's also thought to increase the volatile oils in whichever other herbs it's planted near.

Yarrow grows so easily in California that it is planted in drought areas as a fire retardant. It's also widely grown for use in dried floral arrangements.

Aloysia triphylla
Lemon Verbena

Although there are more than thirty perennial species of lemon verbena, only one will survive an average winter—*A. triphylla*, sometimes sold as *Lippia citriodora*. Even this species is tender, which is perhaps why lemon verbena isn't in wide cultivation. Gardeners who can't overdose on the fragrance of lemons, however, or those who want to blend their own pot-

Consider planting dill just outside, rather than within, your vegetable patch. Plants of *Anethum graveolens* are basically graceful, but they hurl their feathery spikes over your head, and their limbs are languid. Dill's tasty fragrant foliage, however, makes up for any awkward growth patterns.

Yarrow blooms in broad heads of white or yellow that emit a pleasant musk fragrance (the foliage smells nice too). Plants of yarrow make fine neighbors—they repel certain insects and are said to increase the volatile oils of nearby plants. A final plus is how nicely yarrow blooms dry for floral arrangements and potpourri.

pourri, wouldn't consider being without lemon verbena, fussy or not.

Plants grow to six feet in one season. Narrow, three-inch leaves arrange themselves in whorls along branches. During summer, insignificant white or lilac flowers appear in open clusters. Seeds are rarely set.

Since legginess is second nature to lemon verbena's growth habits, plants should be pruned severely before each winter. In spring new growth will appear from old stems (unless frosts knock them to the ground) as well as from the base of the plant. If you worry that plants may not survive your winters, take cuttings each summer and keep them indoors. (Be sure to take twice as many cuttings as you think you'll need, and, for goodness sake, use a root stimulant.)

Leaves may be harvested at any time for flavoring drinks or jellies, brewing tea, or as a culinary substitute for lemon or mint. If you grow lemon verbena for drying, wait until the end of summer to harvest plants. Essential oils will have intensified, and you can enjoy the lemony, fresh scent that lemon verbena freely releases all summer long. If you garden where the summers are extended, you can get two full harvests each season.

If you're interested in blending your garden's own potpourri, by all means plan for lemon verbena. Next to roses and lavender, we've found no plant to be more useful. Leaves dry well and retain good color and strong scent.

Anethum graveolens
Dill

Dill's name is derived from the Saxon *dilla*, to lull. Mothers used to rub their breasts with dill-seed water before nursing their babies, after which infants were said to drop quickly off to sleep. Tranquility was so closely associated with the herb that dill was lavishly planted in cottage gardens as an antidote to witchcraft. Dill seeds freely release their essential oils when infused in hot water, the liquid from which was used as "gripe water" to ease flatulence in children and to quicken sleep at bedtime.

Dill so closely resembles fennel, to which it is related, that, as the famous herbalist Culpeper said, the likeness "deceiveth many." Both have finely cut foliage and make tall, willowy plants. There are a couple of distinct differences though that will allow you to tell one from the other. Dill's foliage is as blue as it is green, and

Lemon verbena usually grows as a loose-headed shrub, but, as shown below, left, also as a neat standard. Leaves of *Aloysia triphylla* are so redolent of lemon that they often serve as a culinary substitute for lemon. Tiny white or lavender flowers (below, right) are insignificant compared to their lemony leaves.

its stems are hollow, whereas fennel's are filled. Dill also almost always grows but a single, thick, round stem, while fennel branches several skinnier ones.

Because seedlings are difficult to transplant, sow dill seeds where you want them to grow. Although they may take two weeks to germinate, your success rate may be 100 percent. Unlike many herbs that prefer poor soil and minimum irrigation, dill appreciates a moderately rich, moist home, especially when plants are young. Dill tolerates partial shade, but prefers full sun.

For some reason, dill is far more popular in Europe than in America. You never see a boiled new potato in Germany without a dill garnish if leaves are anywhere in sight. Scandinavians treasure dill for what it does for fish, especially salmon. The French use it even in baking cakes and pastries.

Dill's delicate foliage, which branches freely from its main stem, is tasty only when young, before the plant starts to concentrate its energies on producing seed heads. As summer heat increases, leaves start to yellow and wither as the plant diverts energy to flat heads of pale yellow flowers atop two- to three-foot plants. As flowers fade and drop, small, bitter, oval seeds form in their places. It's these seed heads that picklers are after.

To satisfy all gourmets who frequent your herb patch, plan successive dill plantings from April through July. Leaves of eight-week-old plants can be harvested for pungent additions to an array of recipes. Sow in May those plants you intend to let go to seed. They'll do it just as cucumbers crop.

People have pickled cucumbers with dill for centuries without altering the procedure much. A recipe from 1640 reads as follows:

"Gather the tops of the ripest Dill and cover the bottom of the vessel, and lay a layer of Cucumbers and another of Dill till you have filled the vessel within a handful of the top. Then take as much water as you think will fill the vessel and mix it with salt and a quarter pound of allum to a gallon of water and poure it on them and press them down with a stone on them and keep them covered close."

Making dill vinegar is much easier. Simply soak leaves for a few days in a salad vinegar of good quality, or insert a feathery dill stem in a bottle of plain vinegar and leave it there until it begins to yellow. Then remove it, leaving its flavor behind.

At season's end, plants of dill set golden yellow heads of delicious seeds, like those below, left. On the way to maturity, plants of dill are particularly happy growing alongside runner beans. To keep your resident cook satisfied, plant dill in successive crops from April to July.

Dill is prolific and reseeds freely. If you carefully choose the spot where you grow it, you may never have to replant.

Angelica Archangelica
Angelica

This Syrian herb was named in honor of when it bloomed—May 8, the day of Michael the Archangel. Pagans believed so strongly in angelica's ability to ward off witches and evil spirits that they tied angelica leaves around the necks of their children in order to protect them from harm.

Angelica is fully aromatic, even the roots, which when freshly cut weep a resinous gum that serves as a substitute fixative for benzoin in perfumes. Absinthe, Chartreuse, several gins and vermouths, and certain Rhine wines owe the essence of their flavor to angelica leaves, roots, or seeds. Some people eat angelica stems as though they were asparagus; others prefer to candy them.

You will have to buy seeds only once, for angelica is a rampant reseeder. A year after you begin an angelica patch, you'll have plants at all stages of maturity. If you prune stalks soon after they flower, or at least before they set seeds, angelica acts the way a perennial does and grows again from its roots. If you let seeds develop and drop to the ground, young plants keep appearing in profusion the following spring.

Unlike most herbs, angelica is perfectly content growing under trees; in fact it thrives best in cool, moist spots. Also unlike its herbal relatives, angelica likes soil rich in rotted manure and compost. If you feed it well, angelica will reward you with lush tropical leaves and thick juicy stems.

Harvesttime depends on what you're after. Leaves can be cut anytime, stems in early summer; seeds should be harvested after they turn from green to yellow. If it's the resinous roots you want, wait until autumn.

Artemisia
Southernwood, Tarragon

Although there are more than two hundred species of *Artemisia*, two are favorites; one

If you're considering a knot garden, be certain to consider artemesia—the quintessential edger. Southernwood isn't popular just because its color is so easy on the eye, but also because plants behave so obediently and their leaves smell lemony.

among gardeners, another among cooks. Gardeners first.

A. Abrotanum, or southernwood, is praised for its easy cultivation; fragrant, feathery foliage; and its yellowish white, button-headed flowers. Southernwood mixes easily in borders of perennials; it looks good with practically everything, and you can always count on redolent fragrance from its grayish green leaves, usually lemon scented, but one form smells of camphor and another like tangerines.

Although herbal lore is fraught with praise for *A. Abrotanum*, much of it is contradictory. For instance, southernwood was so hailed for its ability to relieve drowsiness that parishioners took sprigs of it to church to keep from nodding off during sermons. Quite different worshipers praised *A. Abrotanum* for preventing insomnia and tied muslin bags of dried southernwood under their pillows to insure a good night's sleep. On one attribute all agree: sprigs of southernwood are effective in keeping moths out of closets. *A. Abrotanum* dries nicely and does its duty for blends of potpourri.

Southernwood needs space. Plants get to be four feet tall and almost as wide whether or not you clip them to the ground and mulch each winter. Another southernwood plus is its adaptability. *A. Abrotanum* prefers sunny, well-drained soil and not much water, especially if it's expected to maximize its fragrance.

If you mention *Artemisia* to cooks, they'll assume you're referring to tarragon, *A. Dracunculus*. French chefs don't wonder whether there are any eggs for a Sauce Béarnaise unless they've already spotted sprigs of tarragon. Many people won't touch egg dishes that aren't seasoned with tarragon.

Don't kid yourself by believing that because you're doing the cooks in your house a favor by planting *A. Dracunculus* that it's going to lend beauty to your garden. On the contrary, the plants aren't pretty at all, and you should take care to plant tarragon among other herbs that will mask its rangy growth. Although stems are leggy, they're cloaked in powerfully fragrant, tapering, upwardly curled leaves. Flowers are thoroughly incidental, and you shouldn't see them anyway if you grow tarragon in order to harvest its leaves. Plants should be harvested as soon as their lower leaves start to turn yellow— a telltale sign of age. Mature plants may require three harvests in a single season, new plants maybe only one. In any case, tarragon dies to the ground each winter and appreciates a blanket of straw while it sleeps until spring.

Never plant tarragon from seeds. *A. Dracunculus* has a botanically unnamed, nasty cousin that's commonly called Russian tarragon, and it is a virtual seed factory. Unfortunately, its leaves have no fragrance or flavor. Even if *A. Dracunculus* is allowed to fully mature, seeds are almost impossible to germinate. Don't give a second thought to buying plants instead. You don't need many, and you'll never have to buy plants again, since tarragon roots easily from cuttings, and will even winter-over nicely indoors in pots.

The species of *Artemesia* you select will depend on whether you're interested in landscaping or cooking. Gardeners choose southernwood like that pictured for its fine gray foliage; chefs prefer the tasty leaves of tarragon, which should always be planted from cuttings, never from seeds.

Borago officinalis
Borage

We don't know who first said, "A garden without borage is like a heart without courage," but we know why it was said. Borage has always been linked to emotional strength. Sir Francis Bacon noted that "the leaf of Burrage hath an excellent spirit to repres the fuligninous vapor of dusky melancholie." Charles Dickens poured a bottle of cider steeped in bruised borage into his famous cider punch to lift the spirits of his guests. (His recipe also called for two wine glassfuls of sherry and one of brandy, so success was probably assured.)

Borage has done duty, however, for more than a cocktail. Its flowers and immature leaves were eaten fresh before lettuce took over as the salad staple. When no blooms or tender leaves were handy, half-mature leaves were cooked and eaten like spinach. Borage is more flavorful than fragrant. The blooms and young foliage always taste like cucumber, but only sometimes smell of it.

Borage supposedly originated in Syria, but no one is sure of the precise spot, for once discovered, the herb spread like a weed throughout Europe. Now practically every country claims that borage grows wild in fields, meadows, and along roadsides, as well it might, for it's a rampant reseeder. This hell-bent-for-survival characteristic contradicts borage's classification as an annual. You may be astonished to see vigorous seedlings appear in a circle all around a plant you set out only last spring even before it begins to wither from winter's approach. The first frost will wipe out everything, but the seedlings will pop out again right after the first spring rains.

Don't plant borage if you're afraid of being stung—it's not called "bee bread" for nothing. Bees are gaga over it, probably because the plants stay in bloom practically forever. Piercing blue, fuzzy, star-shaped flowers with jet black anthers adorn plants atop stems two to three feet high. Borage is cousin to the forget-me-not; with a little imaginative effort you'll detect the family resemblance in their blooms.

Because the plant sprouts hair all over, borage parts look thicker than they really are. If you use stems to garnish Pimm's cup, scrape them first. If you happen to want to use borage flowers as a confection, you'll bless their down; it helps to bind sugar and egg whites to them.

The seeds are large and easy to handle, but you must put them where you want the plants to stay. Borage is one of those herbs that literally "puts down roots"; its tap root doesn't transplant well. Place seeds a comfortable distance from nearby plants. Borage grows just as wide as it does tall (about two feet). Strawberries are good neighbors for borage, as both like

Borage isn't nicknamed "bee bread" for laughs; bees are crazy about its fuzzy blue (sometimes pink), star-shaped flowers that are never out of bloom. Because borage forms taproots that resent transplanting, sow seeds where you want plants to remain, and be sure to allow ample space (borage grows as wide as it does tall).

rich, loose, well-drained soil blanketed with moist compost. Mature plants complement each other.

If you've never had borage in your garden, try a few plants in four-foot spots not otherwise reserved. We bet you'll keep it, especially if you worry whether enough bees will come calling to pollinate your less-seductive plantings.

Calendula officinalis
Pot Marigold

Some observant Roman noticed that pot marigolds were blooming on the first day of nearly every month—calends; hence a genus. Another Roman tacked on *officinalis*—any herb with official medicinal value. Today *C. officinalis* is commonly called pot marigold because it numbers among the "pot" herbs—those useful in the kitchen.

Although calendulas really do bloom most of the year, they're at their peak in August, when the sun is in its exalted astrological house, Leo. Calendulas are devout sun-worshipers; they open their petals when the sun rises and close them when it sets—a habit about which many a writer has waxed.

C. officinalis sprouts easily from light yellow, irregularly shaped seeds that can be sown directly where they are to grow. Although you need to keep weeds from competing with seedlings, after calendulas are established, they pretty much take care of themselves. Plants with bitterly pungent, long, sticky leaves reach two feet in height and blossom with daisylike flowers, each up to four inches across. Blooms range in color from orange to cream.

Although pot marigolds try to live longer than one year, you really don't want them to—plants become straggly. You needn't wonder where your replacements are coming from, however, since calendulas are energetic, rampant reseeders.

Medicinally (for everything from toothaches to piles) the only useful part of the calendula is the flower petals that surround a flavorless green center. Petals should be plucked one by one and dried in the shade. If you're drying calendulas for potpourri, of course, that's another matter—flower heads can be dried whole. Although they are still sometimes used in the kitchen to spice a salad or stew, most cooks agree that fresh petals of pot marigolds taste pasty at first, then salty, and are at best a poorman's saffron.

Chrysanthemum Balsamita
Costmary

Costmary is known as Bible leaf because colonials used it as bookmarks in prayerbooks. (If sermons grew boring, churchgoers could revive themselves by bruising and sniffing costmary's leaves.) Though closely related to tansy, also a

Costmary has spiffy relatives, including this one—feverfew. Whichever member of this chrysanthemum family you select, you'll be blessed with a plant that complements everything nearby, and emits a pleasant balsamic fragrance too. Foliage dries nicely and retains a flavorful scent.

member of the Compositae—daisy—family, costmary is more pleasantly scented, mostly of balsam.

Don't look for seeds of costmary; there aren't any. Like mint, plants are propagated by division of their roots. Some leaves grow close to the ground, others on two- to three-foot stems; all are light green, shiny, pear shaped, and finely toothed. In late spring plants of costmary bear small, pale yellow, buttonlike flowers. Leaves should be harvested as soon as they begin to turn yellow.

Costmary is praised by gardeners for deterring weeds and at the same time providing a flattering background for showy annuals. Costmary also flavors teas and the finest of German sausages. Leaves dry quickly and retain much of their scent.

Helichrysum angustifolium
Curry Plant

The only *Helichrysum* one finds in most nurseries is *H. bracteatum*, commonly known as everlasting strawflower. The reason strawflowers are called everlasting is that their papery pompoms seem to last an eternity after being dried. While strawflowers are void of scent, they have some powerfully fragrant cousins.

H. angustifolium, best known as curry plant, is a remarkable feat of nature. While kitchen curry is actually a somewhat complicated combination of spices, *H. angustifolium* somehow manages to capture the precise blend of scents in its leaves.

Although curry plants are native to South Africa, they also grow as perennials in moderate climates, particularly if planted in sandy soil that enjoys full sun. Silvery leaves on plants up to two feet tall smell exactly like curry, most strongly in the evening. In late summer bright yellow flowers appear on foot-long stems. Like their cousin the strawflower, blooms from curry plants are everlasting. There is a miniature species, *H. italicum*, which doesn't grow more than one foot tall, but which also has pungent silvery foliage.

Curry plants make nice edgings and borders. Leaves dry well and retain their powerful scent. Just as when you season with curry in the kitchen, you must be cautious with curry plant when blending potpourri—a little of it goes a long way.

Hyssopus officinalis
Hyssop

Hyssop is derived from the Greek word *azob* (a holy herb); it was the official herb for cleaning temples and other sacred places. Mentioned in the Bible as a purifier, hyssop was used by the Egyptians for cleansing lepers. As far back as there are notes on such matters, hyssop has been praised as a tea, and infusions made from the herb were thought useful in the treatment of numerous diseases of the chest. Essential oils

Curry is a blend of several specific spices, but *Helichrysum angustifolium* (left) manages to combine them all in one silver-leaved plant that sports yellow blossoms. Leaves dry well and make fine additions to potpourri, but be sure you don't use too many, or your entire batch will smell only of curry.

Although hyssop (right) has long been praised for making tea and for curing certain ailments, today it's valued for perennial white, pink, or blue additions to her baceous borders. Foliage is shiny and powerfully aromatic when bruised.

distilled from green hyssop plants were once an essence for English eau de cologne. Today hyssop is valued primarily for its contribution to the garden, particularly to herbaceous borders.

Hyssop is a shrubby, hardy perennial that grows to three feet tall each summer. Leaves are shiny green, thin, long, and powerfully aromatic when bruised. Flowers, which bloom from leaf axils, are either white, pink, or blue (the blue variety is considerably more vigorous than the other two). Hyssop must be grown in full sun, but it isn't fussy about the soil in which it's planted as long as it is kept reasonably dry.

Leaves can be harvested at any time of the year. When plants bloom, however, their flavor diminishes and their stems become woody. If you're growing hyssop for brewing tea, cut some of the plants to the ground before they bloom, and dry the leaves whole.

Lavandula
Lavender

You may think we've blundered in including lavender in this chapter, but we haven't—lavender is officially classified as an herb. Although its leaves are scented and useful in potpourri blends, it's the flowers almost everyone is after, including distillers. Lavender bows only to roses in commercial distillation of essential oils.

Native to southern Europe, lavender was popular with pre-Christian Greeks and Romans as a scent for soaps. In fact, its generic name, *Lavandula*, derives from *lavare*, the Latin verb "to wash."

Although lavender is a genus of more than twenty species, there are only three with which you'll want to familiarize yourself. If volume is your goal, *L. spice* will satisfy you with its prodigious yield and copious oil content. If you're after flowers, *L. angustifolia* is the variety for you. Known as English lavender, it's thought to be the "true lavender" because its oil is the most fragrant. *L. Stoechas* is the Spanish variety, also fragrant and prolific, but partial to temperate climates such as that around the Mediterranean. There are also several dwarf varieties that are perfectly suited for knot gardens. In fact, few plants make a more attractive evergreen hedge. Blooms range in color from white to purple, with all shades of pink, mauve, and lavender-blue in between.

When starting your own lavender, don't begin with seeds; they're difficult, requiring about four weeks, to germinate. Although several may sprout, they'll have a disappointingly low survival rate. It's best to buy young plants, after which you can take cuttings in August of each year for productive plants the following spring.

Lavenders are shrubby perennials and prefer a sandy, coarse, even rocky, soil. They all appreciate reasonable drainage and lots of sun.

Lavender blooms in colors ranging from white to purple, and three species are famed for their sweet, fresh fragrance. Flower spikes can be dried whole, but if you're after maximum perfume, harvest them just before blossoms open. If you're late, pick blooms anyway and sprinkle them over carpets before you vacuum.

The more-robust varieties should be planted three to four feet apart—closer if you want to create a hedge rather than billowing clumps. Compact, dwarf varieties should be planted twelve to fifteen inches apart since they grow only as wide as they do tall.

When it comes to diet, lavender is hardly a gourmet. It doesn't respond well to feedings and never to anything fresh. If you need to mulch because of soil erosion, don't use green manure, but the oldest, most well composted you can find. It's said that lavender growing in poor soil, even those with high chalk content, produces the most fragrance.

Many gardeners suggest discarding or replacing plants after five years, when older plants become leggy. You can extend this period rather indefinitely by giving plants a hard cutting back each March or April. By so doing, you'll not only shape bushes, but also you'll encourage bushy, symmetrical growth.

The leaves of lavender plants can be harvested anytime, but flowers should be gathered just before they open because they lose their aroma quickly after they blossom. Spikes of lavender can be harvested to enjoy as cut flow-

ers, which last well. Or they can be picked and either hung in a dry place or placed on screens to dry. With both techniques, try to keep the spikes in one direction; that way they can later be gently raked off their stems by hand, several stalks at a time.

Lavender retains its sweet, fresh scent when dried, making it a favorite for those who don't want to fuss with essential oils. For centuries dried lavender flowers have been sewn into muslin bags and tucked among linens. Blooms can also be left on their stems for dried arrangements and won't fall off if handled gently. If you're into arts and crafts, you can make lavender balls and tussy-mussies. When you have more blossoms than you know what to do with, try sprinkling some onto carpets before you vacuum—you'll freshen the mustiest of smells.

Majorana hortensis
Marjoram

Although Italians swear by basil, Scandinavians by dill, and French by tarragon, cooks the world over love marjoram. One good reason is that, unlike most herbs, marjoram is at its best when dried, meaning that you can enjoy it year-

Although your garden might not look like Villandry in France's Loire Valley, if you have formal hedges with no plants between them, by all means consider lavender. Bushes of lavender remain compact and in bloom most of the summer.

round. Also, even when sprinkled too liberally, marjoram doesn't dominate the flavor of a dish the way oregano (which marjoram resembles), rosemary, and cilantro do.

In Portugal, where it's native, *M. hortensis* is a perennial. Because it won't tolerate even mild winters, however, almost everywhere else in the world, marjoram is treated like an annual.

Since seeds are unusually small and tedious to tend outdoors, marjoram should be sown inside in starter pots or flats and transplanted after the soil in their future home has warmed. Because it grows from shallow roots, marjoram flourishes in a mulch rich in humus. (If you use manure, said to sweeten marjoram's flavor, be sure that it's well rotted.)

Plants grow upright to one foot with square stems surrounded by short branches cloaked in oval, fuzzy leaves. You'll hardly notice marjoram's white or pink flowers because they're almost entirely surrounded by small foliage.

Although cooks may snip marjoram throughout the year, there should be two main harvests. Plants should be cut to one inch above ground when flowers appear at the tips of stems. Hell-bent to reseed themselves, lopped-off plants of marjoram rebound with new vigor, and the second harvest (again when flowers appear) is better than the first.

Cuttings dry easily on paper or screens in warm, shaded areas. After leaves are dry, they may be crumbled to desired sizes or mortared into powder.

Melissa officinalis
Lemon Balm

Nuns of the Carmelite order used to concoct an invigorating wash that was blended from angelica root, nutmeg, lemon peel, and leaves of *M. officinalis*. Carmelite Water was said to "driveth away melancholy and sadness." Elizabethans added fresh leaves of lemon balm to their bath water to "refresh and comfort" the body. Shakespeare mentions lemon balm in *The Merry Wives of Windsor* by including it among strewing herbs—those you spread around the house to make it smell inviting for guests.

While the flowers or foliage of many plants smell strongly of lemon, none is easier to grow than *M. officinalis*. Although lemon balm is native to southern Europe, it now grows wild both in England and the United States.

M. officinalis will grow in sunlight, but it prefers shade. The soil in which lemon balm is planted should be fertile and friable, and water must be available nearby. Allow two feet between plants so they can spread sideways.

Lemon balm grows two to three feet tall. Leaves are heart-shaped, yellowish green, crinkled, and covered with stiff hairs that release a refreshing lemon scent whenever they're bruised. Insignificant, bluish white or yellow flowers bloom from May until October and are followed by oval, dark brown seeds.

If you want foliage to develop maximum fragrance, don't let lemon balm flower. Instead, harvest whole plants to two inches above ground as soon as you see flower buds begin to form. Dry lemon balm quickly, but out of the sun's fading rays (leaves often turn black if dried too slowly or in the sun).

Bees are particularly attracted to *M. officinalis*, as are cows. In the kitchen, leaves of lemon balm lend zest to fruit cups and salads.

Menta
Mint

When you mention mint to most gardeners, you have a fight on your hands. Mints are nuisances in the garden because they show no respect for their neighbor's soil; if it's available, mint invades it with nasty roots. Mention mint to gardeners devoted to fragrance, however, and they'll take you back to a shady, out-of-the-way spot where mint has been allowed to take over.

Mint is mentioned in the Gospel according to Saint Matthew and by Shakespeare in *The Winter's Tale*. Culpeper prescribed a compress of hot rose petals and mint leaves as a cure for sleeplessness. It is said that bees will never abandon a new hive if it has ever been rubbed

Lavender and rosemary not only look terrific planted next to each other, they like the same lean growing conditions (poor soil and little water). Lavender retains its sweet, fresh scent when dried, making it a favorite for those who want to blend potpourri but don't care to fuss with essential oils.

with mint. A monk writing during Charlemagne's rule said about the number of different varieties of mint that he "might as well try to count the sparks from Vulcan's furnace." That monk would be shocked with the varieties of mint that have come along since the ninth century. Today there are mints that include a wide variety of scents within their complicated overtones. We grow four varieties that are fine both fresh and dried for blending potpourri.

M. x piperita is the variety grown for extraction of the essence of peppermint (one acre can yield fifty pounds of oil per year). Although peppermint flowers on tall spikes, its leaves grow on short, square, black-stemmed stalks. *M. x piperita* is a favorite for brewing mint-scented tea. There is a subspecies, *M. x piperita citrata*, or bergamot mint, whose leaves are flavored with orange.

M. spicata, commonly known as spearmint, comes in two forms—one with narrow, smooth leaves, another that's crinkled. Plants of spearmint are smaller than those of the peppermint, and they bloom with leafy, purplish flowers.

M. suaveolens, often sold as *M. rotundifolia* and otherwise known as round-leaf or apple mint, is actually scented with both apple and mint. Hairy leaves are a lighter shade of green than those of other varieties, and flowers are purplish white. A cultivar, *M. suaveolens* 'Variegata', smells like pineapple.

M. Pulegium, commonly known as pennyroyal, is actually a ground cover. Plants with round leaves that stick up only a couple of inches creep along the soil. Small, lavender flowers appear in dense whorls. Pennyroyal smells strongly of mint and is a favorite in the kitchen.

Although *Mentha* is indigenous to the Near East, it now grows as though it were native worldwide. Unlike most herbs, mint prefers some amount of shade and moderately rich soil. If you're certain of the fragrance or taste you're after, plant mint from runners; seeds don't germinate true to parent plants. Where mint is grown for commercial distillation of its essential oils, runners are sold in bushel baskets.

To combat its invasive growth habits, many gardeners plant mint in pots and submerge them in the ground. While this technique helps, it won't keep mint from spreading; you must constantly be on the prowl for runners that reach out from their containers and root themselves.

Don't plant too much mint. Besides its characteristic of increasing itself so rapidly, you need only a few springs of mint to flavor a drink or to sweeten and "cool" a room.

Mentha needs harvesting as soon as its lower leaves begin to yellow. Plants can be hacked to just above the ground and mulched for winter protection.

Be cautious when you buy *Mentha*; many varieties, like that on the left, show no respect for their neighbors, and will take over their beds. Be specific, too, with the scents you select—from apple to orange. Once you settle on a precise aroma, plant mint from runners, not seeds, which rarely germinate true to parentage.

All parts of bee balm (right) are scented, even the stems. Plants dry well, too, and concentrate the nectars that bees and hummingbirds leave behind. Don't plant *Monarda* from seeds. Besides being slow to germinate, seedlings require more than a year to establish themselves before you dare to snip at their pungent leaves.

Monarda
Bee Balm

Here's a fragrant herb with a host of nick-names. Although it's most often called bee balm, it's also known as bergamot (it smells like the tropical, orange bergamot tree), Oswego tea, gold melissa, Indian nettle, and even as *Monarda*, its proper name.

Bee balm grows all over the world, but its origin is definitely American. It is native to somewhere around the Oswego area in New York. Both the common name for the plant and the town's name were probably suggested by the Indians who inhabited the area before the Shakers took over.

Dried leaves make a brisk, somewhat bitter tea. Because of this, bee balm enjoyed its finest hours during the time of the Boston Tea Party, when patriots stubbornly substituted it for imported varieties.

The Shakers, prominent American herbalists, valued bee balm for medicinal and culinary uses. They concocted infusions to soothe sore throats. They also suggested adding fresh leaves to salads and to flavor fruit cups and jellies.

Plants of bee balm are tall and erect, with stalks topped in clusters of fuzzy flowers that are usually some shade of red (*M. didyma*), but may be lavender or white (*M. fistulosa*). Stems are adorned with dark green leaves four to six inches long.

Monarda is best grown from small plants. Seeds are slow to germinate, and even when they finally sprout, it takes a year for them to establish themselves before you can enjoy a harvest. Established clumps, however, can be transplanted any time of the year except late fall. Another reason for buying plants is to assure yourself you'll get the variety you want. Because bees are so addicted to the flowers, they indiscriminately cross-pollinate bee balm with wild bergamot, producing offspring lacking in both fragrance and flavor.

If you can't stoop or squat to weed, don't plant bee balm. Areas where it grows must be weeded by hand; hoeing severely damages its roots, which grow just beneath the surface. You need only worry about weeding at planting time though; once established, clumps multiply quickly, and their prodigious roots choke out weeds.

Bee balm prefers sunny locations, but it also thrives in partial shade. Wherever you plant, soil should be kept reasonably moist and fertile. You can insure fertility by adding a one-inch blanket of compost in late fall when you cut back the plants to the ground. Mulch not only protects clumps during winter, but it also provides nutrients for shoots that burst upward each spring.

Blooms of bee balm are there for the smell, but leaves must be bruised before they give up their fragrance. Everything is scented though, even stems; and all dry nicely, making bee balm valuable for potpourri.

Bees aren't the only garden visitors attracted by *Monarda*. Hummingbirds love the nectar harbored in the deep throats of the blooms. In case you care, this nectar is much better for hummingbirds than the sugar-syrup concoctions mixed for those feeders that seem out of place in the garden anyway.

Nepeta
Catnip, Catmint

One day a visiting herbalist from Boston, upon spotting catnip among our herbs, chuckled in a way that gave us pause, and asked if we'd read the famous catnip adage before we planted it: "If you set it, the cats will eat it; if you sow it, the cats won't know it." Then she told us about a hard lesson she once learned.

If cats stalk your garden, be careful where you plant *Nepeta*—felines become frenzied over catnip's scent. *N. Mussinii*, commonly known as catmint, makes a fine border plant, especially where lavender-blue flowers complement background plantings. All *Nepeta* species dry nicely, for potpourri or for cats' play pouches.

She lives on one of those city blocks where all houses back onto a common garden. Having long ago squeezed the last possible plant into her own allocated area, she had to search for unclaimed space when a friend who knows how she adores her kittens offered her some catnip plants. When she found a spot, borrowing from a neighbor who had grown weary of replanting annuals, she planted a prodigious number of catnip clumps that very evening.

In the wee hours of the next morning, she was awakened by a loud banging on her back door. When she rushed downstairs, she found a disgruntled neighbor, who told her that whatever she had planted had acted as a summons to every cat in Boston. She grabbed a flashlight, went to the catnip patch, and found chaos and destruction. The cats hadn't just ripped out the patch; they had thrown pieces of plants into areas five and six feet away and then torn up those areas too.

If catnip is planted from seed, cats have no way of finding it. Only when mature plants are bruised or when they begin to dry do they leak the oil that drives cats into a frenzy. Once cats sniff it, they can't get enough. They plunge their noses into it, roll on it, scratch at it, and rip out entire plantings in an effort to rub the oil into their fur. We're talking about all felines, not just domestic ones; mountain lions are said to do the same thing.

The only reason our catnip hadn't been assaulted was that quite by chance we had planted it in the center of a bed encircled with thyme and chives. Even when the catnip became established, our cats didn't find it because it remained unbruised. The very evening our guest told her horror story, we picked some and presented it to our cats. Sure enough, they acted giddier than we had ever seen them. We've now moved the catnip out of the garden entirely. We still grow it, but beneath a windbreak, where the aftermath of an orgy might go unnoticed.

Although you may never relish this herb as much as your cats do, it *is* fragrant, and two varieties deserve credit for their ease in growing, if for nothing else. *N. Cataria* is the classic catnip. A perennial plant, it is covered with downy, gray-green leaves and grows two to three feet tall, with white or lavender flowers appearing every summer in clusters at the stem tips. Although it prefers light soil in a sunny area, the plant is adaptable to most garden conditions and freely reseeds itself. *N. Mussinii*, commonly known as catmint, grows to only two feet (it can be used as a rather tall ground cover). Its foliage is similar to that of catnip, and its flowers are lavender-blue.

The culinary uses for catnip seem limited to teas, although some people go to the trouble to candy the leaves with sugar, lemon juice, and egg whites. Before Europe began trading with China, catnip tea was a favorite among the tea-loving British. It's still popular in some areas, though tea addicts claim that it's a weak second to Eastern teas.

Instead of showing your cats your catnip patch and risking never seeing it again yourself, we suggest you cut, dry, and crumble leaves into muslin pouches, sew them shut, and hand them over. Cats have a passionate affinity for these toys, and you can arrange for them to play where they're not likely to do damage. By the way, dry the leaves out of the sun to retain as much of the volatile oil as possible.

Ocimum Basilicum
Basil

Basil seems to have once been schizophrenic; in the Western world, it was feared and thought to attract scorpions, whereas in its native India, basil was treated with reverence and hailed as a protector. Culpeper, the world's most famous herbalist, said of basil, "Being applied to the place bitten by venomous beasts, or stung by wasp or hornet, it speedily draws the poison to it. Every like draws its like." Meanwhile in the Eastern world, basil was grown in pots to bless temples, and houses built where basil flourished were thought to be safe from harm. Today, thankfully, almost everyone agrees that basil is a must-have herb.

Basil is the epitome of an annual and needs to be started from seed each year (the first hint of winter is enough to cripple year-old plants). Seeds of basil should be sown in rich, well-drained soil.

Since basil's aromatic essence is harbored in its leaves, not in its thoroughly incidental flowers or tiny seeds that follow, your goal in growing basil should be to keep plants from blooming. When plants get to be about nine inches tall, pinch back the main stem, but be sure to leave at least two side shoots. New growth will spring from the sides of bushes, and they, too, should be pinched back, as should the shoots that follow. This constant nipping fosters a round, lush bush that doesn't grow more than two feet tall and never develops a tall center stalk.

As you already know, herbs are as esteemed in the kitchen as they are in the garden. No herb takes a second seat to basil as far as some cooks are concerned. Italians, for instance, couldn't get through an entire summer without pesto for their pasta.

Gourmets will applaud your growing techniques since your busy fingers result in fresh basil leaves all summer long. You should know, by the way, that even healthy basil leaves arch backward from their central spine and sometimes look crinkled. If you worry that they're undernourished, look closely at their color. Dark green is what you're after; yellow leaves are a telltale sign of anemic soil.

Besides ordinary basils, of which there are numerous varieties, from compact and short to leggy and tall, there are now varieties with additional scents, such as anise, cinnamon, and lemon. There is also an 'Opal' variety ('Purpurascens') that's purple-red and looks terrific growing next to its green cousins.

Fresh basil leaves may be preserved for winter use by layering them compactly in olive oil. Leaves will also flavor vinegars if you simply insert sprigs into bottles of plain wine vinegar ('Opal' will turn it a nice shade of red).

Basil dries perfectly well when tied in bunches and hung upside down out of the sun's blanching rays. Although dried basil pales in comparison to fresh, in the winter dried leaves are welcome additions to stews and salads. Dried basil leaves are also good additions to potpourri blends, particularly when you'd like an overtone of lemon, cinnamon, or anise.

Origanum
Oregano

If you're confused between oregano and marjoram, join the club. Not only have the two herbs always been confused, horticulturists can't seem to agree on which species of *Origanum* is true oregano—some gardeners swear that it's *O. heracleoticum*, others that it's *O. vulgare*. Many cooks won't permit oregano of *any* name into their kitchens unless its flowers are known to bloom white. When in doubt, gourmets choose marjoram since oregano has a strong dominating flavor.

O. heracleoticum, native to Greece, is actually a tender, woody shrublet with a complicated, dense root system. Plants with hairy leaves grow close to the ground, but send up foot-long stalks that bear small clusters of white flowers.

Basil is a true annual— plants must be started anew each year even where winters are mild. If you want basil leaves to be as pungent as possible (and no good cook can imagine why you wouldn't), keep plants from blooming by constantly pinching back the center stalk. Nouvelle cuisine is largely responsible for the introduction of basil varieties that smell of cinnamon and lemon, even anise.

O. vulgare is also a perennial native to the Mediterranean, but it differs form *O. heracleoticum* in that it is quite hardy, grows to two-foot heights, and its dull, oval leaves are far less hairy. Flowers may be lilac, pink, purple, or white.

Oregano isn't fussy about the soil in which it grows, nor does it need more water than that in most seasonal rainfalls. If you pick fresh leaves regularly, oregano won't bloom, which is just as well since whole plants should be harvested as soon as flowers appear. Gathering leaves will also keep plants from becoming leggy. Unlike most herbs, oregano can be dried in full sun without losing its scent or flavor.

Pelargonium
Geranium

It's a pity that someone long ago started calling *Pelargonium* "scented geranium." Now few gardeners can explain the difference. *Geranium* is in fact a separate botanical genus, one far less appealing to the gardener interested in fragrance. The varieties we grow and write about are all scented *Pelargonium*, though you may still have to purchase them under the common name of scented geranium. Just remember that anyone raving about the fragrance of their "geranium," however it smells, really means *Pelargonium*.

Pelargonium is a genus of more than two hundred species native to South Africa. There are records that document pelargoniums in London .early in 1632, during the reign of Charles I. For almost two centuries, however, they were enjoyed only by those wealthy enough to afford greenhouses. It seems clear that servants in manor houses snitched leaves to try in pots on their own windowsills, for by the nineteenth century, pelargoniums flourished in cottages all over Britain. Victorians lined their stairways with pots of scented pelargoniums so that their long garments brushed the plants and perfumed the air. In summer the containers were moved outdoors to line paths for the same purpose.

Few plants offer a wider array of scents than pelargoniums. The most prevalent variety is *P. graveolens*, the "rose geranium" that is laden with geraniol, the essence of rose perfume. Other popular varieties include those that smell like lemon, orange, mint (several flavors), cinnamon, nutmeg, filbert, almond, or balsam. (We grow one variety called 'Tutti-frutti' that somehow manages to combine several of these scents all at once.)

When you visit a nursery to purchase pelargoniums, be sure to smell what you're considering purchasing. Ask permission first, explaining that you're not "picking" leaves, just

Pelargoniums are particularly easy to root—just as well since mother plants crumple to the ground each year at the first hint of frost. Pelargoniums grow so quickly, however, that seedlings planted in pots in spring will spill over before summer's end.

rubbing them to release their scent. Also, save some fingers or the back of your hand for last minute decisions. If you squeeze indiscriminately, you'll reek of a spice rack, and you won't be able to identify what you've just bruised.

Although scented pelargoniums blossom, you won't take much notice of their small flowers, whether they're white, orange, or lilac to purple; it's the leaves that matter. Foliage of most varieties is large, midgreen, deeply cut, and covered in down, sometimes oily to the touch, but always fragrant.

Before you take home your first pelargonium, be forewarned that it won't last through winter, unless, of course, you live in the tropics. The first hint of frost turns mature plants to a hideous shade of brown. If you can stand the sight, leave the dead foliage; it will help to protect the roots, which may or may not rebound in spring. Fortunately, rooting pelargoniums couldn't be easier. Slips taken at summer's end will root in plain sand, often without the help of a root stimulant. Cuttings that winter-over indoors grow to maturity the following summer.

Pelargoniums thrive in any soil that drains well. Though they prefer full sun, particularly in coastal areas, pelargoniums accept some, but never full, shade. Flavor and scent increase if plants are kept on the dry side (only the top inch

of the soil should be damp) and feedings should be held to a minimum (no more than two or three times a year).

Pelargoniums are popular among cooks for flavoring ice cream, jelly, cake, and tea. Flower arrangers like to include pelargonium leaves to insure that bouquets smell nice, especially if nothing else in the arrangement is notably fragrant. The French distill scented pelargoniums for an inexpensive substitute for rose attar, and fair-weather gardeners bless pelargoniums for being so free of diseases and pests.

Petroselinum
Parsley

It's no wonder that parsley is so steeped in history, considering how long it has been treasured. Gardeners wouldn't dream of being without a neat, bright, midgreen edging of parsley around their herb patches, cooks won't lift a spoon in kitchens without it, and herbalists consider parsley vital to most brews.

Although said to be native to Turkey, the Greeks were the ones to write most about parsley because they believed it to be the herb of Hercules. Fresh parsley was woven into wreaths to crown the heads of victors at athletic games.

Because parsley seeds are so slow to germinate (they are said to visit and return from the devil seven times before they sprout), all sorts of myths were associated with planting parsley. At one time it was thought that a crop of parsley would flourish only if it was planted either on Good Friday or by a pregnant woman. Today any of us can grow parsley successfully as long as we plant it in early spring in humus-rich soil and give it a fair share of water all summer.

Lists of parsley's medicinal values are long; it was thought to ease the pains of afterbirth and arthritis; to lift the dropsies; prevent halitosis; and to effectively combat coughs, insect bites, and vermin in the hair. Gastronomically, parsley is thought to be an effective antidote to garlic. Above all else, however, parsley is praised as a diuretic, and to "cause urine." In fact, a literal translation of the Greek word for parsley is "stone breaker." Today's herbalists still value parsley as a rich source of calcium, riboflavin, thiamin, and vitamins A and C (more concentrated than in oranges).

Even though it's usually grown as an annual, parsley is actually a biennial. In temperate climates where it doesn't freeze, parsley stops growing during the winter, but leaves one foot of roots in the ground. Early spring triggers the formation of a stalk that develops greenish yellow flowers, then grayish brown seeds. Cooks who are also gardeners treat parsley as an annual

The leaves of pelargoniums are so packed with perfume that distillers extract their essences as substitutes for more-costly oils, including attar of roses. Although varieties of pelargoniums differ widely in their fragrance, they're almost all disease and pest free.

because they're interested only in its leaves, and want them to be fresh (dried parsley pales by comparison).

Because parsley is so slow to germinate, weed well the areas where you intend to sow seeds and hope that your tiny parsley seeds sprout before the weeds do (count on a good three weeks, whether or not you're pregnant).

It's difficult to pinpoint parsley's fragrance. Mostly, fresh parsley smells like just that, fresh. It also has a wholesome, uplifting zip to it, as though you can actually sniff all those nutrients.

By far the favorite variety among Europeans is *P. hortense*, commonly called Italian flat-leaf parsley. For some reason, *P. crispum*, the variety with curly leaves, has caught on stronger in America (at least at the supermarkets). We grow both, preferring to eat the European version and look at the American one.

Rosmarinus
Rosemary

We keep a clump of rosemary near the entrance to our fragrant garden. If we doubt a visitor's olfactory system, we ask him to rake his fingers over a branch of rosemary and inhale. If he gets no smell, the subtly scented violet patch is out of the question.

Rosemary is perhaps the most pungent of all fragrant plants. If you squeeze a sprig, you won't be able to smell anything else from your fingertips until you wash off the essential oil rosemary freely releases. Rub the back of your hand or forearm over the plant instead, and save your fingers for less-robust fragrances.

The name comes from the Latin *ros marinus*, meaning "dew of the sea." Plants indigenous to the Mediterranean have a way of steeping themselves in history, and rosemary is no exception. It became an integral symbol of fidelity and remembrance in wedding and funeral services. Sprigs were interwoven into the bridal bouquet or tied with bright ribbons and given to wedding guests as a reminder of the couple's vows of constancy. At funerals sprigs were thrown into graves to pledge that the deceased's good deeds would not be forgotten.

There is a legend that the healthiest plants get only so tall—to six feet in thirty-three years, the height and age of Christ. At that stage they stop vertical growth, never to stand taller than he did. An amusing belief dates from the sixteenth and seventeenth centuries, when rosemary was prized not only for its fragrance, but also because rumor had it that it could help retrieve missing husbands. If a man left home, the story went, and the wife wanted

him back, she could soak one of his shirts in the water in which rosemary had been boiled and hang it to dry. In four days the wanderer would return.

Rosmarinus is a genus of one species, *officinalis*, although there is a ground hugger, 'Prostratus', with lavender blooms. The form 'Roseus' has pink blossoms, and 'McConnell's Blue' is semiprostrate with brilliant blue flowers. The finest form is the one seen most often, 'Tuscan Blue'. It's rigidly upright, to three feet and taller, with porcelain blue blooms. All varieties have narrow, midgreen to dark green leaves that are silvery gray underneath.

Other than sun and good drainage, rosemary has few needs, and it's almost disease free. Only snails and slugs dare attack it, and they're easy to control with bait spread around the bottoms of the bushes. Rosemary flourishes in poor soil with infrequent waterings. Once established, it requires no irrigation at all, except in the desert. Excess watering and fertilization result in rank, woody growth.

Rosemary responds well to clipping and makes a fine hedge; it is particularly attractive as a background for gray-leaved plants. Established bushes produce side branches that root all by themselves for easy transplants. Otherwise, six- to nine-inch cuttings from mature shrubs can be rooted in the spot where they are to grow.

Both cooks and gardeners praise sage—gourmets for its sharp taste (best when fresh), ornamental horticulturists for its many-colored blossoms. All sages dry nicely, both leaves (invaluable to winter chefs) and flower spikes (handsome additions to holiday wreaths).

Ruta graveolens
Rue

When you change your money for cruzeiro in Brazil and sniff something that doesn't smell good, it will probably be rue. Brazilians believe that rue brings good luck, and keep a sprig of it in their wallets and purses, saturating their cash with rue's earthy aroma. Brazilian men often smell earthy, too, since it's believed that rue placed in a husband's underwear keeps him faithful.

Those who love rue believe that it smells like oranges, while those who only like it say that rue smells more like orange peel. Many people dislike it altogether, claiming that it stinks.

R. graveolens is a hardy, evergreen perennial that grows to three feet and is covered in fern-like, bluish green leaves and greenish yellow flowers. Although rue grows easily from seeds, it also grows well from divisions of its roots. Greeks to this day believe that cuttings from a neighbor's rue grow better than do those plants acquired honestly.

Salvia
Sage

An ancient Latin proverb goes: *Cur moriatur homo cui Salvia crescit in horto?* (Why should a man die when sage flourishes in his garden?) The name *sage* is a spin-off of a once-held fancy that the herb could prolong life. In fact, sage was so exalted for anything that ails you, it was the panacea of herbal medicine in the Middle Ages. As herbs became less prevalent for medicinal purposes, sage stuck around because of its culinary values.

Sage is a shrubby perennial that reaches eighteen inches to two feet. Stems are square and covered in down; leaves are wrinkled, gray-green, and oval. Small, purple blooms appear as whorls at leaf axils during late summer.

There are several species, including ornamental ones. *S. pratensis* grows wild in woodlands in Dalmatia, where it's native. Of the common sage, *S. officinalis*, there are some pretty forms, such as 'Icterina', which has variegated, golden leaves, and 'Purpurascens', which has purple leaves on red stems. These two forms make particularly attractive border plantings not just for the herb patch, but for an entire garden. *S. elegans*, the pineapple sage, isn't as hardy as its cousins, but its leaves really do smell like a ripe pineapple, and it has dazzling, red blooms.

Ornamental sages come true only when propagated as cuttings taken in late summer and heeled into sandy soil. If winters are severe, although most sages will tolerate o° F, plants may be wintered-over under glass and set out in spring. Ordinary sage grows well from seeds that are large and easy to space.

Salvias bloom in a wide array of colors. *Salvia uliginosa* (below, left), for instance, is true-blue, while *S. leucantha* (below, right), better known as Mexican bush sage, is dusty rose. To make certain that you get the color you want, propagate sage from cuttings, not from seeds, which often don't bloom true to parentage.

All sages like to grow in sandy, well-drained soil and in full sun. Plants are shallow rooted and must be kept well mulched. No single sage plant should remain in your garden for longer than four years. After that time, maybe even sooner, stems become woody and tough. To keep plants going as long as possible, simply cut out older stems each spring.

If you've never used fresh sage in your kitchen, you'll be surprised how much nicer it is than when dried. Sage has lots of uses besides the traditional recipes for stuffing, but even fresh it has a pervasive flavor that you don't want to overdo. Try adding just a bit before putting in all you've chopped up, for you can't take it out once it has settled in.

We've started making fragrant wreaths for the Christmas season. That's a good time to harvest rosemary and bay for drying anyway, and they make nice bases for wreaths, over which ornamentals such as dried lavender and whole rose blossoms can be tied. When we first put together one of these wreaths, the combination needed just one more herb—a dried, fragrant one with an interesting shape. We tried everything we grow, but nothing worked out better than a broad-leaf sage tied in small bunches.

Santolina

Santolinas are evergreen herbs native to the Mediterranean. Like other members of the Compositae—daisy—family, santolinas blossom with a profusion of round flowers.

S. Chamaecyparissus, known as *S. incana* in Britain and commonly as lavender cotton, has woody stems that are densely clothed with gray leaves and bright yellow, button-headed flowers.

S. virens is similar to lavender cotton, but its leaves are narrow and dark green. Because the foliage is so intricately textured, whole plants look like poofs of green smoke. Flowers are creamy to faint green.

Santolina is the definitive knot-garden plant, particularly the two varieties we've just mentioned. Although plants can grow to two feet, they respond well to clipping and look best when kept compact. Santolinas make a fine edging for an herb garden, particularly since they like to grow in full sun and couldn't care less how poor their soil is as long as it drains well.

A practical reason for planting santolinas is that, when dried, plants repel moths. If you're not careful, santolina might offend you too.

Left unclipped, santolinas grow to two feet and have yellow, white, or pale green, button-headed flowers. Because their scent can be bitter, when you want to smell santolina, brush, rather than crush, their leaves. When dried, plants repel moths.

Don't bruise santolina's leaves when you want to smell it, brush it instead. When leaves are crushed, they're more bitter than pleasant. Also, be careful when selecting varieties, or you could end up with one species known as *S. neapolitana*; it bears ugly, lime green flowers that smell strongly of human perspiration.

Tanacetum vulgare
Tansy

Tanacetum is derived from the Greek name Athanasia, meaning immortal. From ancient times until the eighteenth century, the essence of tansy was used as an embalming agent and, before refrigeration was available, to preserve meat. Tansy also became irrevocably associated with the holiest of springtime religious rites— Easter. Cakes made from tansy came to epitomize Passover (when eaten, they were said to purify the body after a sparse Lent). Medicinally, tansy has been thought to increase fertility when applied externally, but to induce abortion if consumed.

Seeds of tansy are difficult to germinate. Instead, you can rationalize the expense of buying seedlings when you realize that you must purchase plants just this once, after which you can divide clumps for your whole neighborhood. In fact, to keep its invasive roots from taking over, cautious gardeners plant tansy in bottomless drums that have been submerged into the soil.

Tansy grows on two- to three-foot stems with fernlike, deep green, aromatic leaves that are four inches wide and six inches long. In late summer plants are covered with heads of flat, round, yellow, daisylike flowers. Only the leaves are used in the kitchen or medicine chest, but blossoms last well on or off the plant.

Tansy is reputed to drive flies and ants from pantries, and it's a key ingredient for flavoring the liqueur Chartreuse.

Teucrium
Germander

It's difficult to find a European ruin that doesn't have germander growing in some crevice or all along the cracks in an entire wall. With its evergreen foliage and short spikes of purple, rose, or white flowers, *T. Chamaedrys*, commonly known as wall germander, looks particularly nice growing against stone, also creeping along a craggy path or a rock garden.

Germander once enjoyed a reputation as a medicinal herb, particularly as a diuretic and for the treatment of gout. Culpeper praised germander by claiming that "it is good against

Santolina is the definitive knot-garden plant because bushes respond obediently to clipping and their rich gray or green colors blend well with everything planted nearby.

a continual headache, melancholy, drowsiness and dullness of the spirits." Later, germander was among the "strewing herbs"—those scattered about the house to delight those guests who stepped on them. During the Tudor period, germander was a favorite planting in knot gardens because of its upright growth habits.

Although plants spread more than two feet, *T. Chamaedrys* never grows more than a foot off the ground. Plants are covered in shiny green, deeply toothed, pungent leaves that are attractive to bees. Because it should be clipped twice a year anyway, germander makes a neat edging to herb gardens.

T. Marum is known as cat thyme and is closely related to *Nepeta Mussinii* (catmint). Like catmint, *T. Marum* has pungent leaves shaped like thyme that cats love to roll in and nibble on.

Thymus
Thyme

If you told gardeners the world over that they could grow but a single herb and cooks that they could season their cuisine with only one herb, they would both overwhelmingly choose thyme. Why shouldn't they? By naming thyme, gardeners "restrict" themselves to more than four hundred species—everything from

varieties that creep along the ground to those that grow into perky, upright plants the size of small shrubs. Cooks who choose thyme have singled out an herb that harbors flavors ranging from caraway to lemon.

Since well before Christ set foot on the earth, thyme has been praised for its association with and contributions to honey. The poet Virgil, who was also a beekeeper, said that thyme "yields the most and best honey." From the earliest records of gardening in the Mediterranean, we know that thyme, already proven irresistible to bees, was widely planted in orchards to insure that the fruit trees would be pollinated. Thyme-flavored honey has always been considered to be the most pleasantly flavored of all honeys. In early Greece one of the nicest compliments a man could tell his lady was that she smelled sweet as thyme (as well she might since women then wore oil of thyme as perfume). Sheep were put to graze in fields where wild thyme grew because it was said to sweeten their meat.

Species of thyme are divided into two groups: those that grow upright and those that prefer a prostrate position. Both are useful all around the garden and all over the kitchen.

T. vulgaris, whether it be the English, French, or German variety, is the perennial

Tansy is irrevocably associated with Passover for its ability to flavor cakes and preserve meats. In late summer plants blossom in broad heads of yellow, daisylike flowers that dry well. Because it so faithfully reseeds itself, you need plant tansy only once. Dried leaves repel certain insects and flavor special liqueurs.

thyme most used both by gardeners *and* cooks. It grows to nine inches tall and is covered in masses of pungent, narrow leaves that may be variegated or grayish green and broad or narrow. Most varieties have either soft pink or violet flowers and thin stems.

As you might guess, *T. x citriodorus* smells like lemons: what's more, strongly of them. Leaves of lemon thyme are small, blooms are pale purple, and there are forms with silver or gold foliage.

T. praecox arcticus, also known as *T. Serpyllum*, is a creeping ground cover with a form that is generally mat, but with branches that grow up to six inches high. While it can't be tromped on, creeping thyme accepts light pedestrian traffic (as when planted between stones in a garden path where you don't *have* to walk on it), and it freely releases its pungent scent whenever its leaves are bruised. Flowers of most forms are rosy purple, but at least one is pure white, and another has hairy, silvery leaves.

When you visit a nursery that specializes in herbs, you'll be bowled over by the number of different varieties of thyme. What you've just read here barely scratches the surface. There are *T. pseudolanuginosus*, the woolly leaved ground cover; *T. vulgaris* 'Argenteus', the official silver

Thyme is a notably versatile herb; it can creep along the ground or mature into a billowing bush, and smell like pine or orange. Blossoms, insignificant in fragrance compared to their pungent foliage, are usually soft pink or violet and carried along wiry stems. Like rosemary, thyme is native to the Mediterranean; the two herbs handsomely complement each other.

thyme, and hundreds more. While some forms are thought to smell of pine, oranges, or pineapple, others reek of turpentine.

Fortunately, you don't have to grow thyme from seeds and wonder what it will smell like. Buy seedlings instead and sniff for yourself. Only the most diligent gardeners care to cope with thyme's tiny seeds (more than 170,000 per *ounce*!). Once you establish thyme, you'll never buy seeds for those varieties again, since new plants can be started easily in early summer as cuttings.

Thyme hardly ever complains about the soil in which it's planted or how often it's watered. Except for plants in the hottest of climates, thyme doesn't seem to require much water at all, making it a favorite for gardens that seem to thrive on neglect.

Those same gardeners and cooks who praised fresh thyme will also shout for its dried leaves. Thyme is basic to many potpourri blends, and few herbs rival thyme's ability to harbor culinary flavor. If you're going to harvest thyme for drying, do so before the plant blooms. If you're serious about your crop, hack the plants to two inches above ground level. A second growth will rapidly appear, but it should be left alone for the balance of the year in order to steel itself for winter (if you *must* have some, take only the top third).

Thyme dries nicely on screens, but even newspapers suffice. After branches are dry, leaves rake off easily. Stems aren't fragrant or flavorful, but you might want to leave some as sprigs anyway for a dried herb bouquet.

Tropaeolum majus
Nasturtium

Nasturtiums flourished from Brighton to Edinburgh almost immediately after their seeds first reached Britain in the early seventeenth century. For more than three hundred years, *T. majus* remained a species of only one variety—a climbing plant with bright yellow flowers streaked with red. Then, in 1929, a hybrid cropped up in California that was almost the same color as its predecessor, but noticeably larger and just as sweetly scented. Today nasturtiums blossom in colors ranging from deep orange or red to pale yellow or white on plants that hover a foot off the ground or climb higher than fifteen feet. Even with extensive cross-pollinations, scent has been retained.

Besides their crisp, refreshing scent, nasturtiums have become garden favorites because of some other qualities—they're exceptionally easy to grow, they liberally reseed themselves year after year, and their leaves and blossoms are tasty in salads, while their seeds are delicious when pickled.

Nasturtiums grow best in sunny, well-drained soil. If where you plant them is too

Nasturtiums aren't praised merely for their clean, crisp scent, but also for their ease of cultivation and tasty leaves and flowers. Blooms can be dark orange or white, but are more often red or yellow; mixed colors blend well.

You must admit that the borage lends a flattering touch (nasturtium and borage grow nicely next to each other).

shady or soggy, plants produce mostly foliage and only a few flowers. Unlike many herbs, nasturtiums appreciate fertile soil.

Nasturtiums are good choices for gardeners with children who express an interest in the world of plants. Nasturtium seeds are large and easy to handle, and they sprout quickly. Once you've seen their saucerlike leaves, which look like little lilypads, you'll never mistake nasturtiums for anything else.

Organic gardeners are fond of nasturtiums for keeping aphids off those plants that are particularly susceptible to sucking insects. Nasturtiums don't repel aphids. Quite the contrary, aphids are so attracted to nasturtiums' tender foliage that they race to them rather than to those plants growing nearby, thereby providing a single clean-up spot. Gardeners determined to use no chemical sprays make an infusion of the plant by filling a pot with nasturtium leaves and stems, covering it with water, and bringing it just to the boil. Then the brew is cut four to one with water and used as a spray—a concoction they are convinced repels aphids.

Valeriana officinalis
Valerian, Garden Heliotrope

Valerian is a contradictory herb. It intoxicates cats, but it attracts rats (the Pied Piper supposedly drenched himself in the oil of valerian just before he coerced rats into the river). Though praised for its scent in the Middle Ages, today's descendants don't smell so hot (most people think that valerian actually stinks). Infusions of the herb were once considered useful as treatment for coughs and bruises; now valerian is exalted as a sedative (properly concocted infusions are said to relieve nervousness, even hysteria).

In the garden, valerian grows three to five feet tall and has dark green, lacy, serrated leaves grouped in pairs. In early summer, fragrant, pale lavender (almost white) flowers form on a single stalk. When blossoms drop, they're followed by gray, flat, heart-shaped seeds.

Valerian is thought to be an asset to the vegetable garden because it attracts earthworms. Many herbalists suggest brewing a spray from valerian and applying it to plants and soil where you want earthworms to visit.

Valerian seeds don't germinate easily. Fortunately, plants multiply quickly. The valerian plant develops a crown—short roots shaped like a cone—that needs dividing at least every third year. New plants should be set no closer than one foot apart.

Valerian addicts covet roots and claim that they must be dried at temperatures higher than those for leaves—at 120° F—until brittle. Dehydrated roots should then be stored in moisture-proof containers.

CHAPTER VI

Planting the Regulars: Annuals, Biennials, and Perennials

Although their blooming habits differ and they don't live to the same age or flourish as long as one another, annuals, biennials, and perennials are always lumped together. The one quality they share is temporary—plants in this chapter don't represent commitment the way trees and shrubs do.

Annuals must be planted from seeds each year. Sometimes, however, Mother Nature sows for you by causing year-old, mother plants to scatter their seeds before they die.

Biennials bloom the second year after planting. At first, you may wonder why you should wait a whole year before seeing the blooms of your labors, but your impatience will subside when you witness the glories of biennials such as wallflowers and certain species of *Dianthus*.

Perennials are mother plants that winterover and rebloom each spring. Some are tender, of course, or become woody and must be replaced every few years; others last an eternity.

Several plants mentioned in this chapter have both annual and perennial forms; some are biennial as well. Others are actually perennial, but get treated as annuals because mature plants become leggy. It's really not as confusing as it sounds, and these plants are worthy of deliberation anyway. Since most grow from seeds or cuttings that root easily, experimentation doesn't represent a sizable investment.

Abronia
Sand Verbena

If you've ever visited a conservatory with hanging baskets spilling over with fragrant blossoms that look like verbena, you've seen *Abronia*. Like verbena, *Abronia* species have trailing growth habits and blossoms that are actually clusters of small, tubular, fragrant flowers.

A. latifolia, the yellow sand verbena, is a perennial native to the coastline from British Columbia to Santa Barbara. Plants form sticky mats up to three feet across that are usually covered in dust and sand. Even so, yellow, fragrant flowers break through the crust from spring through fall.

A. fragrans is the upright member of the family—to two feet or more. Pure white blossoms that are powerfully scented of vanilla open at dusk throughout late summer.

A. umbellata is a dwarf, trailing plant that seldom grows taller that six inches. Rose pink, honey-scented blossoms cover the plant from summer through fall, and sporadically all through the year.

Sand verbenas are easy to grow as long as they're planted in well-drained soil that gets full sun. Plants are most easily propagated from cuttings; seeds are slow to germinate (soak them in warm water for several hours before sowing them).

Allium

When most gardeners think of *Allium*, they imagine *A. giganteum*, the giant form with starburst clusters of grayish lilac blooms on five-foot stems. Unfortunately, *A. giganteum* smells much like its cousins—garlic, onions, and shallots.

The massive *Dianthus* genus includes carnations, pinks, and sweet Williams. Although only some of the more than three hundred species are fragrant, those that are smell as strongly of clove as any flower. Pinks make superb plants for edging borders, spilling their flowers into paths, and scenting air over a considerable distance.

Pale-colored alliums are actually fragrant, but blossoms in the deeper hues smell like their relatives: onions. If you want the largest blooms possible, plant alliums in rich, sandy soil and give them plenty to drink.

Probably because their scent is offensive to insects, few pests bother alliums (below, left). Plants aren't susceptible to diseases either, making alliums favored companion plants, especially when their colors blend so nicely with those nearby.

Although some of the pale-colored varieties are actually fragrant, that's not why most gardeners choose to plant *Alstroemeria* (below, right), but rather for their lasting qualities—properly conditioned blooms of Peruvian lilies last far longer than a week in a vase. If you have a greenhouse, you can grow some of the tender varieties (one smells just like cloves).

The alliums aren't praised for their scent, but a few varieties actually have fragrant blossoms without a hint of garlic. True to the rules of perfume by color, the white and yellow alliums have pleasant scents, whereas the blue varieties have no scent at all or smell like onions.

A. Moly has bright yellow flowers on foot-long stems, with leaves almost as tall. Blossoms are mildly fragrant; the rest of the plant doesn't smell so hot.

A. narcissiflorum is native to the Italian alps and looks terrific in rock gardens. Ruby red, pleasantly scented, bell-shaped flowers appear regularly all summer on nine-inch stems.

A. neapolitanum has pure white flowers on foot-long stems. Plants smell nothing like the rest of the genus and are grown commercially as cut flowers and pot plants.

All varieties of *Allium* are easy to grow, particularly if you plant them in rich, sandy soil and give them plenty of water while they're growing. Alliums seem disease free, and insects don't bother them either.

Alliums can be started from seeds. They also multiply as bulbs and need to be lifted and divided every few years.

Alstroemeria

Claes Alstrom, an eighteenth-century, Swedish naturalist, spent much of his life roaming the European countryside in pursuit of his passion—sheep breeding. Once, while in Cádiz, he spotted unusual flowers blooming in a courtyard. Certain that he had never before seen such blossoms and that his friend Carolus Linnaeus, the famous botanist, was sure to like them, he found seeds to prove his hunch. In turn, Linnaeus immortalized his Swedish friend by naming a botanical genus after him. *Alstroemeria* is sometimes called the Peruvian lily, even though it is not a lily at all.

Certain species and hybrids of *Alstroemeria* are fragrant, but it wasn't because of its perfume that *Alstroemeria* caught on so quickly; rather it was because it makes such superb cut flowers (properly conditioned, blooms last well over a week) and because *Alstroemeria* adapts so well to greenhouse culture. Today *Alstroemeria* species are raised from seeds in Portugal, then shipped as small plants to the Netherlands, where commercial growers welcome them with open arms as energy savers. (*Alstroemeria* species grown under glass in chilly Holland don't require heat the way roses do.)

Alstroemeria grows from a mass of tuberous roots. Since it detests being transplanted, *Alstromeria* is usually grown from seeds, but it can also often be purchased at nurseries in one-gallon cans. (When established, plants can be transplanted without disturbing their roots, and they'll bloom more quickly than those planted bareroot.) *Alstroemeria* prefers cool, well-drained, sandy soil with protection from wind and blistering sun.

From a clump of insignificant twisted foliage, graceful slender stems carry trumpetlike flowers in irregular shapes. *Alstroemeria* can be cut when the first blossoms appear; the rest of the floriferous stem will open nicely when placed in a vase.

Although there are now more than fifty known species in every color imaginable but blue, if you're after fragrance, look for *A. Ligtu* and its hybrids in shades of cream, buff, pink, and salmon. Although these hybrids don't tower to five feet the way their more brightly colored cousins do, their stems of two to three feet carry deliciously scented blossoms, smelling not unlike mignonette.

Argument still rages in the horticultural world over the hardiness of *Alstroemeria*. Some American gardeners claim that you shouldn't try to grow *Alstroemeria* north of the Mason-Dixon line. Others claim that if you plant roots a foot deep and mulch what withers in autumn, clumps of *Alstroemeria* will thrive in cold winters. Many people don't care what their winters are like, choosing instead to grow *Alstroemeria* in pots in greenhouses. Plants can be brought into bloom under glass, then moved indoors to enjoy their fragrance and exotic beauty.

If you decide to grow *Alstroemeria* in a greenhouse, there is another tender species you should know about. *A. caryophyllaea*, native to tropical Brazil, is eye-blinking scarlet and smells like clove.

Antirrhinum majus
Snapdragon

A. majus so long ago established itself in Britain that snapdragons are now numbered among England's wildflowers. For years, this member of the same family as foxglove flourished simply because people liked the wide array of colors, certainly not because they were fragrant. Then, in 1963, three fragrant varieties popped off some hybridizer's pollen palette—'Super Jet' (apricot yellow), 'Vanguard' (deep rose), and 'Venus' (peach pink) have a sweet perfume with an undertone of clove.

A. majus got the common name of snapdragon because when the five-petaled flowers of each flower are pressed from the side, they "snap" open. This very feature is probably why *A. majus* was never fragrant until humans, rather than insects, crossed its pollen. *A. majus* is self-pollinating, and its blossoms lock insects out while they fertilize themselves. Since it was pointless to attract insects to where they were off-limits, nature gave the flower no scent.

Snapdragons grow easily from seeds either started early in flats or sown directly where they are to grow. *A. majus* is disease free, except for persistent rust (spores of orange pustules appear first on the undersides of leaves, then spread until they defoliate plants). If you don't care to use fungicides, at least keep plants in good health and never water them from overhead.

Until 1963 no variety of snapdragon was scented. That's because the curious anatomy of *Antirrhinum majus* wouldn't allow insects to cross-pollinate its pollen. Once hybridizers forced blossoms to "snap" open, sweetly scented varieties followed.

Brugmansia, Datura

It's with certain resentment that we include *Brugmansia*, since we can't grow the perennial well in Petaluma—our winters are just cold enough to crumple plants to the ground. So we cultivate *Datura*, the annual. For those of you who live in more-temperate climates, however, you should know about a couple of *Brugmansia* species.

B. x *candida* and *B. suaveolens* both grow quickly into rotund shrubs or fifteen-foot trees, depending on how you train early growth. Foliage is elliptical and oblong, with leaves that are smooth above but downy beneath. Beginning in midsummer and extending late into fall (year-round in their native tropics), shrubs and trees of *Brugmansia* look as though someone has decorated them with white trumpets, each one up to eight inches long. Particularly at night

Unless you live in a temperate climate, you may have to satisfy yourself with *Datura*, the annual form of *Brugmansia*. Several varieties are packed with perfume. Some people believe the trumpet-shaped flowers smell like bath soap (do you suppose that's why *Brugmansia* so often dangles over birdbaths?); others swear their fragrance is lilylike.

the blooms emit powerful perfume. Some people find it overwhelming, comparing its smell to that of cheap bath soap; others find it elegantly lilylike.

There are also *Brugmansia* species in tropical colors, but only the white or near white species are known for their fragrance. Although some blossoms of *Brugmansia* are double, all are poisonous.

The best-known *Datura* species also grow quickly—to three feet each season. In sheltered gardens, they liberally reseed themselves. *D. ceratocaula*, native to Cuba, has purple, downy stems and hairy leaves. White blossoms with purple edging open in late afternoon. *D. Metel*, also a tropical native, has heart-shaped leaves and exotic, trumpet-shaped flowers that are followed by fruits the size of apples.

Because gardeners devoted to fragrance are so addicted to the intoxicating perfume of *Brugmansia* and since they grow so well in containers anyway, *Brugmansia* species are often grown in pots that can be brought indoors during winter. Whether you can grow *Brugmansia* outside or must content yourself with container culture, mature plants should be pruned in February.

Centaurea moschata
Sweet Sultan

Early in the seventeenth century, the sultan of Constantinople was traveling in the Middle East, where he saw *C. moschata* blooming. He took such an immediate shine to it that he plucked a flower, pinned it to his garment, and

asked for seeds he could plant in his homeland. The Turks grew so fond of *C. moschata* themselves, and so appreciative of their leader for having found such a treasure, that they named the flower in his honor—sweet sultan.

C. moschata is an annual whose seeds should be sown as soon as garden soil "can be worked," meaning that you can stand to be outdoors and that weather forecasters aren't predicting more frosts. Plants grow erectly to two feet, with deeply toothed leaves, and from July through October blossom with two-inch, thistlelike flowers. Blooms are most often some shade of lilac or rose, but may be white, yellow, even purple. All smell strongly of musk. One variety, *C. Margaritae* is pure white and said to be the most sweetly perfumed. Another, *C. suaveolens*, is citron yellow.

Sweet sultan makes a terrific cut flower. For the best blooms, plant *C. moschata* where it will receive plenty of heat and no water from overhead.

C. Cyanus, commonly called cornflower or bachelor's button, is first cousin to sweet sultan. Though certainly not known for their perfume, certain *C. Cyanus* plants are actually fragrant, and they certainly are pretty.

Cheiranthus
Wallflower

The first year we planted these cheery flowers, we waited for them to bloom most of the summer before realizing that we had chosen a biennial form that wouldn't flower until early the next season. The delay was worth it; the following spring the sunny border where we had massed them became a sea of color—pinkish reds, warm oranges, and mahogany that blended harmoniously through shades of mauve and yellow. Elizabethans loved combining these colors in nosegays, which is how the wallflower earned its botanical name *Cheiranthus*—hand flower.

During Queen Victoria's reign, the wallflower came to signify that poor girl who sits along the dance floor's perimeter while her friends waltz and polka with prospective beaux. That's an unfortunate association; if anything, she should be the life of the party, clutching such a sweet-smelling nosegay.

C. Cheiri is a species from a small genus of herbs of the Cruciferae family. At home in central Europe, it grows well in a number of areas, especially in the British Isles, where it long ago befriended English cottage gardens. The wallflower has some powerfully scented relatives in stock and sweet rocket, but has its own secret blending of clove and nutmeg.

According to a famous Scottish gardener, Robert Ingram, the wallflower must establish a fibrous, wide-bodied root system. To encourage such developments, he sowed seeds in early April and transplanted seedlings in June and again in August, each time pinching out the taproot and the tip of the central stem to promote a massive root system and bushy growth. In October the seedlings were planted in the ground where they were intended to flower the

Wallflowers are perfectly cheerful all by themselves, but they also blend well with other flowers. At lower left spicy mahogany wallflowers are nicely complemented by lightly scented, creamy French tulips and ever-blue forget-me-nots. Those on the right make a bold golden statement and lend fragrance to an otherwise scentless border.

following spring. This seems like an awfully lot of bother. We don't doubt that it would produce admirable results, but we've had no problem with starting seeds in starter pods and transplanting them once they're established. We do pinch the taproot and the central stem when we transplant, and that is perhaps why we've had enough success to suit ourselves.

Wallflowers should be spaced from nine to twelve inches apart. Mature plants are from one to three feet high, have masses of narrow, lance-shaped leaves about three inches long, and sport dense clusters of four-petaled, individual flowers on multiple stems.

Wallflower plantings are especially effective with tulips and narcissuses. Their bushy habit cleverly conceals the bulbs' unsightly withering after they bloom. Once while in London for the Chelsea Flower Show, the gardeners' mecca, we visited the Royal Horticultural Society's dream garden at Wisley. There we saw the ultimate in companion planting—mahogany wallflowers, yellow tulips, and forget-me-nots. We still wonder how they managed to get everything to bloom at the same time.

Wallflowers were once thought to have medicinal uses, which is probably how they earned the name *chevisaunce*, an old English word meaning comfort. Medicinal values have since been discounted, but not what the wallflower's sweet perfume might do for the ill.

Harvesting the blooms and drying them on screens yield perky additions to dry pot-pourri, mostly because of the wide color range of wallflowers. Be sure to add small amounts of clove and nutmeg to your potpourri mixture, thereby insuring the lasting quality of these trace scents.

Dianthus
Pink, Sweet William, Carnation

What a tribe! There are more than three hundred species of annual, perennial, and biennial members of this genus. Single, semi-double, and double flowers can be of one, two, or variegated shadings of almost every major color except blue. Within species there are hybrids that even *Dianthus* devotees have lost count of. The complex Caryophyllaceae—pink—family deserves texts of its own, not so much for how to cultivate the species as for classifying and numbering them. We refer you to *Carnations: Perpetual Flowering Carnations, Borders and Pinks* by Steven Bailey for one such comprehensive presentation.

The Athenians named the genus with the most highly honored, unused name they could muster—*dianthos*. Flowers were the mainstay for making garlands and coronets, hence, another name—coronation, from which carnation is derived. *Dianthus* was historically associated with libations, and blooms were used to flavor wines and stronger spirits.

All forms of *Dianthus* bloom from grassy tufts of green, gray, blue-green, or blue-gray and are good for cutting. Not all are fragrant

Dianthus species flower each June/July and, if you take the trouble to cut them back, again in September/October. Otherwise, in a supreme effort to please, pinks bloom to death and must be reseeded.

(yet again, hybridizers willingly substituted new colorings for fragrance), but if they are, they smell distinctly of clove.

Pinks were the rage in nineteenth-century England, even among home gardeners. One such horticulturist came up with an especially fragrant variety and named it for his wife, 'Mrs. Sinkins'. It was introduced by Charles Turner, an avid florist who had earlier presented Cox's orange pippin for apple commerce. 'Mrs. Sinkins' is still praised for her powerful perfume.

Garden pinks are classed as either old-fashioned or modern, the latter coming about when an old-fashioned variety was crossed with a perpetually flowering carnation, resulting in the *Allwoodii* strain. Modern pinks make ideal border plantings, flowering in June/July and again in September/October if cut back to the tops of their moundy bases after their first burst of bloom. Otherwise, plants seem so eager to please those who tend them that they will literally flower themselves to death and must be reseeded.

Sweet William is officially known as *D. barbatus* and is believed to be native to southern Germany, from where it quickly spread to neighboring countries. Which Bill was it named for? Not William the Conqueror, as many believe, even though it grows wild in Flanders and the Normandy hills. Others say it was named in honor of Shakespeare. Another opinion gives the credit to Saint William of Aquitaine. Any of these men would have been flattered to lend his name, for Sweet William is sweet indeed.

D. barbatus is usually shorter than its cousins and darker in coloring. Those deeper in hue are less scented than the paler forms. Some of the oldest strains, especially the auricula-eyed, have the most clove perfume.

Carnations are classed as florists' or border plants. Florists' types are usually grown in greenhouses—outdoors in only the mildest of climates. Flowers are large and double on long stems. Border carnations closely resemble pinks and bloom in profusion with shorter stems on bushy plants.

Dianthus species are sun lovers, but appreciate some afternoon shade in particularly hot areas. They prefer soil with lime to those high in acid, but they'll grow almost anywhere except where the soil is waterlogged. *Dianthus* tolerates intense cold and is bothered by few pests or fungi, except rust.

We have pinks of several varieties planted all along the sunny border of our garden, where they spill their blooms over the edge and into paths. Even when the whole border is in bloom, clove is the first thing you smell when you enter the fragrant garden. What a welcome scent!

Erysimum alpinum
Alpine Wallflower

E. alpinum is native to the Norwegian fjords, where they grow as six-inch tufts all along rocky formations and in tiny crevices. Leaves

When it comes to combining bold colors, *Dianthus* has no fears. Unlike other flowers that are heavily pigmented, pinks like these at lower left have discovered how to retain strong scent.

In spite of their minimal needs, alpine wallflowers are rarely out of bloom, and they flourish in the tiniest of places—within rocky crevices and tiny openings in walkways. Not all species of *Erysimum* are fragrant, but those that are smell strongly of spice, most often of cinnamon. Most scented varieties have yellow blossoms, like those below, right.

are covered with down, giving the plants a hairy appearance. Flowers that are usually yellow bloom almost all year long and, like *Matthiola* species (stock), their cousins, smell of cinnamon or cloves.

Alpine wallflowers make superb plants for rock gardens and will sprout from the smallest of openings in walls and walkways. They prefer poor soil and little water.

Be specific when you buy seeds of *Erysimum*. If you're not careful, you could end up with *E. alliaria*, better known as wild garlic, or *E. melicentae*, which has no scent at all. If you're lucky, you might get *E. linifolium*, also known as miniature wallflower and similarly scented, or *E. odoratum*, which has pale yellow, powerfully fragrant flowers.

Hosta
Plantain Lily

One rarely visits a garden in Britain without seeing a handsome stand of *Hosta* planted to conceal the bottom of leggy plants such as rhododendrons or azaleas. Many gardeners plant plantain lilies simply for their foliage, finding the shiny heart-shaped leaves irresistible. *Hosta* species grow in clumps, with distinctly veined leaves that are up to ten inches long and six inches wide.

Although you may detect a trace of scent from a few of the nearly forty species of *Hosta*, the fragrance of only one is worth writing home about—*H. plantaginea*, the true plantain lily. Plants reach two feet, with large, brilliant

Hostas are best known for their pretty foliage and for so nicely concealing the leggy growth habits of several flowering shrubs. When it's time for rhododendrons to shed their blossoms, hostas are well on their way to camouflaging awkward undergrowth. Blossoms of *Hosta plantaginea* look like tiny white trumpets and smell like lilies.

green leaves. As a special dividend to the distinctive foliage, in late summer clumps of *H. plantaginea* send up tall slender stalks topped with drooping, white flowers that look like tiny, white trumpets covered in snow. As do other members of the Liliaceae family, blossoms smell like lilies.

Because hostas are among the few perennials that tolerate dense shade, many people believe that hostas don't like sun. In fact, hostas prefer sunlight at least half the day. During the other half of the day, shade helps to keep leaves from bleaching or turning yellow.

In response to winter's first frost, hostas wither to the ground and remain invisible until spring signals new growth. Hosta roots, however, are tough, hardy to temperatures below 0° F. Especially when grown under a cozy blanket of peat moss, hostas last for years, occasionally requiring dividing. In fact, because hostas won't grow true from seeds, the only way to be certain your hostas will have the exact variegated foliage you like is to buy crowns from clumps that have just been separated.

Hostas are relatively disease free. Their masses of foliage, however, are havens for snails and slugs. If you plant hostas, make a note to spread bait around clumps at least four times each year.

Iberis
Candytuft

Iberis is botanically named after the Iberian Peninsula, but nicknamed for *Candia*, the ancient word for Crete (the more-fragrant varieties are native to Greece). *Iberis* grows both as a perennial and an annual, but only the annuals are noted for their perfume. Although *Iberis* is a member of the Cruciferae family, as is the wallflower, just two varieties carry the sweet scent for which the clan is noted.

I. amara produces round clusters of tight, white flowers that elongate into hyacinthlike spikes. Foliage is narrow and slightly fuzzy. Varieties are available from dwarfs that never get more than six inches tall to giants that grow to two feet tall.

You may have difficulty locating seeds of *I. odorata* because the variety is less well known, but your search will not be in vain. Even though the plants of *I. odorata* don't quite reach one foot in height, their pure white blooms are powerfully scented.

Iberis thrives in any garden soil that drains well. Sow seeds at regular two-month intervals to prolong the blooming season. *Iberis* is generally disease free, and the only regular pest is the rather obscure flea beetle.

Limnanthes Douglasii
Meadow Foam

You will often notice the name "Douglas" or some spelling variation of it, such as *Douglasii*, when you read gardening books. Every reference is to the same person—a young nineteenth-century, Scottish botanist who tragically lost his life in the Sandwich Islands. Although he is best remembered for the Douglas fir, his name was also lent to a charming annual native to California named *L. Douglasii*, or meadow foam.

Because meadow foam doesn't grow much more than six inches high, it makes a fine plant for edging since not only does it stay close to the ground, it also spreads evenly. If seeds for the tender annual are sown in March, they'll flower from June until frost. Where winters are mild, seeds may be planted in the fall for blossoms in the spring.

Flowers that are only one inch across are white with yellow centers. Because the blossom somewhat resembles it, *L. Douglasii* is sometimes called the poached-egg flower. Blooms are sweetly scented and attractive to bees.

Lobularia maritima
Sweet Alyssum

While flowers of white *L. maritima* are said to smell somewhat like honey, most people believe sweet alyssum smells more like new-mown hay, which is how it originally got its

If you plant *Lobularia maritima* where it likes to grow, you may buy seed packets only once, for sweet alyssum liberally reseeds itself. Perfume fanciers claim that blossoms of sweet alyssum (most often white and no taller than six inches) smell like honey; plainer noses say new-mown hay.

country name of sweet Alyson. *L. maritima* is actually a perennial, but because plants get leggy without regular manicures, it's more commonly treated as an annual. *L. maritima* is also a rampant reseeder; not only will new plants sprout in areas where you sowed last year, you'll spot sweet alyssum growing where you never intended to plant it. *L. maritima* has also been known to escape the confines of a garden and, when content, to naturalize itself in the countryside.

If you plant *L. maritima* for its clean refreshing scent, plant the white varieties. Some of the pale pink forms have detectable fragrance, but the heavily pigmented varieties such as the rich purple 'Violet Queen' have no perfume whatsoever.

L. maritima has endless uses in the garden. Besides being the ideal plant for bordering a bed or edging a path, sweet alyssum is helpful in concealing plants with awkward growth habits (or a bulb patch past its glory), and it is ex-cellent as a temporary filler in rock gardens, between stones in paths, and in containers.

Although some varieties of *L. maritima* grow as tall as one foot, the more strongly perfumed varieties such as 'Little Dorrit' and 'Carpet of Snow' grow only to half that height. Plants shower themselves in tiny white flowers from June to November. Because they become rangy when left to their own devices, and since sweet alyssum reblooms so quickly, one month after the first bloom, many gardeners shear plants back by half. In case it matters, be fore-warned that bees are irresistibly attracted to sweet alyssum.

Lupinus
Lupine

If you're a gardener in search of inspiration, plan a European vacation around London during the third week of May, when the Royal Horticultural Society stages its magnificent Chelsea Flower Show—surely the most impor-

Where lupines are content, usually near salt-laden breezes, they will naturalize themselves in meadows and bloom all summer. True to the Legumi-nosae family, most lupines are sweetly scented—from clover to vanilla.

tant annual floral event in the world. Although the Chelsea sports many outdoor landscape exhibits, the horticultural cream of the crop is housed under a series of marquee tents. Under these billowing masses of canvas, awards are given for the best newly introduced roses, sweet peas, clematises, violas, and too many more exotic flora to number. Although we vividly recall several glorious displays, the exhibit that caused us to skid to a halt was the one featuring a new strain of lupine. Something about the stately, staunchly upright lupine demands respectful scrutiny.

Lupinus is a genus of more than two hundred species of annuals, shrubs, and herbaceous perennials. Modern lupines, as most people know them, are actually hybrids and strains of two parents, one scented, one not—*L. arboreus*, the fragrant tree lupine, and *L. polyphyllus*, the scentless perennial.

L. arboreus is nicknamed tree lupine because of its twiggy growth to five feet in all directions. Native to California and naturalized throughout Europe, *L. arboreus* has an affinity for sea-laden breezes. Foliage is light green, with leaves that are divided into six to nine leaflets; all parts are covered in soft, silvery down. Six- to nine-inch racemes of flowers cover shrubs from June through August in white, yellow, lilac, purple, or blue. True to the Leguminosae family, the blooms of most forms of

L. arboreus are sweetly scented—from clover to vanilla.

Lupine flowers are similar to other members of the pea family, but their petals are more compressed. The upper petal, called the "standard," gently folds backward as it develops. The lower petal is called the "keel" because it's so rigidly held between those petals compressed on either side that it actually resembles the keel of a boat.

In the early twentieth century, hybridizers began crossing *L. arboreus* with its sister, *L. polyphyllus*, a scentless perennial with blue or red flowers. Finally, however, it was George Russell who meticulously crossed strains to produce today's revered garden-border *Lupinus*. What set Russell apart from his cross-pollinating peers was that he managed to develop lupines with spikes up to two feet tall and flowers with standards and keels in contrasting colors. Few named varieties have any notable fragrance, nor do they consistently bloom true from seed.

Because lupines require plenty of water but don't appreciate sitting in it, their soil must be well drained; otherwise, roots will rot. Modern strains sometimes contract mosaic virus and powdery mildew, but all *Lupinus* species, regardless of age, are susceptible to aphids.

Matricaria recutita
False Chamomile

The reason that we agree with those horticulturists who refer to the annual *Matricaria* as false chamomile is that we believe *Anthemis nobilis*, the popular perennial ground cover, is the true chamomile. If you grow chamomile for the purpose of brewing tea, however, or if you don't have a large sunny spot for *A. nobilis* to creep over, then *Matricaria* is the one for you.

Seeds of *M. recutita* grow quickly into plants as tall as two feet, with masses of fernlike, pungent foliage. Flowers with a hollow, yellow disk and rays of white petals cover the plants during late summer. Plants of *M. matricarioides* are somewhat shorter than those of *M. recutita*, and the blossoms are greenish yellow.

Once established, *Matricaria* liberally reseeds itself each year and requires little or no irrigation. Along America's Atlantic coast, plants of *M. recutita* grow in mile-long stretches beside roadways; in California, *M. matricarioides* not only thrives along freeways, it flourishes in dry wasteland.

If you intend to make tea from your *Matricaria*, remember to use only thoroughly dried flowers. Brews from *M. recutita* have an overtone of pineapple, whereas those from *M. matricarioides* hint of apple.

All members of the pea family have blooms with thoughtfully crafted petals, but none more cunning that those of modern lupines. The lower petals on spikes of lupines are called "keels" because they're so tightly packed against their neighbors that they actually resemble a boat's keel.

Matthiola
Stock

Although many plants, especially those in the Cruciferae family, produce blossoms that seem perfumed with spice, none smells more strongly of clove than *Matthiola*. At close quarters or under glass, the fragrance of stock can be sweetly overpowering. Although there are more than fifty species to the genus, two are prominent: *M. longipetala*, night-scented stock; and *M. incana*, the grandparent to what is now commonly called garden stock. Though mostly native to southern Europe, from Spain to Greece, certain *Matthiola* species are thought endemic to Britain as well (they've been found growing wild on chalky cliffs in Sussex).

M. longipetala was once called the melancholy gillyflower because of its woebegone appearance during sunny hours. All day long plants of night-scented stock look like sulky balls wrapped around clusters of dusty, brownish lilac flowers. Then, as dusk approaches, *M. longipetala* comes unglued, its blossoms unfolding an intoxicating scent into the evening's air.

Night-scented stocks grow erect to just over one foot tall and have three-inch, lance-shaped leaves. *M. longipetala* should be planted from seeds each year, preferably in full sun.

All *Matthiola* species that we call garden stock, whether they bloom in spring, summer, autumn, or winter, are descendants of *M. incana*. Long ago, there were only white or purple forms of *M. incana*. By the sixteenth century, hybridizers had managed crosses that produced double flowers and colors from red to flesh. Today stocks are available in a wide palette of colors—white, yellow, bluish lavender, salmon, crimson, and all shades in between. Fortunately, most hybrid offspring of *M. incana* have retained their predecessors' scent. Modern garden stocks grow to heights ranging from less than a foot to more than three feet tall.

Although garden stocks grow easily from seeds, you may want to start them indoors and set them out in early winter. Plants will tolerate frost; they just won't set buds until evenings warm up.

The only diseases that affect *Matthiola* are caused by improper drainage. If stocks aren't grown in raised beds or garden spots known to drain rapidly, their roots will rot or their leaves will mildew.

Although stocks rank high among flowers favored for cutting, there's a problem that you should know about in advance. Unlike roses and other flowers with woody stems, garden stocks have green, fleshy stems that ooze if submerged in water. While blossoms remain sweetly scented, stems make water smell foul. If you use stocks as cut flowers, plan to change the water in their vases at least every other day; if you wait much longer, plan to clothespin your nose while you scrub yuck out of containers.

Mirabilis
Four-O'Clock

While *Mirabilis* species grow as perennials in their native tropics, elsewhere they're treated as annuals. *Mirabilis* species are called four-o'clocks because on a warm, summer day that's when their blossoms open (during cool, sunless weather they may stay open all day).

Plants of *Mirabilis* grow quickly from seeds planted exactly where they are to grow. Or you can get a head start by planting them in starter pots indoors. However they're planted (as long as it's in full sun and rich soil), seedlings of *Mirabilis* usually come into bloom after only two

Many flowers smell like clove, but none more strongly than those of garden stock. Before the sixteenth century, there were only white and purple *Matthiola*. Then Renaissance hybridizers crossed pollen until they discovered colors from scarlet to beige. Learn how to treat stocks as cut flowers (if you're not careful, they get messy).

months in the ground. Foliage is dark and formed in bushy clumps up to four feet tall and just as wide.

Although there are more than sixty named species of *Mirabilis*, only two are notably fragrant. *M. Jalapa*, also known as the Marvel of Peru, has trumpet-shaped flowers of rose-pink, yellow, or white. Varieties of *M. longiflora* have lilac-pink or white, narrow, tubular flowers that can be up to six inches long and redolent of orange blossoms. Except for aphids' inevitable attack on young plants, *Mirabilis* is virtually pest and disease free.

Nicotiana

If you sit nervously in your office fretting that the flowers in your garden are wasting their fragrance while you are at work, plant nicotianas, for they hold off until you get home. Only as dusk approaches do the blooms open and release their perfume, closing again against the irksome morning light.

Another plus for nicotianas is how easily they grow. After you garden for a while, you'll find yourself kindly disposed to plants of such temperament. Nicotianas top our list of carefree annuals. They seem indifferent to the soil in which they grow (though they love leaf mold), and they freely reseed themselves.

Jean Nicot, an ambassador to Portugal in the midsixteenth century who seemed to have liked snuff, planted *N. Tabacum* in the garden of his Lisbon embassy. Early cigars were made from drying Nicot's "tobacco plant," and appreciative nicotine addicts named the genus for him. Our advice, though, is if you like snuff, buy some, and plant nicotianas for the extended, sweet-smelling blooms.

Nicotiana is classed as an annual, though it could easily qualify as a perennial, since you plant it only once. It will religiously reseed itself ever after. In fact, if you like it, you can have your fill because each spring tons of new seedlings push up in last year's nicotiana areas. Thin and replant them; they don't seem to notice their new surroundings as they scramble to four feet and taller.

Hard-nosed fragrance seekers will tell you to plant only white varieties. That's nonsense— all the colors are deliciously scented. Besides, an assortment of colors may prove to be your preference, especially since they look so nice together. A seed mix will include white, several shades of pink, lilac, lavender, and tobacco red. When you transfer seedlings, you won't know which colors they are and will wonder if you're creating a pleasing mix or a cacophony of color. The latter is never the case.

Nicotianas would just as soon grow in full sun, but will happily tolerate some shade, especially in particularly warm areas. In fact, they're so obedient that you'll find yourself transplanting them, with good results, into areas that are marginal, at best.

Nicotiana leaves are large and undivided. Trumpet-shaped blooms cluster at the tops of long stems. If you have hummingbirds anywhere near, they'll find your nicotianas when they bloom. The flowers can be cut for lasting indoor enjoyment, but they too will shrink from harsh light in their environment—if you want them to stay open, put them in low light.

Papaver alpinum
Alpine Poppy

Poppies are garden favorites the world over. Even those of us devoted to fragrance find it difficult to resist Iceland, Oriental, and Shirley poppies. One species of poppy is actually fragrant, however—*P. alpinum*.

Seed packets of nicotianas are among the few you should buy in mixes—their natural colors look nice together, and all blossoms sweetly scent the air from cocktail hour until dawn. If you decide to plant nicotianas in your garden, you'll probably never get rid of them, nor will you want to. Before dying back each winter, nicotianas liberally scatter their seeds.

Modern species of *Phlox* aren't always fragrant, which many people believe is a blessing (the scent of phlox isn't a resounding winner). At least while they're fresh, however, phlox blossoms often smell like new-mown hay. This variety, 'Bright Eyes', shown on the left, below, is appropriately named, and blooms during more months than it doesn't.

Frenchmen in Provence so love its smell that they plant mignonettes (below, right) in pots, with an eye toward enjoying them indoors.

Alpine poppies are botanically classified as perennials, but are more usually treated as annuals because plants aren't long-lived, and they liberally reseed themselves every year anyway. From a basal rosette, *P. alpinum* grows to about ten inches tall, with leaves that are bluish gray and finely covered in hair. White, yellow, pink, and salmon flowers about an inch wide bloom each spring.

Gardeners disagree on what alpine poppies smell *like*, though everyone concurs that they are fragrant. Some claim that blossoms have an undertone of musk, others swear they smell like new-mown hay, most say that they sniff something earthy but pleasantly scented.

As you might have guessed from both its proper and common names, *P. alpinum* makes superb rock-garden plants. While they prefer full sun, alpine poppies don't ask for more than ordinary soil, though they like it to drain well. Don't feed plants at all until they're well established, and don't stop picking flowers until you're ready for seeds to set.

Phlox

Phloxes are a classic example of how greedy hybridizers eliminate scent. Once upon a time, two species of phloxes native to the United States were powerfully scented. Since the flowers of *P. maculata* and *P. paniculata* were only purple or white, however, breeders crossed them with scentless phlox in order to extend the color range. Because fragrance was of no significance, new colors emerged in blossoms with no trace of perfume.

Loss of scent in phloxes suited many people just fine, for while everyone agrees that phloxes smell, many people find their "perfume" objectionable. One famous gardener described the phlox's scent as a blend of pepper and pigsty. Whether you think of phloxes as smelling like new-mown hay or just fresh earth, you probably will like the scent best when flowers are fresh. As blossoms age, they take on a rancid quality.

P. maculata grows to two feet and is covered in purple flowers arranged in pyramidal panicles. There is a 'suaveolens' variety with pure white flowers that is thought to be the most sweetly scented of all phloxes. *P. paniculata* grows considerably taller (to more than five feet) and blooms with flowers ranging in color from purple through lilac to white.

These two species, both perennials, grow easily as long as they're planted in full sun. Most garden soils suffice, but plants should be well mulched to keep their roots cool. Plants of phlox can live a long time, but they should be lifted and divided every few years, especially those varieties you want to keep (phloxes don't always bloom true from seeds).

Reseda odorata
Mignonette

While Napoleon was campaigning in Egypt, he noticed a flower that grew like a weed, but was remarkably fragrant. Imagining that Josephine, known to be hooked on scent, might like it, he sent seeds to her. The empress didn't just fancy *R. odorata*, she was so mad for it that she began a fad of growing *R. odorata* in decorative pots on balconies and terraces. It was Josephine who gave *R. odorata* its common name—mignonette (little darling). Mignonette reached Britain at about the same time and was even more popular there than it was in France.

What attracted everyone to mignonette was certainly not its blossom—spikes of insignificant, brownish gray and greenish yellow, loose flowers. Mignonette became an instant hit for sheer perfume power—the same reason we treasure it today.

It's no wonder that the sweet scent of mignonette has eluded the perfume industry; no one can agree on just what it smells *like*, only that it's habit forming. Whatever else it is, the perfume of mignonette is both sweet and clean at the same time.

Seeds of *Reseda* can be started in pots in September and set in sunny windows for spring bloom. Outdoors, seeds may be sown in early spring for blooms from summer through fall.

The scent of mignonette is strongest when plants grow in full sun and poor soil. Recent hybrid varieties are better colored than their ancestors, but not nearly so fragrant.

Scabiosa
Pincushion Flower

Although most species of *Scabiosa* have no notable fragrance, we decided to list the genus because of the scented *S. atropurpurea*, the most famous member of the entire genus. *Scabiosa* is called pincushion flower because its perfectly straight stamens protruding beyond curvy segments look like pins stuck in a cushion. *Scabiosa* is also commonly called mourning bride because of its somber purple coloring.

Seeds of *S. atropurpurea* are ordinarily sown in spring for late summer–early fall bloom, but it's also possible to start seeds in August. Even in moderately severe winters, seedlings will winter-over to bloom the following early summer.

Scabiosa would rather grow in poor soil in full sun than in rich soil in partial shade. Many gardeners claim that the chalkier their soil, the better their *Scabiosa*. Seedlings develop into rosette clumps of narrow, deeply cut leaves. From this mound rises a slender stem strong enough

If you want to make a fragrance fancier squirm, ask him to tell you exactly what mignonette smells like. The scent is elusive, hard to define, but habit forming. It's said that plants of the most sweetly perfumed mignonette bloom in full sun and poor soil. Recent varieties of *Reseda odorata* are more nicely colored than their ancestors, but they don't smell as fresh.

to support a two-inch flower. Colors range from purple through blue, red, pink, lavender, and salmon to pure white, although the almost black 'King of the Blacks' and the pale blue 'Azure Fairy' are said to be the most sweetly scented.

Gardeners who make their own potpourri wouldn't consider omitting pincushion flowers from their annual crops, for few other flowers dry better or more perfectly retain the precise form they had when they were fresh.

Smilacina racemosa
False Solomon's-Seal

S. racemosa is one species in a small genus of herbaceous perennials with blooms that resemble those of Solomon's seal (*Polygonatum*—also slightly fragrant), hence the nickname false Solomon's-seal. Besides its gentle, sweet perfume, *S. racemosa* is a favored border plant because it blooms when so little else does, from the beginning of March through May.

S. racemosa grows to three feet, with arching stalks that support leaves up to ten inches long. Foliage is light green and downy on the underside. Fluffy, conical clusters of fragrant, creamy white flowers appear at the tops of stalks and are followed by red berries. Plants prefer partial shade and a cool, leafy soil.

There is a lesser-known species, *S. stellata*, that has white, star-shaped flowers. Blooms of this species are called star-flowered lily of the valley because the flowers are powerfully scented, like other members of the Liliaceae—lily—family.

Plants of *Smilacina racemosa* grow to three feet and sport leaves almost a foot long. During late winter and early spring, fluffy clusters of creamy white flowers scent the air with a perfume not unlike that of lilies, only softer. False Solomon's-seal caps off the year with red berries.

Trillium
Wake-Robin

Trillium is so named because it grows with leaves arranged in whorls of three and because its flowers usually have only three petals each. Besides being called wake-robin, *Trillium* is sometimes known as the wood lily and is native to the woodlands of North America. Planted in fall, *Trillium* blooms in spring.

Unless you're into kinky scents, stick with lightly colored trilliums, usually white, pale pink, or greenish yellow. Those with dark blossoms, often purple, actually stink. *T. erectum*, for instance, smells so strongly of decaying meat that it's pollinated by flies.

T. chloropetalum, also known as *T. sessile californicum*, has oval, mottled, dark green leaves and sweetly fragrant, white flowers that snuggle themselves within whorls of foliage.

T. cernuum has long, tapered leaves that almost hide its fragrant, white or pale pink flowers; hence the name bashful Ben.

T. viride was discovered in Indian reservations in North Carolina. Plants have purple, mottled leaves and greenish yellow flowers that have a refreshing lemon fragrance.

Trilliums are useful in shady parts of the garden rich in peat, particularly among ferns and azaleas. Plants multiply nicely if never allowed to dry out completely.

Viola cornuta
Viola, Violetta

V. cornuta, the fibrous-rooted, tufty annual with heart-shaped leaves, is sometimes called the horned violet because the petalage of its blooms embraces an awl-shaped spur. If you stimulate plants of *V. cornuta* by vigilantly cutting their blooms, pale blue, sweetly scented flowers regularly repeat themselves from April through September. As with several other species whose palest colored petals are the most heavily perfumed, *V. cornuta* comes in a white form, 'alba', that is more sweetly scented.

Immediately after it was introduced into Britain in 1776, *V. cornuta* was a hit in English cottage gardens. Almost one hundred years later, in search of colors to relieve the light blue, rarely white monotony, a Berwickshire County gardener began mating his violas. Writing in *Pansies and Violas*, this Dr. Stuart wrote, "In 1874, I took pollen from pansy Blue King, a bedding variety then in fashion, and applied it to *Viola cornuta*. There was a podful of seed which produced twelve plants and which were all blue in colour, but with a good tufted habit. I then took pollen from a pink pansy and fertilised the flowers of the first cross. The seed from this cross gave more variety of colour and the same tufted habit of *Viola cornuta*." He didn't stop there. Before he finished scrambling pollen, Dr. Stuart hybridized a whole new strain of violas worthy of a name all its own. Through the auspices of the Royal Horticultural Society, the gardener's find was promptly named violetta. As if their varied colors weren't enough, violettas also carried a strong vanilla perfume like that of sweet peas.

Today there are more than one hundred varieties of violettas, from the cream-colored 'Little David' (said to smell like freesias), through 'Buttercup' (rich, butter yellow), to the deep blue 'Jersey Gem'. Not only are almost all varieties deliciously scented (particularly in the evening), they're almost never out of bloom. Just like their cousins *V. odorata* (sweet violet) and *V. Wittrockiana* (pansy), *V. cornuta* and violettas thrive in full sun or partial shade as long as the soil is well drained.

The only secret to keeping violas in bloom for more than half the year is to keep their blossoms picked. Josephine noticed that characteristic and planted blue-to-lavender violas under her standards of roses at Malmaison, the home she briefly shared with Napoleon. (This particular bush looks as though it might have been planted by the empress herself.)

CHAPTER VII

Bulbs, Corms, Rhizomes, and Tubers That Produce Scented Blooms

More people begin gardening with bulbs than with anything else. Bulbs are substantial, definitive, easy to plant exactly where you want them to bloom. Then the reward comes so quickly, particularly with those bulbs known as "early bloomers," which may blossom only weeks after planting.

Everyone knows of the reputed fragrance of hyacinths, peonies, and tuberoses, but few people know that there are varieties within these families that have no perfume whatsoever; fewer still know that certain varieties of tulips, irises, and daylilies are sweetly scented.

Depending on your climate and how your bulbs and corms are treated after they bloom, many will naturalize themselves and multiply each year. Even though it's a pain in the petunia, certain other rhizomes and tubers should never be left in the ground and must be lifted and stored after their foliage has died back.

If you plant bulbs to enjoy the fragrance of their blooms, you'll learn that some make good cut flowers. To enjoy fragrance indoors, you may decide to plant others in pots that can be brought inside. Or you may opt for both.

Acidanthera

Acidanthera looks like nature's cross between *Gladiolus* and *Ixia*. Often called fragrant gladiolus, *Acidanthera* has swordlike leaves and blooms that appear from sheaths. Like *Ixia*, *Acidanthera* has long tubular blossoms flared at the top that last well as cut flowers.

Native to Tanganyika, *Acidanthera* naturalizes only in mild climates. Elsewhere, the corms must be lifted after winter's first frost and stored in a cool, dry place. Although there are several species, only one is notably fragrant— *A. bicolor*. Thankfully it's also the hardiest member of the family.

Late in spring corms of *A. bicolor* should be planted four inches deep. Growth that follows consists mostly of tapering, swordlike leaves. Early in autumn eighteen-inch, slender, arching stems bend over from the weight of up to six flowers that are creamy white with a chocolate maroon base. *A. Murieliae* is the most de-liciously scented of all, smelling like violets, only sweeter.

Acidanthera looks best when grown in masses where one's lanky growth will camouflage another's. For a succession of blooms, plant bulbs at three-week intervals.

Amaryllis Belladonna
Naked Lady

When you mention *Amaryllis* to most people, they think of *Hippeastrum*, those plants commonly called amaryllis. One could almost be grateful that *Hippeastrum* isn't fragrant, for common amaryllis is an awkward plant with coarse blossoms. It's true that some of the near white and pale salmon forms are pleasant, but their tastelessly striped brothers and sisters are downright garish, and none of them smells any better than does the dark green plastic pot in which they grow at breakneck speed.

A. Belladonna is another curious plant, also boldly colored. It, however, unlike common

Monet was very fond of his garden at Giverny, just outside of Paris, particularly the paths that he lined with the flowers he most liked to paint. This inviting path, right in the middle of the garden, is bordered with bearded irises, many of which are deliciously scented.

Blossoms of *Acidanthera* appear from sheaths that arch over clumps of swordlike leaves. *A. bicolor* has creamy white and brownish red blossoms that scent the evening air with a violetlike perfume. Like *Ixia*, which also has tubular flowers, *Acidanthera* is a splendid cut flower.

Hippeastrum, is powerfully fragrant, with a scent often compared to that of apricots. The reason *A. Belladonna* is nicknamed naked lady is that without benefit of foliage she blooms on slender, reddish brown, two- to three-foot stems without a stitch on them. Four to ten rosy pink, trumpet-shaped blooms are carried on top of each naked stalk.

During fall and persisting through winter, naked ladies develop two-foot clumps of strap-like leaves that form in mounds. After spring and early summer, all foliage disappears. In late summer *A. Belladonna* begins to stand and, seemingly embarrassed by her bare stems, quickly blooms, as though to hurriedly conceal her naked torso.

A. Belladonna will tolerate almost any soil that drains well. Once established, naked ladies will thrive without even an annual top dressing of manure and with practically no water at all.

In fact, some gardeners swear that the hotter and drier the summer, the lustier the naked lady will be.

If you want to plant naked ladies, you must do so at the right time of year and to the correct depth, depending on where you live. Wherever you reside, whole clumps of *A. Belladonna* should be planted just after they have finished blooming. (If you separate clumps when there's no foliage, your bulbs may not bloom for several seasons.) Because winters are mild where we garden, we plant bulbs of naked ladies flush with the ground. Where winters are severe, gardeners plant bulbs up to six inches deep along sunny walls.

A. Belladonna should be planted in masses. Otherwise, they'll look more like flashers than naked ladies. Remember that their pink is strong, so mix *A. Belladonna* with low-growing annuals in complementary colors.

Amaryllis belladonna is nick-named naked lady because she blooms without a stitch of foli-age. The rosy pink flowers of naked lady look like trumpets and smell like apricots. If you want to divide your *A. bella-donna*—a good idea since it multiplies quickly—be sure to dig clumps when foliage begins to conceal the naked lady's slender torso.

Crocus

Although everyone associates them with spring, it's possible to have crocuses in bloom half the year. If you want to grow only scented varieties, choose your crocuses precisely, for they're not all fragrant (some even stink).

Crocuses that bloom in the fall and during early winter must be planted in June; the spring-blooming varieties should be sown in October. Crocuses aren't fussy about the soil in which they grow as long as it drains well. Corms grow into low clumps of grasslike leaves. Crocus blooms develop from slender tubes that look like stems (the actual stems are quite short and mostly underground). Blossoms have broad, flaring petals that close at night, protecting clusters of brilliantly colored stamens.

If you're on a budget for spring bulbs, consider buying more crocuses and fewer tulips. Crocuses are much easier to grow than most bulbs and cost a fraction as much. And, unlike many bulbs that only shrivel in size each year, crocuses multiply like rabbits. Keep in mind, however, that you should plant masses of crocuses rather than just a few. They look wonderful growing in lawns just under the spread of a large, deciduous tree, but only if they take up at least half the space. Remember, too, that crocus leaves must be left on the plant if their corms are to mature and multiply; if you plant your crocuses in the middle of your lawn, you'll just have to mow around them until their foliage yellows and shrivels to the ground. If you choose some of the rare varieties or those known mainly for their fragrance, you might want to plant them in pots, either because they're expensive or because it takes only a few blooms of some species to scent an entire room with the smell of ripe plums or honeysuckle.

C. longiflorus is both the first to bloom and perhaps the most strongly scented species of the genus. Blooms appear simultaneously with foliage. Blossoms have deep violet petals and brilliant orange anthers.

C. laevigatus is another early bloomer—beginning in November, even on winter's coldest day. Violet-veined tubes of white develop into blooms that are brown outside, with pure white anthers inside. *C. laevigatus* grows well under glass, and only a few bulbs per pot are needed to perfume an entire greenhouse.

C. sativus, commonly known as the saffron crocus, is more famous for its culinary uses than it is for its sweetly scented fragrance; it's also one of the few species that don't fold their petals each night, probably because of the large stigmata that protrude from each blossom. When dried, those stigmata are a source for the saffron used to flavor and color baked goods. Blossoms are reddish purple, veined dark violet.

C. vitellinus begins flowering in December and persists through February. Blossoms have sweetly scented, golden yellow, tapered petals feathered with bronze.

If you're on a budget for spring bulbs, you should reconsider your order—more crocuses, fewer fussbudgets. Crocuses aren't nearly so particular about soil as tulips and hyacinths are, and bulbs multiply quickly. If you want your harbingers of spring nicely perfumed, be certain you buy the right crocuses; some varieties don't smell so hot.

C. chrysanthus wasn't always fragrant. Early members of the species were a lovely golden yellow, but void of perfume. Then, in the 1920s, hybridizers began cross-pollinating scentless *C. chrysanthus* and ended up with lovely, colored, fragrant varieties such as 'Snow Bunting'—white, stippled pale blue. *C. chrysanthus* begins blooming before the end of January and continues through March.

Freesia refracta
Freesia

Freesias are native to South Africa, the exact spot being somewhere around the Cape of Good Hope. The first known species, *F. refracta*, was brought to England in the midnineteenth century in hopes of a warm reception because of its sweet perfume. It received no such welcome, probably because of its color—cream with a deep orange throat (orange wasn't in vogue). Then, at the very end of the 1880s, a certain Mr. Armstrong brought a pink variety to Kew Gardens and was met with open arms. It was classed as a new species almost on sight, named *F. Armstrongii*. The British crossed it with its predecessor, then bred the offspring that followed. Although wild bursts of colors followed, and eventually twenty species came into being, hybridizers got just what their repetitive

incestual matings deserved: pigmentation replaced fragrance in the freesia. Many dark reds and oranges have no fragrance at all. Early forms, especially the whites, creams, and yellows, are, thankfully, heavily perfumed with a fragrance like that of ripe plums.

Freesias can easily be grown from seeds, but it's probably not worth your while, as corms are so readily available and they bloom much sooner. Seedlings don't transplant easily, so if you do try growing them from seeds, sow them where they are to flower.

In mild climates corms that are to bloom in late spring should be set out in late fall. Plant the pointed ends up, two inches deep, in light, well-drained soil. Corms can be lifted after foliage yellows and dries, but they can also be left to multiply right where they are.

In climates too cold for outdoor planting, freesias can be satisfactorily grown in pots in sunny windows, where they'll bloom without a lot of bother. Flowers last well, and their fragrance is strong enough to scent an entire room.

Most freesias grow to between one and one and one-half feet, though some are slightly taller. Their foliage is so grasslike as to be almost unnoticeable in beds with other plantings. Five or six tubular flowers appear on slender stems that have an enchanting habit of

Freesia blossoms, which many people believe smell like ripe plums, are carried on slender stems that nod above grasslike foliage. If you want maximum perfume, stick with the lightly colored freesias; the deeply pigmented varieties have little or no fragrance. Freesias can be sown from seeds, but corms are inexpensive and bloom much sooner. However you plant them, put freesias where they are to stay—they dislike being transplanted.

bending over for easy viewing, as if proudly showing off their blooms.

Freesias' needs are few; they don't even demand a lot of water, probably no more than what you'll plant them next to. Their only pests seem to be aphids, which, as you know, munch indiscriminately on anything succulent within their disgusting sight.

Roy Genders, in *Scented Flora of the World*, says that freesias "carry a sweet, refreshing perfume, to the author one of the most exquisite of all flower scents." When we read those words, we put down his excellent text and ordered the varieties he's partial to—early, pale colors. They're wonderful. Do try them if you haven't already, but reserve dark colors for some other flower.

Galtonia candicans
Summer Hyacinth

Galtonia is named after Francis Galton, a horticulturist devoted to the flora of South Africa (where *Galtonia* is also known as cape hyacinth). Two fine attributes of galtonias are their height—sturdy stems up to four feet—and their blooming season—late summer through early fall. True to the family of which they are members, galtonias smell like certain other lilies.

Straplike leaves up to three feet long mound in clumps to form a footing for thick stems that reach four feet. Each spike blossoms in drooping clusters of funnel-shaped, white-tinged-green, fragrant flowers.

Because the large leaves look floppy when they mature, plant galtonias at the rear of a flower bed or behind low-growing bushes. They also grow well in containers.

Bulbs should be planted six inches deep in well-drained soil. If given an annual mulching, galtonias needn't be disturbed for years. Summer hyacinths make it through average winters as long as they're given a warm blanket of mulch. Where winters are brutal, bulbs should be dug up each fall and stored at moderate temperatures.

Hemerocallis
Daylily

If you're interested in fragrant daylilies, it will help if you like yellow and can remember the difference between *flava* and *fulva*. *H. flava*, a yellow daylily native to central Europe, is sweetly scented, as are many of its modern offspring, usually yellow, beige, or golden, but sometimes pale lavender. Descendants of *H. fulva*, however, harbor no perfume whatsoever in any of their madly colored blooms, from pink through orange to blackish red. In the United States, *H. flava* is often sold as *II. Lilioasphodelus*, commonly known as lemon daylily.

Daylilies are perennials and grow from fleshy, tuberous roots. Plants form mounds of narrow straplike leaves above which two- to three-foot stems carry clusters of funnel-shaped flowers. Individual blossoms last only one day, and each one is smaller than its predecessor on the same stem, but they follow one another in rapid succession. Daylilies are favorites among flower arrangers because there are varieties ranging in height from dwarf to giant. Blossoms of *H. flava* and her descendants are thought to smell like honeysuckle.

If there is some out-of-the-way spot in your garden where you want to plant something and forget about it, or if you're just a fair-weather gardener to begin with, consider daylilies, for few plants are tougher or more disease free. *Hemerocallis* accepts almost any garden spot— full sun or moderate shade. Watering is required mostly when plants are in bloom, and feeding is suggested only twice each year (spring and midsummer).

Daylilies multiply quickly. Ideally, roots should be divided in late fall. If you forget, plants can still be separated safely in early spring, but no later.

Hyacinthus orientalis
Common Hyacinth

When you ask gardeners hooked on fragrance what their pet spring bulb is, they almost always name hyacinth. Many think hyacinth's unique balsamic perfume qualifies it as the most cherished of scented flowers.

Hyacinths have long been treasured for growing indoors. Blooms kept intact on the bulb retain their fragrance longer than those cut from the garden. Bulbs forced indoors can grow either in soil or water. If planted in pots, bulbs should be secreted for two months in a cool, dark room before being brought into full light at room temperature. Glass containers for growing hyacinths in water are commercially available, but any vessel will do if it provides adequate neck room with water beneath into which roots can plunge.

There are some things you should know before you plant hyacinths in your garden. First, bulbs left in the ground produce successively smaller flowers each year. To prevent that, apply an all-purpose fertilizer right after bloom. We've tried it; it works. This feeding gives bulbs the replacement nourishment they need to plump out to the size they were before blooming undermined them.

Second, hyacinths don't look good spread around the garden. Their blooms seem rather stiff and embarrassingly formal next to anything else. They look much better in clumps, particularly in areas with ground covers or fluffy annuals nearby that help conceal hyacinth's post-bloom droop. When bulbs finish blooming, they must not only be kept watered; they must not be lifted until their leaves signal it's okay by yellowing, then drying.

Finally, think about how you mix colors. The tried-and-true pale hues of blue, yellow, pink, and white look like a kindergarten setting if you don't separate them.

H. orientalis, the common hyacinth, seems common indeed when compared to its offspring, the Dutch varieties. It has one-foot slender stems with widely spaced, white or blue, fragrant flowers.

The Dutch seemed obsessed with making the hyacinth uncommon. They certainly succeeded, first by extending the color range to include deep shades of purple and red, then by figuring out how to pack longer stems with more flowers. During all this messing around, the hybridizers managed, thankfully, to retain powerful scents.

Holland's rule over the hyacinth extends to its rating all bulbs by circumference. Top of the line is exhibition grade, lowest is miniature. If you're on a budget, and bulbs are usually dear, you'll still be happier with the larger ones.

You're already on an uphill battle to keep them from getting smaller each year.

The planting technique we use with hyacinths is a spin-off of that for sweet peas. Start by digging a foot-deep trench in the area you're going to mass with bulbs. Fill the bottom two inches with a compost considerably enriched with an all-purpose fertilizer. Over this "goodie" layer, put back the same soil you removed when digging the trench. Bulbs should be five to six inches deep and covered with soil to ground level. If you fertilize after blooming is finished, the bulbs won't just come back next spring—they'll multiply. With that in mind, plant bulbs nine inches apart.

The bulbs of older varieties produce multiple floriferous stems. Modern varieties almost always produce one bloom per stem. Cutting them seems extravagant. However, to deny oneself the pleasure of having their irresistible aroma in the house seems masochistic. Either plant twice as many as you first considered, planning to smuggle half of the blooms indoors, or plant bulbs inside to begin with.

Iris

The genus *Iris* includes more than two hundred widely diverse species divided into two groups, dependent on whether they grow from rhizomes or bulbs. The majority of irises bloom in spring or early summer above swordlike clumps of tapering leaves.

The balsamic fragrance of hyacinths (left) is perhaps the most irresistible of all spring bulbs. Probably because they perform best during their first growing season, hyacinths are favorites among indoor gardeners. If you plant them outdoors, there's an easy trick to coaxing hyacinths to bloom, even multiply, in subsequent years; just fertilize them after they finish blossoming.

You may suspect that we grow the iris 'Mary Frances' (right) simply out of devotion to our good friend M. F. K. Fisher. Actually, that would be reason enough, but, as good luck would have it, the variety, like the lady herself, is sweetly scented.

Some iris "expert," who proved not to be a pro, told us that hardly any irises are thought to be fragrant anymore and that we should simply plant *I. florentina*, commonly called orrisroot, not for its flowers, but rather for its scented roots. The thought of our own fixative for potpourri was appealing, that is, until we learned how long it takes to process orrisroot—forever (at least two years). The violet scent harbored in the roots of orris intensifies as rhizomes dry, and the longer the better. By the time they're at their most redolent, roots are shriveled and almost impossible to powder, even with a mortar and pestle. No, thank you. Powdered orrisroot is cheap compared to your valuable time. If you're serious about making perfume, however, you might want to learn how the Italians extract orrisroot's expensive, powerfully violet, essential oils.

Blooms of our *I. florentina* weren't what we call strongly scented, but their slightly lemony scent was pleasant. Even so, they didn't satisfy our noses, and we continued our search for fragrant irises. Some better-informed gardeners told us that some bearded irises, which we longed to grow, were fragrant and suggested

Irises make fine companions to other flowers. This variety, 'Lacy Snowflake', grows almost as tall as giant foxgloves and softly perfumes the entire bed. Bearded irises like to grow in full sun and better-than-average garden soil.

that we contact Shreiner's Gardens in Salem, Oregon, famed for their fabulous collection of bearded irises. Their lovely catalog arrived, filled with handsome photographs and enticing descriptions. Alas, not a word about fragrance. We wrote back to Schreiner's staff, asking whether they might tell us on the sly about varieties that some people believe have fragrance. In response, we received a thoughtful letter explaining that, much to everyone's chagrin, fragrance had just about been hybridized out of bearded irises, with emphasis instead being placed on color and form. (We were in total sympathy; similar greed had led to scentless roses.) On a cheerful note, however, our iris specialist told us that he was a member of the British Iris Society, whose members had published an article on bearded irises praised for their fragrance. He kindly forwarded us a copy.

What tempting claims! Unfortunately, most of the varieties that were highly praised in England weren't available to us here. Thankfully, a handful were: 'Blue Lustre' was said to smell like lilac, 'Blue Reflection' like honey, and 'Pink Sleigh' like sweet citrus. How could we go wrong? Besides, according to their pho-

tographs, these irises were worthy additions to the garden, whether or not they smelled. Then there was a variety called 'Stepping Out', which looked positively garish with its bold combination of white and purple-blue, *but* it was touted by the British to smell like honey in the morning and spice in the evening! We ordered them all, plus some that laid no claim to fragrance, but which were irresistibly colored.

When our irises bloomed, we found, to our regret, that our sense of smell is considerably less keen than that of our British peers, though we agree that the varieties we planted are indeed fragrant. We've concluded, however, that none of our irises is strongly perfumed, nor, to our noses, do they smell different during the day than they do at night. As for 'Stepping Out', I fear its days are numbered, especially since a white iris called 'Lacy Snowflake' and an apricot hybrid named 'Liebestraum' are much easier on the eyes and smell just as nice, particularly in the evening.

Bearded irises like to grow in better-than-average garden soil, and they demand good drainage; otherwise, their roots rot. They prefer full sun, tolerate a half day, and won't bloom in shade. Bearded irises don't require much fertilizer, only some bonemeal at planting time and an October dressing of well-composted humus. If you feel an urge to remove leaves after irises have flowered, resist it. Leaves store food and shouldn't be cut from the plant until late fall or early spring. You can, however, remove dead brown tips anytime they appear; they won't turn green again.

When you talk about irises, basic terminology helps. Blooms of irises have six petals, three flaring upward, called standards, and three arching downward named falls. If an iris is said to be bearded, it means the falls sport tufts of hair.

There is a host of irises known best by their common names, no hybrids of which are thought to be particularly fragrant—English iris, Dutch iris, Louisiana iris, Siberian iris, Spanish iris, and Wedgwood iris. Many come in dwarf and intermediate heights.

Lesser-known species of *Iris*, especially those growing from bulbs rather than rhizomes, are perhaps the most strongly scented of the entire family. Iris in the Reticulata family are good in rock gardens because they don't get large (flower stems are rarely more than six inches) and come in a mad array of colors, including purple-red with an orange splash and ultramarine spotted with black. Most varieties are said to smell strongly of violets; some bloom more than once a year.

Blooms of *Iris florentina* might not smell as sweetly as their cousins, but they *are* lemony. And their roots are the source of orrisroot—a treasured violet-scented fixative for potpourri.

Leucojum vernum
Spring Snowflake

The reason gardeners keep confusing *Leucojum*, snowflake, with *Galanthus*, snowdrop, is that they closely resemble each other. Besides both being members of the Amaryllidaceae family, both snowdrops and snowflakes bear white flowers tinged green on short stems surrounded by tufts of straplike, glossy green leaves. Gardeners devoted to fragrance, however, know that, pretty as they are, *Galanthus* smells no better than fresh moss, whereas *Leucojum*, precisely *L. vernum*, is powerfully scented. In fact, *Leucojum* derived its botanical name because of its reputed fragrance. Because they believed *L. vernum* smelled like violets, only stronger, Greeks commonly called it the white violet—*leucoion*. The scent of *L. vernum* is often compared to that of stocks, only sweeter.

Stems of snowflake are hollow, but reach to one foot and during March carry solitary, dangling bells that are snow white tinged green. Because its fragrance is intense and since it adapts nicely to container culture, *L. vernum* is often planted in decorative pots for indoor enjoyment.

Leucojum likes to grow exactly where daffodils thrive—in moisture-retentive, free-draining soil. Also like daffodils, snowflakes shouldn't need dividing more than every three years, longer if they're still blooming instead of just growing foliage. When it's necessary, lift, divide, and replant bulbs as soon as the foliage dies down.

People confuse snowflakes and snowdrops because they so closely resemble each other. If it's fragrance you seek, however, make certain you can identify *Leucojum vernum*, the snowflake reputed for its strong violet scent. Then plant the bulbs where daffodils thrive.

Lilium

Lily

Except for roses, no flower is more strongly steeped in history than the lily. *L. candidum*, the cloyingly fragrant madonna lily, was thought to have sprung from the milk of Juno. When purity was the finest of virtues, white lilies were regarded as the epitome of grace, and old masters painted their regal forms while poets extolled their glories.

Not all lilies are fragrant; in fact, Gertrude Jekyll accused *L. pyrenaicum* of smelling like a mangy dog. The species and varieties that are actually pleasantly perfumed, however, handily make up for their scentless kin. Many people believe that lilies rank just under tuberoses on a scale of perfume power. But not even everyone finds the scent of *fragrant* lilies agreeable. A seventeenth-century gardener who esteemed many flowers as cures for ailments said of *Lilium*: "Notwithstanding the sweet and delicious odour of the Lily of the garden, it becomes deleterious when freely inhaled in an apartment. Grave accidents and even death itself is reported to have resulted from individuals having remained exposed to the emanations of Lily flowers during the night." Many people still find the scent of lilies overpowering in a closed room, but refreshing in an open garden.

If you mention lilies, most people think of Easter and pots of *L. longiflorum* that have been forced under glass to bloom whenever the full moon and vernal equinox occur. *L. longiflorum* has little modesty where perfume is concerned, smelling irresistibly of jasmine, with maybe a touch of honey. Although some forms are native only to Okinawa, *L. longiflorum* is grown commercially all over the world. To make certain no pollen will blemish their dazzling, pure white color, some growers remove each blossoms' terra-cotta–to–crimson anthers before they have a chance to ripen, spill, and stain.

L. auratum ranks closely with the madonna lily where elegance is concerned. Plants soar to more than six-foot heights to sport racemes of sweetly scented, white blooms (sometimes more than thirty per stem) edged in gold and freckled with crimson.

If you mention lilies to florists, they'll brag about their *L. speciosum*, the 'Rubrum' lily. Forms within this species may be pure white or seductive pink spotted crimson-purple. Whatever their color, most are powerfully fragrant. Since *L. speciosum* grows well under glass, the blooms are available for purchase throughout the year.

All species of *Lilium* mentioned so far like to grow in sun, or at least no less than high shade. The lilies we personally prefer, because their

After growing numerous lilies, we've decided on Orientals as our favorites. Varieties like these below are seductively fragrant without being over-powering. 'Journey's End', on the left, is dark pink with a crimson center and chocolate spots. 'American Eagle', on the right, blooms with ten-inch, white flowers heavily covered with maroon spots. All lilies make good container plants.

perfume is the quintessence of lily, are commonly known as Oriental lilies. Actually, Oriental lilies are modern hybrids of *L. auratum*, *L. speciosum*, *L. japonicum*, and *L. rubellum*. Oriental lilies prefer some degree of shade—as much as a half day where summers are hot; they should also be planted deep.

When we decided that we wanted to include lilies in our fragrant garden and started reading up on them, we were overwhelmed with the genus's diversification. We learned that what smelled like one thing to one person smelled quite different to another and that, to be absolutely certain, it was best to smell for ourselves before buying costly lily bulbs. We contacted a local lily society and went to a meeting, then to an exhibition. While we admired almost all of the species and their various forms, the Orientals were our favorites—diversely but always richly colored, and seductively fragrant without being overpowering.

We were advised by Oriental-lily fanciers to order bulbs from specialists, and we sent for catalogs. Although we were tempted to try more, we settled on three varieties. 'American Eagle' is particularly vigorous and bears clusters of translucent, ten-inch, white flowers heavily covered with maroon spots. 'Everest' is also white, but it has a light green center and lavender freckles. 'Journey's End' is crimson pink with a chocolate center. While all three are fragrant, the two white varieties are more strongly scented—never overpowering, but always robust.

Lilium should be grown in neutral or slightly acidic soil (a pH between 5.5 and 6.5 is ideal). Good drainage is essential; otherwise, bulbs rot. If you buy your bulbs from specialists, instructions will accompany your order, telling you how deep to plant—bulbs that develop roots on stems that grow above the bulb's crown must be planted more deeply than others.

Keep beds of lilies well mulched. Where winters are hard, mulch softens the blow from sudden freezes. Where summers are hot, mulch keeps plants cool. Besides, *Lilium* species need nutrients if their bulbs are expected to multiply; and mulch, particularly leaf mold, provides plenty of nutrients. Since lilies grow constantly, they should be kept well watered; always water at root level, since sprinkling the foliage encourages the spread of disease spores. Aphids are fond of *Lilium*. If you spray your roses for aphids, spray your lilies with the same formula. If you refuse to use chemicals, plant lots of garlic around your lily patch; aphids shy away from members of the onion family.

Lilium is a favorite for container planting, not just because lilies grow well in pots, but also because they don't naturalize easily. We've mentioned that drainage must be perfect; that remains true, even after you annually incorporate plenty of leaf mold into your lily patch. Where lilies grow contentedly, however, they multiply, but don't lift and divide them prematurely; wait instead until one year's bloom is noticeably skimpier than the last and stems are distinctly shorter. Then separate bulbs after all foliage has turned yellow.

Lycoris
Spider Lily

Lycoris is called spider lily because its blooms of long stamens and petals curved backward into wavy segments actually resemble spiders. *Lycoris* blooms in a wide array of colors, including scarlet, but only the soft pink species

Many lilies have no fragrance whatsoever, but those that do are packed with perfume; some smell like jasmine, others like honey. Most species of *Lilium* prefer to grow in full sun; some accept high shade. Wherever lilies are planted, they should be well mulched; and since they never stop growing, lilies must be regularly irrigated at root level.

have any notable fragrance. There are two: *L. incarnata* and *L. squamigera*. The scented sisters differ only by their shade of pink. While *L. incarnata* is simply pink, *L. squamigera* is definitely lavender as well.

Lycoris is often confused with *Amaryllis Belladonna* (naked lady), which it closely resembles. Like naked ladies, spider lilies bloom with no foliage in sight. Straplike leaves that flourish in early summer die at the thought of autumn and wither to the ground. Very quickly, during August, stems grow to two feet and boast ten to a dozen blooms per stem. A clump will drench a garden with sweet fragrance.

While spider lilies need plenty of irrigation while they're growing, the water should be cut off entirely when they go dormant, just after they bloom. *Lycoris* grows best in sunny locations, but it tolerates shade without a fuss.

If you're a fair-weather gardener who likes flowers that have the scent of both honey and musk, grape hyacinths are the bulbs for you. Although most *Muscari* are short and fat and bloom in shades of lavender or blue, some are tall, skinny, and pure white.

Muscari
Grape Hyacinth

Gardeners who appreciate fragrance would not consider being without grape hyacinths in spring. First, little else blooms with purplish blue flowers. Second, few garden plants, certainly no bulb, are more adaptable to where they grow or so oblivious to the soil in which they are planted. Mostly though there's that delicious honey-musk perfume.

Muscari is often confused with common hyacinths, to which it is closely related. There are, however, some basic differences. Besides never growing as large as their relatives, grape hyacinths have grassy, thin foliage that appears in fall and winters-over in clumps. Then there are the blooms themselves. Blossoms of grape hyacinths remain pinched together at their tips, whereas those of common hyacinths flare and reflex into stars. Although there are more than fifty species, only five are in general cultivation in the United States.

M. botryoides (Latin for a "bunch of grapes") is the most popular and readily available species. Also known as the Italian grape hyacinth, each spring—*M. botryoides* blooms on six- to eight-inch spikes. Ruskin spoke of these delightful flowers as "if a cluster of grapes and a hive of honey had been distilled and pressed together in one small boss." There is a pure white form called 'Album'.

M. armeniacum has azure blue, dense racemes on short stems. Modern strains of this species are more sweetly scented than are their ancestors, and they come in varying shades of blue.

Some gardeners think of *M. comosum* as a quaint monstrosity. It's odd, indeed, with its greenish purple, shredded flowers and bright blue, twisted filaments growing on foot-long, brown-spotted stems. Besides not caring for its color scheme, we've not planted *M. comosum* because it's said to be difficult to grow.

M. Tubergenianum is sometimes called the Oxford-and-Cambridge grape hyacinth because it embodies both schools' shade of blue. Bells at the top of eight-inch stalks are dark blue (Oxford), while those at the bottom are pale blue (Cambridge). Don't let the precious nickname keep you from buying bulbs of *M. Tubergenianum*; the effect is handsome.

M. moschatum is the species that smells most unmistakably of musk. Otherwise, blooms are unappealing—purple grapes that, as they age, first turn gray, then yellowish brown. Because it is fragrance that many gardeners are after, this species is often planted in pots and used to scent, rather than decorate, rooms.

Although the blooms of most varieties will please you, their foliage is likely to annoy you. Leaves of grape hyacinths appear in profusion in fall and insist on remaining throughout winter, even if covered in snow. Each spring flower spikes blind you to the somewhat unsightly clumps from which they rise, but after the blooms are gone, there it is again—spindly foliage that seems to take forever to die back.

If you like grape hyacinths, you can have sheets of blue all over your garden. Unless you're certain of the varieties you want to cultivate, don't buy too many bulbs of any one species; they multiply quickly on their own.

Grape hyacinths make terrific companion plants. They look nice beneath daffodils, tulips, and other spring flowers that bloom at the same time. *Muscari* also looks good encircling rosemary.

Narcissus
Daffodil, Jonquil

Most gardeners call all *Narcissus* species daffodils. That's better than calling them jonquils, since only one particular species is actually named *N. Jonquilla*. Whatever you call them, *Narcissus* species are those dependable spring flowers that have a perianth (six symmetrical petals) and a corona (cup or trumpet rising from the middle of each blossom). Most *Narcissus* specialists list eleven divisions; for our fragrant purposes, there are seven.

Members of the Tazetta narcissuses are probably the most powerfully fragrant of all *Narcissus* divisions. The division is best known for *N. papyraceous*—paperwhite. If you get no scent from paperwhites, you have just cause to worry about your sense of smell; *N. papyraceous* is so

If you want to naturalize flowers in woodland areas, by all means consider narcissuses. Not only will daffodils multiply quickly, they'll deter gophers wherever you plant their bulbs. Divide narcissuses only after one year's bloom is noticeably skimpier than the last.

Narcissuses are those dependable spring flowers that have a perianth (six symmetrical petals) and a corona (cup, or trumpet, rising from the middle of each blossom). Bulb specialists list eleven divisions, seven of which are fragrant.

Daffodils are so popular in Britain that it's hard to spot a bobby's station that doesn't have a pot of cheerful yellow flowers. All narcissuses grow well in pots.

powerfully fragrant that many people become nauseated if they try to inhale perfume from more than one blossom at a time. Paperwhites are often grown in water between pebbles in saucers, then temporarily placed all over the house to perk things up. Although each stem carries only five or six starry white flowers, a few of them will sweetly scent an entire hall with intoxicating perfume.

Double narcissuses are distinguished by having more than one layer of petals. One variety has orange-red in its color scheme, but most are shades of white on white. Blossoms are often compared to gardenias, and their scent to orange blossoms.

N. Jonquilla has yellow, cup-shaped blossoms that smell distinctly of orange. Cups range in color from light pink to bright red.

Blooms of large-cupped *Narcissus* species are carried one to a stem, usually with light petals and a cup from pink to orange-red. Few of the forms are known for their fragrance, but 'Louise de Coligny', with overlapping white petals and apricot-pink trumpet, is one of the smelliest.

Small-cupped *Narcissus* species are among the last members of the *Narcissus* genus to bloom. The more-noted fragrant varieties are white, but some are white and yellow with a colored cup.

N. poeticus is also known as pheasant-eye narcissus because it has a tiny, red corona chock full of yellow stamens, the coloring and pattern of which resemble a pheasant's eye. Although only one blossom is carried per stem, they're showy and sweetly scented.

Trumpet daffodils are best known because of the 'King Alfred' form—large, bright yellow flowers that look exactly the way daffodils are *supposed* to look. Other members of the trumpet family are white or bicolored white and yellow. Although trumpet daffodils aren't known for their fragrance, the freshness of their smell is definitely appealing—something like baby's talcum powder.

There are plenty of reasons to grow *Narcissus* species—they're almost trouble free, and they multiply quickly. *Narcissus* withstands bitterly cold winters and suffocatingly hot summers, and they adapt well to containers and to either shade or sun. As a real bonus, *Narcissus* species are among the few plants that gophers won't munch. In fact, daffodils so strongly repel gophers that they're often planted as a protective ring around precious sapling trees.

Although *Narcissus* bulbs prefer rich, sandy loam, they accept heavier soil that drains well. If you suspect that your soil retains too much moisture, add some humus to the whole planting area and a layer of sand underneath each bulb. Plant bulbs between September and November and keep them watered until rains begin. If spring brings no rain, keep the hose out; it's almost impossible to overwater *Narcissus* species while they're growing.

If you plant *Narcissus* bulbs to the right depth and far enough apart, they will be content for several years. Number-one grade bulbs, called double nosed, should be planted six inches deep and eight inches from their neighbors. Smaller bulbs should be planted four inches deep and six inches apart. When flowers become smaller and fewer, it's time to divide clumps. Wait until foliage ripens thoroughly, then lift and separate bulbs and keep them dry, dark, and cool until it's time to replant them.

Even though the most sweetly perfumed varieties don't retain their fragrance after they wither, dried blossoms (particularly those from the miniature varieties) make distinctive additions to blends of potpourri, and essential oils refresh lost scents.

Paeonia
Peony

When you mention peonies, most people start to swoon. After roses, peonies are considered among the most fragrant of all flowers. More than that, it's the form and size that peony blossoms assume: they're downright decadent.

Peonies are sharply divided into two groups: tree peonies, which are really deciduous shrubs, and herbaceous peonies, which die (or get cut) to the ground each fall. If you live where it never freezes, your world of peonies may be limited to the tree versions because herbaceous peonies bloom most profusely after moderately severe winters. Where we garden in temperate northern California, we're right on the peony border—colder than it needs to be for tree peonies and not as cold as herbaceous peonies would like. So we grow both. Our vast preference is for the herbaceous varieties, not because tree peonies don't bloom in nice fragrant colors, but rather because the last thing our garden needs is another ugly deciduous shrub that we have to worry about wintering-over.

Tree peonies reach heights of more than six feet and need evergreen plants around them to conceal their severe growth patterns. When you plant tree peonies, be sure *not* to set them facing due east because their tender shoots, if frosted from the night before, can't be thawed too quickly; the early-morning sun may cause their tips to burn and shrivel. While tree peonies tolerate cold to -40° F, they have to warm up slowly, never in direct sunlight.

If you can meet these conditions, you have a wide selection of colors and scents from which to choose. Although the blooms of most tree peonies are light in coloring, they're often larger (to more than a foot across) and just as fragrant as the herbaceous varieties.

Because they're long-lived, tree peonies should be planted in well-prepared holes that will keep plants happy for a long time. Spring pruning should consist of dead-heading blooms, shaping plants, and cutting back to fresh wood.

Herbaceous peonies grow in clumps, usually about three feet tall with as much girth. Buy peonies only from specialists, preferably those you can visit when their demonstration gardens are in bloom. When you plant, remember that peonies resent being disturbed—place them where you want them to remain.

Herbaceous peonies grow in clumps, usually about three feet tall with as much girth. Foliage is attractive, with large, nicely divided, dark green leaves. Clumps grow from tuberous roots that thicken and spread as they grow. When you plant, remember that herbaceous peonies resent being disturbed. Set tubers three feet apart, leaving ample room before clumps begin to collide underground. When they must be divided, lift them, hose them off, and be sure to leave three buds on each tuber you separate from the mother root.

Buy peonies only from specialists, preferably those you can visit when their demonstration gardens are in bloom. Besides looking closely at varieties in flower, smell them. Not all peonies are fragrant; in fact, scented varieties are in the minority. Also, there's a curious component to the perfume of peonies. Louise Beebe Wilder called it a "sub-odor," explaining that while the more sweetly scented varieties smell somewhat like roses, "back of this is something indefinable that is a little rank." Be certain that you like the smell of the varieties you purchase, remembering that, properly cared for, they'll flourish in your garden for fifty years. If peonies are content where they're planted, they'll bloom during their first season.

In 1987 we visited the famed Bois de Boulogne in Paris, hoping to see the lovely rose garden at its peak. As it happened, the roses were late, but the peonies were in their glory. We knew how widely peonies are colored (from pure white to black-purple), and we had been told that they came in every form from singles to double-doubles, but we had no idea just how diverse peonies really are. Some had thick clusters of stamens that were more vividly colored than their six petals. Petals of the double varieties intensified their colors as they swirled themselves across blossoms the size of cabbages. Although most varieties were scentless, several were powerfully perfumed, though a few did harbor that elusive but surely unpleasant subscent. Almost all were irresistible.

Polianthes tuberosa
Tuberose

When we have a profusion of blooms from any of the plantings in our fragrant garden, more than we can handle for drying or extracting essential oils, we take them, along with our roses, to the wholesale flower market in San Francisco. When we asked our wholesaler which of the many flowers he sells is considered to be the most fragrant, he assured us the question wasn't a close one. "Tuberoses are the hands-down Big Bertha of fragrance," he said, and went on to tell us that many florists include tuberoses in almost all their arrangements, just to insure that customers will smell something even if nothing else in the bouquet is scented.

Purists consider the tuberose to be the most strongly scented of all flowers. Its heavy, heady fragrance is enough to bring on nausea in some people, while others can't get enough.

A native of Mexico, the tuberose requires heat and doesn't winter-over where frosts are likely. In such places bulbs are begun in pots indoors and set out in early summer for blooms

When you ask devotees of fragrance to name their ten favorite flowers, they almost always include peonies. If nothing else, peonies *look* fragrant. In truth, many modern varieties have a rank undertone that makes them more smelly than perfumed. Visually, of course, peonies are knockouts.

about two months later. Although they demand heat (in fact, tubers won't grow at all until the soil warms), tuberoses also want partial shade—a dual requirement not easily met in most gardens. Next, they must have copious waterings as they grow. Finally, drainage should be thorough, and soil must be rich. Then, just when you despair at owning the most persnickety plant in creation, they bloom, and you're ready to go through it all again. When flowering stops, water should be withheld to let the leaves dry and yellow, after which bulbs should be lifted and stored. Tuberoses can be grown indoors, though they're fussy there too.

Leaves of tuberoses are slender and grasslike. Flowers are waxy, funnel-shaped blooms that arrange themselves loosely on three-foot stems. As the flowers age, they flatten into star shapes. There are thirteen species, but only one is in general cultivation—*tuberosa*, which includes a couple of varieties, including a double form called the 'Pearl' that is perhaps even more fragrant than the single types.

If you grow fragrant plants because you intend to extract their essential oils, then you'll want to find a way to plant tuberoses in your area, because no flower is more turgid with perfume essence than the tuberose (its attar is more costly than that of roses). You may go so far as to grow them indoors in specially equipped greenhouses. Be advised that the blooms turn an unappealing yellowish tan when dried and don't look pretty in potpourri blends.

Tuberoses blossom with flowers that are waxy and funnel shaped. As they age, blooms flatten into star shapes. Purists consider the tuberose the most strongly scented of all flowers, but a few poor souls are nauseated by the heavy, heady fragrance.

Scilla
Bluebell

Although *Scilla* species bloom with purple, pink, and white flowers, they're commonly called bluebells in honor of their exalted color and, it seems, because the blue varieties yield the strongest, balsamic, hyacinthlike perfume. In spite of there being more than eighty species of *Scilla*, except through the catalogs of bulb specialists, you're likely to find only two for sale in most nurseries.

S. bifolia is native to the mountainous regions of southern Europe, where it blooms just after the snow melts. Its brilliant blue or turquoise blossoms are borne on six- to eight-inch stems. Individual flowers shaped like stars are only an inch across, but there are usually six per stem.

In England, where *Scilla* species are properly appreciated, bluebells regularly cast drifts of azure mist under deciduous trees. Besides blooming when so little else does, bluebells (that can also be white, pink, or purple) scent the air with balsamic, hyacinthlike perfume.

S. siberica, the Siberian squill, is indigenous to the northern shores of Russia. In long succession from March through May, it bears its dangling flowers of electric blue on three- to six-inch stems. Bees are irresistibly attracted to the blue pollen of *S. siberica*. There is also 'Alba', a pure white form, and 'Spring Beauty', thought by some gardeners to be the finest *Scilla* because it grows to twice the height of other varieties with double-size, delphinium blue flowers.

For some reason, *Scilla* has never caught on as a popular spring bulb in America the way it has in Britain, where the blooms cast drifts of blue mist under trees and beneath deciduous shrubs. *Scilla* species multiply quickly, but bulbs shouldn't be lifted and divided until they are disagreeably overcrowded. It's also wise not to plant *Scilla* too near other blue flowers, which will only pale by comparison.

Tulipa
Tulip

Many people don't think of tulips as fragrant, probably because most gardeners rarely buy from bulb specialists, choosing instead to buy from neighborhood nurseries. If you bother to look beyond mass bulb bins, however, you'll find fragrant tulips in several species and varieties. Tulips are one of the few flowers whose dark-colored varieties are as fragrant as the lighter shades. Like most other flowers, however, double forms are more strongly perfumed than the single versions.

Species of the genus *Tulipa* grow naturally in countries that border the Black Sea and the southern Mediterranean. Tulips are also native to Persia; in fact, the tulip takes its name from the Eastern headdress *tülbent* (turban). The first tulip reached England in 1577—*T. Gesnerana*, a sweetly scented, scarlet bloom that is the great-grandparent of modern cottage tulips. Although several tulips are still marketed by their species names, such as the yellow *T. Celsiana* and *T. sylvestris*, or the clear lilac *T. saxatilis*, most tulips are marketed by their common names.

Single tulips are among the first to bloom, in April, and many descendants of *T. suaveolens* are sweetly scented—the butter yellow 'Bellona' smells like orange blossoms, the perfume of the ox-blood 'Doctor Plesman' reminds many people of lily of the valley, and the terra-cotta 'Fred Moore' smells of honey. Single early tulips are ideal for growing in containers because they are easy to force after being refrigerated a few weeks before they are planted.

Four types of tulips bloom in May—double, cottage, parrot, and lily-flowered. The double

varieties blossom first and are the most fragrant; colors range from crimson red to pure white, perfume from lily to honey. Cottage tulips are so named because they were first discovered growing in old English cottage gardens. While cottage tulips are available in a wide assortment of colors, the most fragrant varieties (some are said to smell like almonds) are usually orange or yellow. Parrot tulips have large, fringed, ruffled petals. Several named varieties are fragrant, including the ever-popular, "black" (really dark purple) parrot. Lily-flowered tulips are so named because their blooms, with pointed reflexed petals, actually look like lilies. The most-fragrant varieties are usually orange or scarlet-rose.

Breeder tulips bloom in early summer. Flowers that are usually some shade of orange, copper, or bronze are enormous and carried on long stems. Those that are fragrant smell like lilies.

Darwin tulips are the last to bloom—as late as the end of June. Blossoms are large, oval or egg-shaped, with stems up to thirty inches. Although the range of colors includes everything from pure white to almost black, the few fragrant varieties are either white or some shade of violet or purple.

During the late eighteenth century, an unusual horticultural event caused tulips to develop stripes and feathered streaks. A highly contagious virus caused tulips to "break" their colors. Those varieties, called bizarre or Rembrandt tulips, were an instant hit, virus and all. Florists were eager for them because of their unusual, thoroughly random patterns of color. Variegated or "broken" tulips can still be purchased and admired for their mad coloring, but you should be aware of two things. First, none is considered to have any notable fragrance, and second, the virus remains. Unless you want your solid-colored tulips to "break" as well, don't plant variegated forms near them.

As peonies, tulips like cold winters and benefit from regular deep freezes. If you live in temperate climates, you will have an uphill battle when you try to naturalize tulips in your garden. Unlike daffodils, which are oblivious to winter temperatures, or hyacinths, which respond well to feeding after they bloom, tulips in moderate climates get smaller each year if left in the ground, no matter how you treat them after they bloom. Digging them up each year seems like a special chore, especially when you consider that after you lift and dry them, bulbs should be refrigerated at temperatures between 40° and 45° F for at least six weeks before being replanted in the fall. Such nuisances are probably why tulips have become such favorite bulbs for planting in pots, to be enjoyed indoors or outside. If you simply can't tolerate the waste of discarding bulbs after only one year of bloom, locate a gardening pal who lives where winters are severe and send your yearlings to be naturalized where they have a chance at multiplying.

Tulips prefer a rich, sandy soil, but will grow almost anywhere as long as the soil drains well. Bulbs should be planted to a depth two and a half times their width. If you live in a borderline-moderate climate, try planting bulbs deeper, where the soil is cooler—to six or eight inches below soil surface.

Tulips bloom in a multitude of colors and shapes. These, which look like lilies, are nicely complemented by a background of periwinkle blue wallflowers. Although they're in the vast minority, several varieties of tulips are notably perfumed, with scents ranging from orange blossom to honey.

Gophers consider tulip bulbs a great delicacy. To keep them and other gnawing rodents away from the luscious, tender, brown-skinned bulbs, use wire or nylon mesh in the holes where tulips are expected to remain.

CHAPTER VIII

Covering the Ground with Fragrance

Ground covers are just as advertised—plants that crawl over garden surfaces. Ground covers are perfect for masking naked plots, for providing a lush foreground for stately plants at the rear of a border, or as a solution to awkward gaps between stepping stones.

There are more plants to cover your ground than those we suggest in this chapter. Herbs such as thyme and mint and annuals such as candytuft and pinks have creepy relatives too (we mentioned them when we spoke about their upright cousins).

While you won't want to trample over most plants that obediently cover your ground, you will over some—such as chamomile, which actually appreciates foot traffic as a chance to release its pungent scent.

Anthemis nobilis
Chamomile

Although there are numerous species of this useful fragrant plant, just two are in general cultivation, and only one will cover your ground. *A. nobilis*, the perennial Roman version, is the ground cover, whereas its German relative, *Matricaria Chamomilla* (said to make finer tea, with an overtone of pineapple), is an upright annual. It's not because we prefer perennials to annuals that we favor *A. nobilis*, since both are powerfully fragrant, but rather because one can inhale chamomile's delightful scent so much more easily in a ground cover. You shouldn't walk on the three-foot-high German chamomile, but you're welcome to tromp the prostrate Italian variety. Bruised by footsteps, Roman chamomile willingly releases its earthy scent. Once established, chamomile welcomes pedestrians and appears to benefit from their traffic.

The word *chamomile* is derived from the Greek *chamai* (on the ground) and *mēlon* (in this case meaning ground apple). For years, people have said that chamomile smells like trodden apples. For us, that comparison is contradicted by a strong camphor aroma apples don't have.

The first consideration of planting should be sun—as much as possible. Chamomile will tolerate some shade, but it will never like it. The lack of strong, regular sun is why chamomile doesn't grow particularly well in Britain, where gardeners are enamored of it.

We first saw chamomile at Sissinghurst, Vita Sackville-West's inspiring garden, in an 18-inch-by-2-foot patch planted as a seat for a bench (a wonderful use). A large sign said "Please Do Not Touch": Sackville-West never had enough sun to grow chamomile well as a ground cover, though she often mentioned how she'd love to.

Robert first planted chamomile in our garden with only two flats of seedlings. We thought we were rather ambitious going after a whole knoll of chamomile by setting plugs nine inches apart over a large area in front of some magnolia and birch trees, but by midsummer the knoll was blanketed with chamomile, except for a few random blank patches. Early that fall, Robert took plugs from the established area and planted them near the edges of adjacent paths. By early summer they, too, filled in.

Realizing that we could probably have a whole chamomile lawn, since we had the ideal place to sow it—a sunny, 20-foot-wide stretch of perfectly drained sandy soil between two 80-foot long parallel rows of hawthorn trees—Robert began investigating growing chamomile from seed.

If you have a sandy stretch of barren soil in full sun and near a source of water, consider a chamomile lawn. You'll bless your efforts when you tromp over chamomile, releasing its lusty scent. Here chamomile provides a handsome footing for a splendid chaste bush.

If you mow chamomile, you may never see its blooms, which are either white or yellow button-headed flowers. If you plant chamomile for making tea, however, you want to encourage the blossoms.

We had read that chamomile seeds are tiny, and we imagined that they'd be hard to come by. They were. After two months of talking with every seedsman Robert could locate, he finally discovered someone who could "special order" *A. nobilis* for a price just a little less than that for rose attar. Imagining that the chamomile seeds would flourish as had their plugs of predecessors, Robert ordered six ounces of the tiniest seeds either of us had ever seen. In March he tilled the would-be lawn, leveled it as best he could (there's a natural contour to our garden that we don't care to alter), and pulled every weed in sight.

Because the seeds were so fine and costly, Robert didn't dare distribute them from a conventional seed spreader. Instead, he mixed them with white river sand left over from a masonry job and gingerly broadcast the mixture off the tip of a square-nosed shovel. The area was then covered with a thin layer of nitralized sawdust that was pressed firmly into the sandy soil with a water-filled lawn roller.

In three weeks there were sprouts everywhere. Some were recognizable weeds; others, well, we couldn't be sure. It took another two weeks for the chamomile sprouts to make themselves unmistakable (by exposing their masses of featherlike, tiny branches). It took two more weeks for every friendly ranch hand we could find to painstakingly weed out everything else.

By the end of summer, the lawn was entirely established, with even fewer and smaller bald patches than when we had planted from plugs of chamomile. By fall the lawn required regular mowing. What a sight, and an even better smell; but best of all was walking across it, trampling out sweet whiffs of camphor. Sackville-West would have loved it too. We can just imagine her, tumbling irresistibly to the ground to saturate her jodhpurs in chamomile's lusty scent.

Chamomile grows upward before it spreads along the ground. Early growth will be wiry compared to later feathery development. When chamomile first gets to a height that you think merits a haircut, don't mow it. The wiry growth will bind in mower blades, and whole tufts will get yanked out. Use shears for early trimming. Don't worry though; once chamomile is established and thickly lush, you can mow it to your heart's content (although you should plan to use a push, rather than a rotary, mower).

Chamomile blooms are usually deep yellow—a few are white—buttons (small wonder, since chamomile is a member of the Compositae family, as are daisies and sunflowers). While the whole plant smells nice, only the blossoms are used in the various chamomile concoctions, including teas. If you mow, by the way, you won't have flowers at all, unless you mow infrequently. That probably won't worry you much, especially if you plant chamomile

It's only fair that we are permitted to grow certain plants better than Vita Sackville-West could. Poor Vita; the best she could do with chamomile was a tiny bench with a "Please Do Not Touch" sign—nice place to sit if she didn't catch you.

mainly as a luxurious ground cover. If you're not going to make teas or use the blooms for other reasons, forget about the flowers. Don't even wonder what they look like; we promise that they're nothing compared to the emerald moss of the plants.

Over the centuries chamomile has had countless uses. It was praised by the earliest Egyptians as a diuretic. Chamomile is highly esteemed for its soothing medicinal values, mostly for calming nerves, but also for preventing nightmares. More-recent reports claim that an infusion of the entire plant is a good hair rinse, especially for blondes.

Chamomile has had various other names. In Spain it's called *manzanilla*, and its flowers flavor the driest sherries. The quintessential companion, chamomile is also known as the "physician plant," because it has often mystically relieved sickly neighbors. Plants growing next to chamomile are thought to be healthier than those growing next to other plants, so much so that gardeners sometimes put chamomile plugs near plants that are ailing.

Asperula
Sweet Woodruff

Before we tempt anyone to choose this charming perennial ground cover, we must warn you that it grows only in shade. You should also know that sweet woodruff releases no scent until after its harvest. Even when the healthiest plants you can imagine are massed with the white blooms of late spring and early summer, you will inhale in vain. Coumarin, woodruff's essential oil, is liberated only when plants are dried. Then lost time is made up as clippings smell increasingly like sweet, newly mown hay, stirring memories of warm days on the farm even in born-and-bred city dwellers.

A gardening friend of ours has thumbs so green that she rarely bothers to read up about anything she decides to grow. That is, she used not to bother. She said that she once planted two flats of sweet woodruff under a birch grove at the back of her garden. When the blooms first appeared, she bent to bury her nose in them, eagerly anticipating that smell she had come to love from sweet woodruff sachets. When she detected no scent whatsoever, she concluded all on her own that her plants were among those fractious kindergartners who don't behave properly during their first season. She waited patiently until the next year, only to be disappointed again. By the end of that season, she was so annoyed with having "bought the wrong variety" that in a fit of pique she ripped out her well-established woodruff patch and tossed it on top of her compost pile.

The next week she was greeted with the unmistakable aroma of sweet woodruff wafting from her compost heap. As she got closer, the fragrance increased. Only then did she bother to refer to a text that told her exactly what she

Keep in mind that low-growing plants mentioned throughout this book also make fine ground covers, especially in areas where you don't intend to walk. Thyme, for instance, has several species that grow prostrate and bloom in gay profusion.

learned the hard way. She replanted the next year and read up on drying.

Asperula is a genus of ninety species, member of the Rubiaceae—bedstraw—family, as are gardenias. All woodruff varieties form leaves in whorls like tiny ruffs all along their stems. The tiny flowers that bloom at the tips of the stems are either white, some shade of pink, or sky blue. Heights vary, but the shorter forms are the most popular for carpeting woodland areas, edging shady paths, and bordering sheltered rock gardens.

A. odorata is by far the most popular woodruff species. Plants are short (rarely taller than six inches), flowers are white, and all parts of the plant are scented when dried.

Woodruffs can be started from seeds, but coverage is faster with seedlings set out from flats. Woodruffs also root from cuttings taken from mature plants. In either case carpets spread quickly in rich, moist soil.

In Elizabethan times dried sweet woodruff was strewn on floors to sweeten smells in whole banquet halls. Before air conditioning, woodruff bundles were hung to "cool" rooms. Even today bags of dried sweet woodruff are hung in linen closets to discourage moths, or layered in drawers to sweeten their contents. While other plants in your garden may have handsomer bushes or prettier blooms, none is more valuable at season's end than sweet woodruff.

Gaultheria procumbens
Creeping Wintergreen

Although there are more than one hundred species of *Gaultheria*, ranging in size from mats of aromatic hairy leaves native to the Himalayas to ten-foot, billowy shrubs indigenous to Santa Barbara, California, one species stands out from the rest because of its unique growth pattern and powerful fragrance. In keeping with its nickname of creeping wintergreen, *G. procumbens* is a ground cover that is redolent of wintergreen scent.

Native to New Jersey and the pine forests of Canada, *G. procumbens* is happiest in dapple-shaded woodlands rich in peat. Although plants of *G. procumbens* hug the ground over a three-foot area, they also send up masses of six-inch-long branches clustered at their tips with thick, leathery, oval, finely toothed leaves. The small, drooping, waxy, white (sometimes pink) flowers that bloom in summer are followed by large, crimson, edible berries that persist through winter.

Except for wanting more-than-average water and soil rich in acid, *G. procumbens* has few needs and is generally trouble free. All parts of *G. procumbens* are fragrant. While neither the flowers nor the berries dry well, leaves and stems dry nicely and retain their strong wintergreen bite.

Several ground covers look nice growing together. These faint yellow violets, for instance, look fetching next to stark white chamomile blossoms with golden centers.

Viola odorata
Sweet Violet

If you have a grove of trees with bare soil underneath or a shady, unclaimed garden nook, consider *V. odorata*, for few plants are as carefree or consistently attractive. Sweet violets are also early bloomers—from January to June, depending on climate. When clumps of *V. odorata* are content, established plants often repeat their bloom in autumn.

V. odorata grows quickly from shallow roots that multiply by runners. Foliage is dark green, heart shaped, and toothed along the edges. Established plants rarely exceed a foot in height, but easily spread to two feet. *V. odorata* is hermaphroditic and self-pollinating. Sweet violet's magic number seems to be five—each blossom has five sepals, five petals, and five stamens.

V. odorata is sold by its varietal names. 'Coeur d'Alsace' is rose-pink, 'Princess of Wales' is a brilliant shade of violet-blue, and 'Christmas' is white. At one time sweet violets had stems no longer than three inches; now modern hybrids such as the deep purple 'Royal Robe' have cutting stems that measure more than six inches long.

Horticulturists don't agree on ideal soil for *V. odorata*. Most gardening reference books advise planting sweet violets in rich soil, whereas many hands-on gardeners assure you that the leaner the soil, the better the violet. Before you water or fertilize your *V. odorata*, decide first why you want to grow it. If it's lush, green, year-round foliage you want, plant sweet violets in soil rich in humus. If you're after fragrant blossoms, keep plants hungry and thirsty. Regardless of how you maintain them, clumps of *V. odorata* show their appreciation for a fall shearing by forming perfectly shaped mounds by spring.

CHAPTER IX

Choosing Unusual Plants

WATER PLANTS

Since fountains, ponds, and bogs are the exception rather than the rule, most gardens have no place for water plants. Water is such a natural in the garden, however, that it's becoming increasingly popular, even on tiny plots, to install inexpensive small preformed pools. Ponds are also on the rise, particularly with the encouragement of water conservation. At Garden Valley Ranch we haven't tackled a pond yet, though we're about to since we know precisely what we'll grow there—the plants that didn't succeed in our pool.

When the fountain was installed, with its 2-foot-deep, 1,500-gallon water pool beneath, the only aspect of its use about which there was no question was which plants would float on the water's surface. They just *had* to be lotuses; we had swooned over them in Australia, Britain, New Zealand, and in certain American display gardens. The scent is indeed heavenly, and the way lotuses thrust their blooms above their massive pads is exquisite.

Although we had read that they resent running water, we never imagined that the steady drops from our modest fountain would bother our lotuses. We sent for *Nelumbo nucifera* 'Alba Grandiflora' from a water-pond specialist and followed the planting instructions to the letter, including sinking the weighty containers to the specified depths and fertilizing them with the tabs that accompanied our order.

The lotuses grew, but they never seemed happy. We later found that the steady trickle of water coming off the top of our fountain was just enough to keep our *Nelumbo* plants from flourishing (lotuses depend on heat reflection from the surface of calm water). Their little pads would develop, begin to look sickly, and finally go belly-up before they matured. We also learned that even if our Japanese variety *had* prospered, it would have grown too large for our modest pool (content plantings of lotus reach ten feet in diameter). There are miniature varieties, but they, too, are bothered by flowing currents of water.

Out with the lotuses, in with water lilies—*Nymphaea*. While they certainly fared better than our lotuses, water lilies also no longer flourish for us. When we finally decided that it was koi rather than flora that we *really* wanted in our pool, we learned that any plant sub-merged in a container filled with soil will eventually tilt a pond's ecological balance as far as koi are concerned. On our way to learning that inevitable fact, we stumbled upon fragrant water plants that will flourish for your calm-water gardens, particularly if you don't also want to keep fish there.

Nelumbo
Lotus

No flower is more steeped in history than the lotus. Not even records of the early cultivation of the rose predate those of *Nelumbo*. Egyptians chose the lotus to fashion headdresses for their sphinxes. In India and Tibet, the lotus was considered so revered that Buddha himself is traditionally found sitting upon one of its blossoms, specifically *N. nucifera*, the sacred lotus. Pale pink flowers shaped not unlike hybrid tea roses have a strong scent, also similar to that of roses. There is a Japanese variety, 'Alba Grandiflora', that blooms huge, pure white, deliciously scented flowers; and a Chinese 'Pekinensis Rubra' whose rich red, goblet-shaped blossoms are pungent with perfume.

Roots of *N. lutea*, native to the United States, were once eaten like potatoes by Indians. Today they are cultivated for their golden yellow blossoms, which, although not as sweetly scented as the Asian varieties, are noticeably fragrant, particularly in the evening.

Several lotuses bloom from the middle of a network of gigantic leaves that are actually capable of supporting a small child. The blossoms of certain lotuses not only resemble hybrid tea roses, but they also smell like them, particularly in the evening.

Hybridizers have been so busy cross-pollinating *Nymphaea* that few modern water lilies can be traced to their exact parentage. When reading a specialist's catalog, pay attention to what time of day certain varieties relinquish their perfume: some are nooners; others prefer evening.

Nymphaea
Water Lily

Nymphaea species share several qualities with *Nelumbo*, including where they prefer to grow, but they bloom in a wider array of colors and have more-versatile qualities (including closing at night or reaching peak of perfume during midday). Hybridizers have recently been so possessed with developing new varieties and colors that few modern hybrids of *Nymphaea* can be traced to their true parentage. The following varieties, however, are somewhere in the lineage of all modern fragrant hybrids.

N. albida is the largest water lily. Exotically fragrant, pure white blossoms that look as though they've been waxed bloom above complementary bottle green foliage.

N. capensis 'zanzibariensis', also known as the African royal water lily, has dark green leaves blotched brown and sharply fragrant, star-shaped, rich blue blossoms and golden anthers.

N. odorata is a multivariety, North American native. No single variety, however, is as showy or as powerfully scented as 'gigantea'. Mature blossoms look like ice white peonies and smell like them as well, only stronger.

Finally, there's the tender but sweetly scented *N. caerulea*, the blue lotus of the Nile; *N. tuberosa*, with pure white, wavy-petaled, six-inch blossoms that smell like ripe apples; and *N. tuberosa* 'Richardsonii', shell pink and seductively perfumed.

Some modern water lilies are white and smell like peonies; others have exotically fragrant blue petals that look as though they've been waxed. Before deciding on any water plants, make certain that the water in your pond doesn't flow too swiftly; neither lotuses nor *Nymphaea* like moving water.

FRAGRANT GRASSES

If you have an area large enough to grow scented grasses, you're probably going to opt for wildflowers instead, which are much more colorful than grasses. Somehow the fact that the vast majority of wildflowers have no particular aroma doesn't seem to matter, even to fragrance fanciers. Should you insist on cultivating only scented plants, however, here are a couple of grasses to consider.

Acorus Calamus
Rush, Sweet Flag

Acorus, a herbaceous plant that prefers to grow near water, is actually a rush with flaglike leaves, hence its two nicknames. Plants are multiplied by division of their creeping rootstock.

Because both the leaves and roots smell strongly of cinnamon, *Acorus* species have been esteemed since the Middle Ages. Today leaves of sweet flag are distilled for their volatile oils—popular in perfumery and a must for flavoring certain vinegars. Other parts of the plant are a source of drugs or a means of clarifying beer. And even though they don't fade to a pretty color, dried *Acorus* leaves lend spice to potpourri.

If your plants of *A. Calamus* bloom at all (most don't unless they grow near streams or ponds), you're not likely to be swept away by their blossoms of greenish brown with a golden

mosaic overlay. However, if you take the time to rub the somber blossoms, you'll find that, like the roots and leaves from which they've sprung, they also harbor a refreshing cinnamon scent.

Melilotus
Clover

Gardeners interested in fragrant plants may be unaware of *Melilotus* for two reasons. First, clover is so common that one doesn't consider cultivating it, rather merely allowing it to grow wild in ditches along roadsides or as a ubiquitous cover crop. Second, *Melilotus* isn't fragrant when it's fresh; just like sweet woodruff, clover releases its perfume only when plants are dried.

M. officinalis grows to about two feet tall, and in late summer blossoms with nectar-laden, yellow flowers. In Switzerland *M. officinalis* is planted as fodder and said to be what gives Gruyère cheese its distinct flavor.

M. alba, sweet or Bukhara clover, may actually be a form of *M. officinalis* (the only major difference is that its flowers are white), but is classified as a separate species. Sweet clover is praised by bees and their keepers.

Although you may not landscape with *Melilotus*, you might designate an otherwise useless garden spot as your clover patch. In Europe, where *Melilotus* is native, whole plants are dried and placed in drawers to sweeten the smell of their contents.

Fragrant grasses are favored plants for hillsides already dotted with flowering shrubs. Foliage of sweet flag smells like cinnamon, whereas clover, widely planted as fodder, is said to season the meat of lamb, flavor milk from goats, and sweeten honey.

SCENTED ROOTS

When you admit that you're interested in plants that have scented roots, people give you strange looks. While being hooked on fragrant foliage or blossoms is acceptable, cultivating plants for their roots suggests that one has gone overboard where perfume is concerned. Fortunately, however, the species we suggest appear quite at home in fragrant gardens; only keen visitors understand that you grow them not for how they flourish above soil level, but rather for what they produce underground.

Asarum
Ginger

Asarum is a genus of more than sixty species of perennial herbs that have creeping rootstock and long-stalked, heart-shaped leaves. Although most *Asarum* species are native to the tropics, the most pungently scented species are native to Canada and California.

A. canadense, the Canadian snakeroot, grows to one foot tall with kidney-shaped leaves borne in pairs. In early summer brownish purple flowers have such an unpleasant smell that you may well believe that no part of the plant is nicely scented. The roots, however, especially when dried, smell strongly of ginger.

A. caudatum, native to California, also has reddish brown flowers that are unpleasantly scented. Unlike its Canadian cousin it blooms earlier and its roots are not so pungently scented, though they still smell like ginger.

Asarum grows best in humus-laden, well-watered soil. Plants are considered a delicacy by slugs and snails.

Inula Helenium
Elecampane

Elecampane was botanically named *Inula* because its roots yield a starch called inulin, from which certain sugars are obtained. The species *Helenium* was named in honor of Helen of

Elecampane is a good-looking herb—upright to five feet, with yellow or orange fringed blossoms that resemble sunflowers. Britain's most ubiquitous wildflower, elecampane is praised for its perfumed roots, which at first smell like ripe bananas, then like violets.

Troy, so as you may imagine, elecampane is steeped in history; it's also the largest of all British wildflowers.

Elecampane is a striking herb—regal and tall, with oversized, pointed leaves that are covered in fine hair, similar to those of comfrey and horehound. Generally, elecampane grows to four or five feet, but if planted in a shady spot in rich soil, plants may tower to more than ten feet (yes, you'll need to stake them). Flowers that appear in summer are yellow to orange, daisylike, and fringed; they have been compared to miniature, double sunflowers.

Elecampane harbors its strongest scent in its roots, which at first smell like ripe bananas, then like violets as they age. At one time roots were eaten as vegetables or candied as sweetmeat; powdered roots of elecampane have been praised in the treatment of bronchial ailments.

Vetiveria zizanioides
Vetiver

In America vetiver was one of the most popular scents for men's cologne during the 1950s and 1960s. In India *V. zizanioides* formed the base of a substance called mousseline, named for Indian muslin that had been doused in its perfume. Although *V. zizanioides* is a perfectly good-looking plant with agreeably green, swordlike, tapering leaves, it's not the rushy foliage that perfume fanciers seek, but rather the violet-scented, rhizomatous roots.

Unless you plan to cultivate *V. zizanioides* commercially, for the extraction of its essential oils, the best way to enjoy its pleasantly scented roots is to grow plants in plastic containers that can be sunk into the garden and camouflaged with mulch. Average soil and moderate light suffice, but vetiver will also thrive in poor soil and full sun. Once each year pots should be lifted, plants removed, roots trimmed, then the plants potted back up and resunk. Adult plants produce abundant, dense, fibrous mats that are easily harvested and dried. If you're adept at and have the patience for weaving roots, fragrant (particularly when moistened) baskets and sun blinds can be made from vetiver roots. Otherwise, roots of *V. zizanioides* provide blandly colored but distinctively scented additions to potpourri.

CHAPTER X

Landscaping with Fragrance

Focal Plants First

Back when we decided to establish a one-acre fragrant garden, we knew only a small number of the plants listed in this book. More important, we had no firm concept of the design of the garden at large—which trees, shrubs, and hedges had to be planted first (or would appreciate having choice spots saved for them)—nor how to specify the placement of plants. As we admitted in the preface, we solicited the help of a landscape architect who is, fortunately, fond of fragrant plants anyway and followed his design to the species. If you're planning a garden in a new site, we would encourage you to do the same, or at least to have a master plan in mind. Later you can add, remove, or substitute according to the personal preferences you develop. At the beginning, however, consult those who not only have expertise in garden design, but those who can tell you which plants are likely to perform well where you garden.

Henry Mitchell, a fine gardener and a regular columnist for the *Washington Post* has told many an amusing story about gardeners who plant with no eye toward the future. In *The Essential Earthman* he had this to say about planting a new garden:

"There is no such thing as laying out a garden from scratch that will look all right in three years and also look all right in fifteen years. It is a continuing process of digging out and chopping down. This boils down to thinking clearly which plants you want in the garden 'forever,' and then planting so that whatever else comes and goes, they will have room to develop.

"Permanent plants—plants that require years to show their true beauty—should not be planted in the first place unless you are convinced you cannot live without them. It is a cruel thing to stick in a little magnolia and let it develop for ten or twelve years and then have to face the crisis of whether you keep the magnolia (which of course has grown faster than you were counting on) or the double-flowered pink plum (which has also quite surpassed itself). You should have planted them twenty-five feet apart in the first place and put in a couple of lesser things to take care of the first few years."

When planting annuals, biennials, perennials, or bulbs, of course, you can afford snap judgments, even mistakes. If something hasn't suited you this year, try another variety next year. When considering focal plants such as trees, shrubs, or hedges, however, satisfy yourself that you want them forever, be certain to pay close attention to how large they become, and also learn whether other plants like to grow beneath or around them.

Consider Color

Color in your garden is as personal as wallcovering in your bedroom, skillets in your kitchen, and tiles in your shower. Coloring your garden is yet another chance to stamp your personal mark on your home.

Novice gardeners usually commence gardening with a total disregard for color, falling easily for pretty packages of seeds marked "mixed colors" (they're sometimes nice, but usually not). Beginners don't usually consider colors of companion plantings either: if a garden spot has been cleared and readied for sowing, they put there whichever seeds are "next," no matter what color the plants bloom. Only after spring tattles on them do gardeners who plant without regard to color notice that red salvias clash offensively with mauve chaste bushes and orange daylilies with pink carnations. Sights like these are enough to make you swear never again to appear oblivious to pigmentation. In fact, cacophonous color schemes have driven many a gardener to theme-by-color gardens. One of the more successful was Vita Sackville-West. Read what she had to say about color in the garden:

"Provided one does not run the idea to death, and provided one has enough room, it is interesting to make a one-color garden. It is something more than merely interesting. It is great fun and endlessly amusing as an experiment, capable of perennial improvement, as you take away the things that don't fit in, or that don't satisfy you, and replace them by something you like better.

"I should like to use the old word garth for the white garden at Sissinghurst, meaning a small piece of enclosed ground, usually beside a house or other building, for it is entirely enclosed, on one side by a high yew hedge and on the other sides by pink brick walls and a little Tudor house. It is divided into square beds by paths edged with lavender and box. But, as it is difficult to convey any impression of a place

Here at Garden Valley Ranch, we've learned to group plants that like the same growing conditions. These beds are massed with *Cistus*, rosemary, lavender, and thyme—all of which prefer poor soil and infrequent irrigation. We've similarly grouped thirsty plants.

without the help of photographs, it would be wiser to confine myself to a list of the plants used to produce the cool, almost glaucous, effect we have aimed at."

She then goes on to enumerate the plants she chose for her white garden: dozens of southern-wood, *Cineraria maritima*, *Santolina*, *Achillea ageratifolia*; drifts of various lilies, delphiniums, foxgloves, gypsophilias, anemones, and dahlias; bushes of hydrangeas, cistuses, peonies, buddleias; and an assortment of roses that climb and gobble up old almond trees.

We've seen Sissinghurst's white garden for ourselves and can attest to Sackville-West's triumph. One of the reasons the all-white garden is so successful is that it's not really all white. Of course, there's the ice white, Iceberg rose, but planted right next to it are peonies that are so off white they're beige. Then there are numerous annuals and perennials planted

Although our white garden doesn't rival the one at Sissinghurst, we, too, have incorporated silver- and gray-leaved plants beside those that blossom pure white. If you're fond of a particular color scheme, try restricting a section of your garden to a "room" landscaped in your favorite hues and shades.

not for their insignificant, white blossoms, but instead for their attractive gray leaves. To plump out Sackville-West's favored skewed end of the color spectrum, there are many plants, even trees, that have distinctive silver foliage. The total effect, especially in late June and early July, is dazzling.

We have friends who have gone bonkers over other colors, restricting sections of or their entire garden to their favorites. Some insist on red and pink, several on blue and purple, and a few demand yellow. Although it's unlikely that many of you will limit your gardens to any specific shades, at least pay attention to which ones please you when mixed with which others, and take notes on combinations that offend you.

When planning your garden, you're likely to discover that there's more to the use of a basic color wheel than you thought. On the one hand, colors right next to one another in the spectrum really *do* look nice with one another; on the other hand, if it's drama you seek, opposing colors planted right next to one another create focal points that you and anyone visiting your garden cannot ignore. A blue-purple buddleia planted in the midst of drifts of yellow pansies, for instance, will pop into focus every time you glance its way. If you want to carry your daring scheme to tasteful fruition, add yellow pansies that have eyes the same shade of blue as your butterfly bush. To cap off your tasteful decorating, add summer-blooming wallflowers of the same shade as your buddleia.

While experimenting with color, always remember that any solid color, such as white, can unify a too-colorful bed and bail you out of a color crisis. When you learn that the reds, oranges, and yellows that you planted are considerably more intense than you imagined from their shot-through-silk catalog pictures, tie them all together with a plant such as alyssum that blooms white in a hurry—the color riot won't disappear, but it will stop screaming so loudly.

The fine gardeners in Britain keep coming up with color combinations that Americans never seem to dream of. Gertrude Jekyll was foremost, of course, known as well for her adventuresome color combinations as for her garden design. She loved pots of long-stemmed, eye-blinking, red tulips with electric blue lobelias growing at their feet, and luxurious beds of yellow and orange rhododendrons with light and dark blue forget-me-nots camouflaging their leggy bottoms.

Don't test your color palette by installing permanent plants—those that should stay where you first place them. Experiment instead with annuals and ephemeral perennials; then, it won't matter if you don't like your color schemes—just start over. Mix as you like; there are no unbreakable rules. Keep in mind, however, that if you decide to encircle your bush of mauve Angel Face with orange marigolds, people are either going to say that you have no taste or, as they've always supected, that you're at least *partially* color-blind.

Good Neighbors

Throughout this book we mention plants that like to grow next to one another because they favor identical growing conditions. No plant requires a unique spot; all happily coexist with *some* others. Learn who lives well with whom before you restrict your garden's neighborhoods.

Gardeners designate areas to herbs not because they don't care to mix them with flowers, but rather because the majority of herbs thrive under identical growing conditions. Rosemary, lavender, and thyme, for instance, are often planted together in complementary-colored, long borders because they all prefer soil on the poor side, relatively small amounts of water, and full sunlight.

Rhododendrons prefer to grow in acid soil beneath dappled shade. Because most rhododendrons have leggy growth habits, gardeners search for plants to grow around their bases, thereby concealing rhododendron's awkward habits. Fortunately, there is an abundance of plants that likes the exact conditions. *Pieris* and *Gaultheria procumbens*, for instance, will thrive anywhere rhododendrons flourish.

If you don't understand the importance of, or don't care to mess with, soil analyses even though you know you should, at least notice how much water certain plants like—you simply can't change their drinking habits. Tuberoses, for example, rarely get their fill of water. Sweet violets, however, should be kept thirsty if you expect them to bloom. Should you decide to plant tuberoses so that they will blossom through the leaves of your sweet violets, you're headed for trouble. Quenching the constant thirst of tuberoses spells doom for violets,

which, if regularly irrigated, produce only foliage, no blossoms. Plant your tuberoses next to something else, such as lilies or lupines, which also like copious amounts of water to drain through their well-mulched beds.

If you're fortunate enough to have inherited a garden with adult native trees, be sure to understand their water needs. Several oaks native to California, for instance, won't tolerate even infrequent watering. Rather than kill your oaks by insisting on color underneath them from plants that demand water, choose a colorful, fragrant plant such as *Romneya* instead, which, like native oaks, doesn't require a drink all summer long.

Some plants make good neighbors not only because they like the same culture, but also because they look so nice together. Borage and strawberries look terrific side by side, and their mature leaves complement one another's. Similarly, *Choisya* and *Asperula* (sweet woodruff) both have white flowers and similarly shaped whorls of foliage. One's green color flatters the other's.

Then there are plants that actually help one another. Chamomile is the classic, of course, since it's thought to benefit everything it grows next to. Nasturtiums are valued companions because they entice aphids away from less-hardy plants nearby.

Companion planting is so in vogue that whole books are written about plants that reciprocate benefits with others. Dandelions are said to help trees set fruit, forsythia is considered beneficial when planted near almond trees, feverfew supposedly wards off bugs, and roses appreciate having garlic planted nearby because members of the onion family are reputed to repel aphids (if you spray your roses, however, don't eat the garlic).

When choosing large plants, particularly trees, decide first if you also want something to grow beneath them. If you do, steer clear of trees such as poplars, which are known for their invasive roots. Consider birches and decorative fruit trees instead, whose roots plunge deep into the ground, leaving ample room for shallow-rooted, flowering plants.

CHAPTER XI

Preserving Your Bounty

People have always favored fragrant plants to their scentless relatives. During ancient times, perfumed plants were burned as offerings at temples and holy places. The Egyptians were the first to extract essential oils from fragrant plants because they wanted something special to scent their palace halls, to garland their priests, and to prepare their dead for the hereafter. On the way to creating perfume, they discovered moist potpourri—when they crammed rose petals into giant crocks filled with salt, oils, and spices and left them to slowly "cure" (rot, actually). In time, the Egyptians shared their knowledge with the Greeks, who told the Romans, who carried perfume secrets to Europe. By the Elizabethan period, people so fancied potpourri that they built entire rooms in their houses and devoted them to the preservation of scent. Stillrooms, as they were called because regulation size specified space for a small still, were cherished getaways for sixteenth-century housewives. Stillrooms were always warm, therefore an ideal place for hanging fresh bouquets to dry and for grinding dried herbs with mortars and pestles.

Dry potpourri reached its heyday during the nineteenth century. No longer satisfied with concoctions that simply smelled good, Victorians wanted visual appeal—the gayer the better. They devised screens and complicated racks that fit in secret, dark places so that every shred of fragrant plant could be dried at the peak of its color.

Advocates of dry potpourri say they favor it because it's quicker to make and prettier to look at. Those who prefer moist potpourri point out that, in their method, petals retain more of their volatile essences and slowly blend them with essential oils during an extended curing period. Although we make mostly dry mixtures, we also like moist potpourri and offer recipes for both types.

Gathering and Drying

Materials for potpourri should be gathered at the peak of their fragrance whether they are to be partially dried for moist potpourri or dehydrated for dry potpourri. Ideally, flowers, herbs, and foliage should be dry to begin with, not moistened with dew. If mornings are arid, pick as early as possible; if they're damp, harvest as soon as materials feel dry to the touch.

Familiarize yourself with peak harvesttimes for various plants. Rose blossoms can be cut for drying almost any time, but blooms of sweet woodruff should never be cut—they aren't fragrant. Plants of sweet woodruff should mature each season before they are sheared for drying. Herbs such as parsley and basil can be manicured at regular intervals; others such as dill and curry plants should mature before being lopped to the ground. Some herbs signal harvesttime by forming flower buds.

In choosing your drying areas, make sure first that they're out of the sun. Materials for potpourri should be dried in the dark, since sunlight bleaches their colors and depletes their essential oils.

After finding dark areas for drying, consider ventilation. Ideally, plant materials drying for potpourri shouldn't touch one another, and air should circulate freely between them (if crammed into musty spaces, petals rot).

If you plan to dry only small amounts, newspapers will do nicely, especially laid over carpeting. If you dry nowhere in the house but under your bed and those of your guests, you'll be amazed at how many papers you can spread out.

When you have no more newspaper space, don't consider stacking new materials on top of those already laid out to dry; they'll mildew from lack of ventilation. Consider investing in window screens instead. You don't need new ones or matched sets, and it won't matter what the frames look like, even whether or not they're painted. All you care about is providing a surface that is reasonably rigid and well ventilated. As long as screens are kept at least six inches apart, with blocks to separate them, racks can be stacked to any height.

When we began making potpourri commercially and had no more space for laying newspapers or stacking screens, a carpenter working at the ranch devised an ingenious adaptation of a solar food dehydrator. Outwardly, the solar oven looks like a 6-foot highboy on 18-inch legs. The two front doors open to reveal two banks of screened trays that are 2 inches apart. The fifty drying racks (twenty-five on either side) slide easily for loading and unloading. There is a 4-inch, rectangular opening along the back side that is attached to a sloping 4-foot-by-4-foot box lined with corrugated metal painted black. Four inches above the metal is a double-layered pane of thermal glass.

Air heats quickly between the thermal glass

If you have an old shower stall or an unclaimed closet in your home, put it to good use by stringing lines in it for drying whole bunches of flowers and foliage. Many herbs retain their strongest scent if allowed to dry on stems left intact. Should you not like the look of a plant dried whole, crumble it into a potpourri blend.

and the black metal. Because heat rises, warm air flows constantly through the trays of petals and carries their moisture out an adjustable lid on the top of the oven. During warm weather, the solar unit dries two hundred square feet of materials every two days.

Another good way to dry is on temporary clotheslines that can be stretched high, near ceilings. Clotheslines are particularly helpful when harvesting plants such as lavender, rosemary, and thyme, which should be left on their stems anyway. Handfuls can be bundled and tied at the base with garden twine (you may decide to dry whole, little, mixed bouquets this way). Bushy plants such as mint, lemon verbena, and pelargonium can also be dried intact, especially since they're so abundant.

Whole flowers dry nicely too, particularly miniature roses and pansies, which make wonderful decorations for clear containers that will later house your potpourri blends. If you dry larger flowers whole, remember that they take longer to dehydrate than petals do.

If you dry your own citrus rind, be sure to cut it into little pieces while it's still pliable. Otherwise, you'll need a cleaver to break it into segments after it has dried tougher than leather.

If you're drying for moist potpourri, petals must reduce their bulk by at least one-third. If you're making dry potpourri, materials should become as parched as cornflakes. When you store them, use tightly sealed, opaque containers; clear glass or plastic allows light to bleach the colors. Cardboard boxes with lids also work well, as do plastic trash cans.

A carpenter working at our ranch in Petaluma devised a solar oven for drying rose petals, fashioning it after a food dehydrator. During warm weather, the solar unit dries two hundred square feet of materials every two days. Gardeners with smaller crops can dry their bounty on newspapers and screens hidden under beds.

Fixatives and Essential Oils

Fixatives actually have the inherent ability to absorb oils and scents and suspend them in time. Besides that difficult-to-grasp accomplishment, fixatives also contribute a distinct scent all their own, which becomes an integral part of the entire potpourri blend. In time, of course, fixatives weaken their grasp, and scent begins to fade (there are ways to revive them, and we'll tell you about them). Still, all potpourris—wet or dry—will weaken into scentlessness without the magical qualities of fixatives to bind their fragrances.

Most fixatives are derived from resins and are sold by names such as sandalwood, cedarwood, patchouli, tonka bean, storax, gum benzoin, and the ever-popular orrisroot. As you know from reading about irises, you can grow your own orris by planting *Iris florentina*. You'll need patience, however, for after digging orrisroot, you must peel and carefully store it in a dry, well-ventilated spot for at least two years. You may derive consolation by remembering that the longer the roots of *I. florentina* age, the more pronounced their violet scent becomes. Orrisroot is readily available for purchase in powder, slices, or irregular chunks, and it's inexpensive. Although powders provide the most-binding fixes, they're not recommended for dry potpourri because they dull colors and cloud containers. For moist potpourri, of course, powders are ideal fixatives.

Gum benzoin is derived from a tree native to the Far East. Gum benzoin has a pungent aroma all its own, but it also blends well, particularly with orrisroot.

If a recipe specifies tonka beans, you must grind them before adding them to your potpourri; otherwise, tonka beans can't release their nutty scent.

If patchouli leaves are called for, experiment with less than the recipe specifies—a little patchouli goes a long way. Although recipes vary, you should figure about a tablespoon of fixative for each quart of dried materials.

Essential oils are the final additions to potpourris and the key ingredient for the basic aroma of a blend. Most herbalists and hobby shops carry essential oils, as do many old-fashioned drugstores. There are also mail-order houses with catalogs that list more than one hundred scents; some are extracted naturally, others are man-made.

The first potpourri recipe we tried called for oil of neroli, obtained from the unopened flowers of the bitter orange, *Citrus bigarradia*. Oil of neroli seemed particularly appealing, probably because our *C. bigarradia* trees had twice frozen to the ground and were eventually replaced by apples. We feared that real oil of neroli would be expensive because we knew that it was the active ingredient in eau de cologne, but we didn't want anything synthetic for *our* potpourri. We soon changed our minds after learning that naturally distilled oil of neroli sells for three to four thousand dollars per kilogram! Synthetics aren't all bad; neither are they as good as the real stuff. Some people swear they can't smell the difference.

For some fragrances, such as almond, coconut, eucalyptus, certain orange, and mint, you can buy true oils for little more than the cost of synthetics. When it comes to rose, gardenia, honeysuckle, tuberose, and violet, however, the truly fine sources are distilled, not man-made, and their prices are dear.

Until you master the techniques for extracting your own, experiment with some of the synthetic oils. At first, try using less oil than the recipes call for—you can always add oil if you want stronger fragrance, but you can't remove the scent from potpourri that has been overdoused.

Moist Potpourri

Besides fragrant plant materials, there are two essentials for moist potpourri: a wide-mouthed, straight-sided crock with a cover and a long wooden spoon. The first step involves alternating thick sheets of rose petals with layers of common, noniodized salt. Ideally, crocks should be filled to three-quarter capacity and left to cure. Crocks shouldn't be so heavy that you can't lift them, because they should be uncovered daily and their contents thoroughly stirred—from the bottom up, then weighted down with whatever is heavy and handy.

After a few days of curing, foam may appear, which should simply be restirred into the mixture. An overzealous crock may form a crust. If crusts develop, remove them whole and break them into small pieces before returning them to the brew.

In three weeks, preferably a month if you have the time, the petals will be ready for fixatives, spices, and essential oils. Stir them in, and set the crock to cure for another month, again stirring every day. At the end of this curing period, moist potpourri is ready to be spooned into the containers you have selected. Fresh batches always smell a bit raw, but mellow in time.

Recipes often call for bay salt. To make your own, add torn bay leaves to salt and grind as finely as possible with a mortar and pestle.

Brandy is a popular additive for many moist potpourris. Besides a scent all its own, because of its alcohol, brandy coaxes latent molecules to release their scent (so does vodka, which has no lingering aroma).

You'll rarely find a recipe for moist potpourri that demands precision. Most blends end up being called "millefleur" because countless materials can be used, depending entirely upon what's available. As for fixatives and essential oils, they're fair game too, dependent on what you want to smell. Some recipes call for sugar, a few suggest brown.

The following is one of our favorites from *Potpourris and Other Fragrant Delights* by Jacqueline Heriteau:

ROSE AND SPICE POTPOURRI

8 cups rose petals
¾ cup kosher salt
¾ cup table salt
2 tablespoons ground mace
⅔ cup orrisroot powder
2 tablespoons ground cloves
2 tablespoons ground nutmeg
2 tablespoons ground allspice
1 stick cinnamon, crushed
1 cup dried rosebuds
5 drops rose oil

Dry the petals to a leathery texture. Combine coarse and fine salt. In a 3-quart, wide-mouthed crock, layer the petals with the salt, each layer about a half inch deep. Set in a dry, airy place for ten days, stirring daily. When the mixture is dry, crumble it and add the remaining ingredients. Add the rose oil a drop at a time and mix well. Cure, sealed, for six weeks. Transfer to a decorative container and keep covered except when in use.

The ideal container for moist potpourri is one with two lids. One is solid, and it is used when you don't want scents to waste their wafts. The second lid, used when you want to perfume a room, should have holes in the surface. Many antique stores, even junk shops, have old-fashioned jars with tops that have movable slots that can be opened or closed by turning a knob on the lid. It is said that moist potpourri made from good materials and properly aged can last more than fifty years without even a rejuvenating shot of brandy or vodka.

Dry Potpourri

Before blending ingredients, decide if you want to look at your dry potpourri after it is completed or whether you want to enjoy only its scent. If you want visual appeal, you must then decide on a color scheme. Rose petals dry to shades of black-red, red, magenta, pink, rose, lavender, and yellow through orange. Petals from white roses end up some shade of chamois or flesh, never pure white. Should you decide to forget about a color theme and use instead everything you have dried, increase interest further by incorporating a variety of shapes, including whole flower buds, seeds, grasses, and roots.

Leaves of some fragrant plants, such as lemon verbena, sweet woodruff, bay, and myrtle, not only retain their scent after drying, but look pretty too. Others, such as mint, pelargonium, and most wide-leaved herbs, retain their fragrance, but dry to unappealing colors. If you don't like the way a nicely scented plant dries, think of it as a spice and crumble it before incorporating it into potpourri.

Recipes for dry potpourri usually specify one tablespoon each of fixatives and spices for each quart of dried material. Mix well all dried materials and apply essential oils. If you doubt the scent of a liquid fragrance, test its oil on small samples before committing the whole batch. When all additions are blended, store the mixture in an airtight, opaque container, planning to mix it thoroughly once a week for at least six weeks. Sometimes when you retoss your blend, you'll be convinced that you've created a brand-new, fragrant masterpiece; other times, your brew will smell like dirty socks. Don't despair until the mixture is thoroughly aged.

The three dry potpourris we blend are the ones we've found most popular and those for which we have all materials in abundant supply. The first is made mostly from garden rose petals. Roses also form the basis of the second recipe, but the blend is enriched considerably with bay leaves. The third blend features rosemary and other robust herbs and vivid rose petals.

GARDEN ROSE POTPOURRI

4 quarts whole rose petals
1 cup sweet woodruff, cut into pieces
1 cup rose-scented pelargonium leaves, well crumbled
¼ cup orrisroot
½ ounce rose oil

If roses are what you yearn to smell, it's hard to beat this simple recipe. The blend is particularly pretty when petals in a single color range are used—your choice.

BAY-ROSE POTPOURRI

3 quarts rose petals
12 torn bay leaves
1½ cups lavender blossoms
1 cup orange blossoms
2 ounces orrisroot
1 ounce ground nutmeg
¼ ounce nutmeg
¼ ounce cinnamon
¼ ounce ground cloves
1 ounce neroli fragrance (or ½ ounce oil of neroli)

This blend is for those of you who crave the smell of citrus and lavender, but want to add a zesty herbal scent.

ROSEMARY POTPOURRI

1 quart rose petals
2 pints lemon verbena (whole leaves, tenderly crushed)
1 pint crushed leaves of rose-scented pelargonium
1 pint crumbled rosemary
1 tablespoon benzoin
1 tablespoon orrisroot
¼ cup angelica
1 tablespoon lemon or orange peel
½ teaspoon cinnamon
1 teaspoon nutmeg
1 tablespoon gingerroot
6 drops rosemary oil
½ teaspoon oil of neroli (or its synthetic equivalent)
2 ground tonka beans

This potpourri is not for the faint of nose, not because it's too strong, but because, just as it is when fresh, rosemary is a powerful scent. The other ingredients help to diminish rosemary's overtones of turpentine, but there's still plenty of zip left.

There are almost limitless good alternates for several dried plant materials. If you like a culinary trace to your blend, crumble in a few leaves of curry plant or substitute mint for rose-scented pelargonium. Use what you have

Before blending potpourri, make certain you have everything you need—dried materials, essential oils, fixatives, measuring spoons, mortar and pestle, and a bowl to hold your brew. Once you get a whiff of what you can make at home, you'll never buy commercial potpourri again (if you do, please buy ours).

plenty of; if you like the fresh smell of certain plants, you're odds-on to like them dried too.

If you want your potpourri to last as long as possible, keep it sealed in a container. As I said before, opaque containers are best, but clear ones allow you to look as well as smell, and if you keep them out of direct sunlight, colors won't fade quickly. Open the container only when you want to enjoy the smell of its contents.

Many people insist that their homemade potpourri remain visible and available for tossing by hand to punch up its aromas. If you keep your potpourri in open bowls or baskets, you can help revive lost scents by occasionally removing the blend to a large porcelain (never metal) bowl, adding a few drops of alcohol (vodka is best), and tossing it thoroughly with a wooden spoon.

In time, of course, all scents will be lost or so faint that they no longer please you. When you see how easy potpourri is to make yourself, however, you'll have many more batches aging in storage.

Sachets

While sweeping up after blending potpourri, people noticed that they were wasting a lot of dried plant material; it was then they thought of sewing the fragrant, powdery residues into sacks and pouches. These sweet bags and sachets had countless uses. At first they were put only in linen drawers and under pillows, but by the sixteenth century, sachets were so popular that women tied little pouches on their underskirts and to sewing baskets so that perfume followed them everywhere. During Victoria's reign, bags of sachet were placed behind leather-bound books to perfume whole shelves, and they were sealed inside linen envelopes to scent stacks of writing paper.

Because you'll probably never again see the sachet material once you've sewn it in a pouch and since dried fragrant material is most strongly scented when powdered, sachet material should be ground with a mortar and pestle or at least worked through a fine screen (twigs pierce bags and cause them to leak). As for dry potpourri, sachet materials must be thoroughly dehydrated; otherwise, they won't reduce themselves to powder.

Silk is the perfect sachet holder since it's woven tightly enough to contain powder, but is sufficiently loose to let blends breathe and release their treasured scents. There are less-expensive materials available, such as muslin, and they work perfectly well as long as they're tightly woven. If you ever find a great sale on silk, buy it—even an off color. You'll probably end up putting silk bags in larger pouches of a fabric you would rather look at.

Classic sachet recipes call for no fixatives or essential oils, but there's no question that sachets will remain pungent longer if they've been fixed and oiled. Once you identify those scents you favor, you don't need recipes for your own sachet blend. Use whatever you want your linens, underwear, books, or stationery to smell like. Our favorite recipe calls for equal parts of rose petals, lavender, and rosemary and a generous amount of ground orange peel. To this, we add orrisroot and our favorite (of the moment) essential oil.

Sachet blends should be stirred frequently and allowed to age a month in an opaque container before being sewn up. Good blends last several years.

Culinary and Fragrant Wreaths

While many flowers such as roses and lotuses and herbs such as rosemary and lavender are

Other than for potpourri, you'll find no better use for year's-end bounty than fragrant culinary wreaths. If you use the correct forms and the right perfumed and tasty plants, you can fashion a wreath from fragrant leaves and flowers that smells good for weeks and flavors stews for months. The possibilities for scented decorative garnishes are almost endless.

steeped in history, nothing dates back further than fragrant wreaths. Dried circles of plants were discovered in Egyptian pyramids from more than four thousand years ago.

The Greeks so inextricably associated crowns of laurel with victors of athletic events, fine writers, and military heroes that by the fifth century artists began immortalizing their idols with the ultimate wreath—a halo. While living, Roman emperors wore crowns of laurel and roses; after deification, they were painted with a nimbus of radiating light. Today wreaths are placed on coffins and grave sites to symbolize the continuous ring of life.

Although wreaths are woven throughout the year all over the world, more are made at Christmas than at any other time. Wreaths have become as much a part of the holidays as decorated trees and poinsettias. Just as was true more than forty centuries ago, fragrant wreaths today are favored over those with no perfume.

Wreaths can be made from any fresh or dried plant material that can be tied over a ring or twisted into rope. We've experimented with almost every plant we grow, but have found nothing better than wreaths of *Laurus nobilis* (sweet bay), with stems of scented foliage beneath and bunches of fragrant decorative herbs on top.

Although you can weave a perfectly good wreath form with pliable woody branches, such as whips from young poplars, it's much easier and quicker to use a metal form. When you finish making a wreath, no part of the form is visible from the front, and wire bases are godsends when you want a wreath in an unusual shape (such as a heart for Valentine's Day).

Metal forms are either flat (double wire) or "pinecone" (triple wire). Flat forms are ideal for kitchen wreaths, when you want only culinary materials. Pinecone forms have a half-circle, hollow cove just under the top surface. It is in this space that bunches of fragrant materials are looped with wire.

Two other essentials are thin (22- to 26-gauge) florist's wire on paddles rather than spools and a small pair of wire cutters. Craft and hobby shops carry all these supplies, as do many florists. Always buy dark green materials.

When using a flat form, your goal is simply to tie on enough materials to completely camouflage all wire. You can pile materials on as thickly as you like, even decorate the mounded surface with herbs such as rosemary and sage.

Pinecone forms give you the chance to use those pungent herbs that dry to insipid colors (basil and tarragon, for instance), or those that lose beyond recognition their fresh form (parsley and borage). Even more important is the opportunity to utilize the intensely fragrant, diversely scented, pelargonium. Myrtle and long strands of poorly colored thyme are also good, as is any plant material that is better smelled than seen.

Once fragrant wreaths have their pinecone bases filled, you can wire above anything you like. If your finished wreath is to have a theme (predominant element), those strands should outnumber all others.

Materials for potpourri look so at home in wicker baskets that you may decide to leave them right there. Certain herbs, like lavender, rosemary, and thyme, retain their fragrance and release it without help from fixatives and essential herbs.

Fragrant wreaths are useful both fresh and dried. Culinary materials are often at their best when dried. When still-useful kitchen wreaths become unsightly because their herbs have tell-tale gaps from continual snitching, just hang them inside a pantry door, where you don't have to look at them. Fragrant wreaths retain their odors long after they have turned from fresh to tired. Hung at the rear of closets, they'll freshen musty odors.

These suggestions for dried fragrant plants don't exhaust the list of their uses. You can make perfumed wands by twining ribbon around and through whole stems of lavender. Tussy-mussies made with linen doilies backing a clutch of fragrant herbs and flowers are popular, and pomanders concocted from oranges or apples pierced with cloves and dusted in fragrant powders still hang on Christmas trees and in doorways. You can even make your own bath sachets, perfumed soaps, and candles. Don't throw away anything you've taken the trouble to dry. If an immediate use doesn't occur to you, store potpourri materials in airtight containers. You'll find a use for them someday and bless your perfectly aged leftovers.

Extracting Essential Oils

When we began making our own potpourri, we declared that we must also extract our own essential oils. After all, we had bushels of extra rose petals and leaves from fragrant herbs. Fortunately, we decided to begin small and read about a "simple" homemade still that required nothing more than two glass jars with lids that could be pierced to hold copper tubing. The larger jar was placed in a pan of water on the stove; the smaller jar sat in a small pan of cool water. The jar on the stove was filled with two quarts each of flower blossoms and distilled water and one quart of pure alcohol (vodka was suggested).

The idea was to gradually heat the water on the stove until it barely moved the flower petals, then to keep the temperature at that level. Supposedly, steam laden with essential oils would rise, pass through the copper tubing, and drop into the cool pan.

Our first attempt was not only a failure, it was a mess as well. Impatient to bring the brew to a simmer, we heated the pan too quickly, and the glass jar cracked and spilled its contents everywhere.

We didn't crack anything during the second attempt; neither did we distill any oils. Although we kept the simmer exactly as described, no steam ever traveled anywhere we could notice, certainly not through our carefully sealed tubing. And we had wasted another perfectly good bottle of vodka.

Later we learned that even if we had succeeded, the essence of our labors would have been only a fragrant "water" that needed further distillation before being suitable for dousing potpourri. We decided to leave extraction to the pros, at least until we get a proper still and clear instructions for safe operation.

CHAPTER XII

Buying What You Grow

There are four major sources to consider when buying plants for the garden: catalogs, specialists, growers, and nurseries. While there are advantages to all, there are pitfalls to some.

Catalogs

The easiest way to choose and procure plants for your garden is to sit back comfortably in your easy chair, look through tempting glossy catalogs, and fill out an order blank. Then either write a check or divulge your credit card number and post your order, after which you may rest again and wait for your selections to arrive by mail. General-purpose garden catalogs have a lot going for them, not the least of which is the listing of everything from acacia saplings to zinnia seeds. But before you divulge your ZIP code to just any mass-mailing list, consider some advice for coping with that jungle of gardening hyperbole.

Catalogs can be exceedingly misleading. Swayed by fancy writing or a supersaturated Kodachrome print, you may order some plant touted for fragrance and learn months later, after you've pampered it into flower, that as far as *your* nose is concerned, it smells about as tempting as cardboard. Or you'll purchase a variety because your garden could use off white blossoms and instead find yourself nurturing a plant that blooms pink. Varieties said to be floriferous may peter out after only two weeks of spindly blossom. A tree reputed to scramble to thirty feet may huddle at four. Such deceit and trickery are enough to make you swear never again to order from those braggarts.

Learn to read between the lines of catalog lingo. Something "slow to bloom" guarantees a three-year wait. You can depend on smelling blossoms said to be "powerfully fragrant," but you'll need a bloodhound's nose to sniff perfume from blooms that are only "lightly scented." If a catalog confesses that a plant is "disease prone," prepare for it to crumple before every ailment known to your area. When someone admits that a variety is "tender," you can bet it will either freeze in winter or wither in summer.

Don't despair, however. Good news, too, is dribbled throughout catalog jargon. "Reseeds freely" implies that you'll probably buy that particular seed packet just this once, after which only a compulsive weeder could keep out volunteer seedlings every spring thereafter. "Drought-resistant" plants are for those of you who don't want to leave your air-conditioned houses during a hot spell, even if your plants need a drink. Although plants promoted to "thrive on neglect" can't be abandoned, they somehow flourish even at the hands of fair-weather tenders. Something said to "grow in any soil" is meant for those content with the dirt they already have and refuse to fuss over additives.

If you worry that catalog writers are out to fool you, get a look at what their camera-clicking sidekicks are up to! With clever air-brushing, photographers can make crabgrass look like the White House lawn. With the assistance of complementary background colors, blossoms can be made to appear more brilliant than they'll ever look in *our* gardens. (The wrong shade of canvas stretched in the distance can also make blossoms look hopelessly frumpy.) A macrolens gives camera buffs all the help they need to make blooms look like dinner plates when they're really only the size of demitasse saucers.

As if the photographers themselves aren't enough, they conspire with those who develop their film. "Make this more red than it already is," they instruct. "Something was wrong with the light or the exposure, and it doesn't look right." Yes, it does; that blossom was as red as its variety gets, just not scarlet enough for what the photographer wanted to portray or what his boss wanted to sell.

The ever-growing confusion over how to shop from catalogs prompted Katherine S. White to write a series of articles for *The New Yorker* between 1958 and 1970. Later the collection was published in a delightful book entitled *Onward and Upward in the Garden*. Read what she had to say about new, got-to-have introductions:

"Let us consider the hybridizers and the horticulturists in general. Their slogan is not only 'Bigger and Better' but 'Change'—change for the sake of change, it seems. Say you have a nice flower like the zinnia—clean cut, and of interesting, positive form, with formal petals that are so neatly and cunningly put together, and with colors so subtle yet clear, that they have always been the delight of the still-life artist. Then look at the W. Atlee Burpee and the Jo-

Although you'll eventually purchase plants from specialists, growers, and nurseries, you may first fall in love with fragrance by buying flowers. This Parisian kiosk is scented from top to bottom.

seph Harris Company catalogues and see what the seedsmen are doing to zinnias. Burpee, this year, devotes its inside front cover to full-color pictures of its Giant Hybrid Zinnias, which look exactly like great, shaggy chrysanthemums. Now I *like* chrysanthemums, but why should zinnias be made to look like them? From Harris, you can buy seed of what it calls New Super *Cactus* Flowered Zinnias, and they certainly do look like cactuses, or you can buy the seed of Fantasy Zinnias, which are the counterpart of Asters. And both companies offer zinnias that look like dahlias. It is all very confusing."

White penned these words in 1958. Today's hybridizers are still at it—making marigolds, daisies, and goodness knows what all bigger and "better"—still dressing flowers in each other's petals. Even so, you need to order from some place.

Specialists

If you know which plants you want, first try to remember whether gardeners you know already grow those plants, and ask them where they buy. Chances are they'll tell you they purchase from suppliers who specialize in flowers—such as roses, wisterias, honeysuckles, daphnes, lilies, and geraniums; or herbs—such as sage, rosemary, mint, and lavender.

If you yearn for some plant that no one you know already grows, consult a book such as *The Mail-Order Gardener* by Hal Morgan. Besides mentioning generalists, books such as these list sources that specialize in almost every family of plants you've ever heard of.

By far the best way to choose the plants that will best suit your eyes and nose is to visit a public garden where new hybrids are under evaluation. This tulip test bed in Britain's fine garden at Wisley gives a preview of what you can order by mail next year.

The greatest asset of specialists is that they really do specialize in the plants they cultivate. Besides offering more varieties than you're likely to find available from a generalist, specialists' catalogs tell you exactly how to best cultivate their prized plants, usually with detailed, to-the-point instructions. They also specify the best time to plant where you reside and deliver accordingly, often with a written, money-back guarantee.

Growers

Growers are specialists who don't ship, selling directly instead to those close enough to have a look for themselves. With some plants, such as rhododendrons and azaleas (which can be planted while in full bloom), visiting growers allows you to smell those plants you're considering buying. Calling on growers also provides an opportunity to admire beautifully grown adult specimens of varieties that interest you. Finally, growers can tell you that extra planting or maintenance tip that never gets mentioned in written instructions.

Often small-scale growers don't advertise. Your local agricultural agent, however, usually knows of their whereabouts.

Nurseries

Even if you locate specialty catalogs and growers, you may, for convenience alone, end up buying more than 90 percent of your plants from your local nursery. If your local outlet stocks plants that interest you, there's the advantage of getting to select them yourself rather than relying on what might randomly be sent by mail.

For those of you who refuse to grow plants from seeds, preferring instead to buy seedlings in flats, nurseries are godsends. Nurseries are also advantageous when you decide to spring for the extra cost of adult specimens that you haven't the patience for maturing in your own garden.

Remember to be specific as to the botanical name of the plants you purchase from your nursery. Don't, for instance, buy something called simply "myrtle" if it's *Myrtus communis* you want, or a plant named "bay" when you know that only *Laurus nobilis* will satisfy your nose and palate. Be even more demanding when purchasing plants that don't bloom until they reach a certain stage of maturity; you don't want to pamper a plant for three years only to learn that it's not what you believed you were buying (neither will you care to uproot it after all your loving care *should* have paid off). Get assurance in writing up front.

Epilogue

Mistakes

If you've purchased some plant because it was touted to be fragrant and have nurtured it into bloom only to learn that as far as you're concerned it's not scented at all, welcome to the world of fragrant gardeners. It's bound to happen, especially until you become sufficiently persnickety to demand the variety you specify. When you err, you have two choices: keep it or get rid of it. You can assuage your guilt over the unfriendly uprooting by finding a home for your scentless error. You can always locate someone who'll take it off your hands, for as much as you may dislike admitting it, most people don't give a hoot about fragrance. If a plant hides a water spigot, utility meter, or anything else people don't care to look at in their yards, they'll never even wonder whether or not it also smells.

One Person's Rose Is Another's Stinkweed

Because I like to start projects at their actual beginnings, when we began this book, I first wrote the preface. As a result, I was held to much of what I admitted early on, including that I can't smell *Boronia megastigma* (brown boronia). Robert had long since quit assuring me that perfume really was there, "it just has to be inhaled at the right distance." One day, another friend stopped in his tracks just as he entered our border of yellow and chocolate flowers.

"What's *that* smell?" he asked.

Bob told him it was that plant whose fragrance eluded me.

"You're kidding," my friend replied. "Why, I think it's *strong*." (There was then a race to see who could first regale me with this tiresome tale.)

I still believe, by the way, that they were both inhaling the intoxicating golden wallflowers that completely surround the brown boronia. They swear not, and we've simply formed a truce not to talk about it anymore.

No matter how deeply you fall in love with the fragrance of some plant, learn not to argue about it with those who don't share your rapture. Even though I bite my tongue, I feel only sorrow when people admit that they can't smell the roses that make me dizzy with their bawdy perfume. Still, there's that damned brown boronia whose "fragrance" escapes me to this day. Then again, after all is smelled and done, whose nose knows?

If you're lucky, roses and rosemary will still be blooming when hawthorn berries begin to redden. After gathering materials for potpourri, take a well-deserved break and enjoy the season's end.

Index